D1518387

Italian Politics

ITALIAN POLITICS:
A REVIEW

Books in This Series

Italian Politics: The Stalled Transition, edited by Mario Caciagli and David I. Kertzer

Italian Politics: The Year of the Tycoon, edited by Richard S. Katz and Piero Ignazi

Italian Politics: Ending the First Republic, edited by Carol Mershon and Gianfranco Pasquino

Italian Politics

The Stalled Transition

EDITED BY

Mario Caciagli
and David I. Kertzer

A Publication of the Istituto Cattaneo

WestviewPress

A Division of HarperCollins*Publishers*

Italian Politics: A Review, Volume 11

Copyright © 1996 by Westview Press, A Division of HarperCollins Publishers, Inc.

Published in 1996 in the United States of America by Westview Press, 5500 Central Avenue, Boulder, Colorado 80301-2877, and in the United Kingdom by Westview Press, 12 Hid's Copse Road, Cumnor Hill, Oxford OX2 9JJ

A CIP catalog for this book is available from the Library of Congress.
ISSN 1086-4946
ISBN 0-8133-3186-2 (hc)—0-8133-3187-0 (pb)

The Istituto Cattaneo, founded in 1965, is a private, nonprofit organization. It aims to promote, finance, and conduct research, studies, and other activities that contribute to the knowledge of contemporary Italian society and, especially, of the Italian political system.

Istituto Carlo Cattaneo, Via Santo Stefano 11, 40125 Bologna, Italy

The paper used in this publication meets the requirements of the American National Standard for Permanence of Paper for Printed Library Materials Z39.48-1984.

10   9   8   7   6   5   4   3   2   1

Contents

Chronology of Italian Political Events, 1995

2   Lamberto Dini seems to be favored as leader of the new government. Carlo Scognamiglio and Mario Monti are also still in the race.
The lira is at its lowest point ever at the beginning of 1995.
The Lombardy region is in the center of a storm after publication of the text of a telephone tap proving the existence of deals between the parties for nominations to the USL (local health committees).

3   Sudden drop in inflation, which falls to a level of 4.1 percent annually. The prosecuting magistrate Carlo Nordio sends notifications that they are under judicial investigation to the President of the League of Cooperatives, Giancarlo Pasquini, who suspends himself from office, and to the President of the Veneto Commettee of the League of Cooperatives, Giuseppe Fabbri.

5   While the government crisis continues, Rocco Buttiglione does not exclude the possibility of his *Partito Popolare* forming an alliance with the PDS in the case of immediate elections.

7   Recovery pushes up imports, but the commercial balance stays in the black.

8   Tension within the *Lega* rises. Roberto Maroni meets with dissidents of the League from which another six parliamentarians have defected.

9   The long discussion between President Scalfaro and Silvio Berlusconi has not helped to find a solution to the crisis; in the meantime, the "doves" from *Polo* affirm that the new government could be led by some members of the majority other than Berlusconi, if the date of the elections is fixed as soon as possible.

10 *Polo delle Libertà* changes its position on the government crisis: either a second Berlusconi government or immediate elections. PDS, *Popolari* and *Lega Nord* ask for a *super partes* government to address the most urgent questions.
New low for the lira. In New York it falls to L. 1,061 against the mark.

11 The Constitutional Court judges as admissible referendum questions on the Mammì law, union fees, liberalization of shop hours and the extension of the majoritarian electoral system to local elections.

13 The President of the Republic charges Lamberto Dini with the task of forming a new government. Dini declares that his ministers will be technicians free of party ties, and that the executive will have a well-defined program: budget adjustments, reform of the pension system, a new electoral law for the regions, and the reform of news services.

14 Dini announces that he will reduce the number of ministers. Antonio Di Pietro will not be part of the executive. The two major alliances approve the choice of Dini, with only *Rifondazione* against his appointment.

16 The Mibtel stock index rises by 4.5 percent, on the crest of the wave of enthusiasm following Lamberto Dini's appointment.
Official figures show that the GNP has grown by 3.7 percent over the same period in 1993.

17 The Dini government is sworn in at the Quirinale. It is made up of twenty-two technicians, for the most part university professors.
Massimo D'Alema and Achille Occhetto go before Roman prosecutors investigating the "red co-operatives".

23 Dini declares to the Parliament that his will be a government of truce and that he will consider his mandate finished as soon as he has accomplished the four specific tasks of his program.

25 The Dini government obtains the confidence of the Chamber of Deputies with 302 votes in favor, 270 abstentions, and 39 votes against.
At Fiuggi, the last congress of the MSI is held, and *Alleanza Nazionale* is born; the break with the past causes a division with the faction headed by Pino Rauti and Giorgio Pisanò. For the first time, representatives of the PDS are guests at the Congress.

30 The INPS (national health service) decides neither to reimburse arrears nor to raise payments for 1 million pensioners affected by decisions on these issues by the Constitutional Court.

31 Open conflict in the *Partito Popolare*. Buttiglione meets Berlusconi, but excludes a move to the Right for the PPI. Beniamino Andreatta claims to have convinced Romano Prodi to enter politics as the leader of a Center-

Left alliance and, with the "Left" of the PPI, asks for the resignation of the secretary.

February

1 The Dini government wins the confidence vote in the Senate. The prime minister announces immediate consultations with unions and business to discuss and finalize social security reform.
After the meeting with Buttiglione, Berlusconi declares that there is an agreement between the two for a common path and announces plans for elections in June.

2 Romano Prodi, ex-president of the national holding company IRI, announces his candidacy for the next elections as leader of the Center-Left against Berlusconi. Buttiglione opposes Prodi's candidacy and accuses him of pushing the PPI into the arms of the PDS.

3 Prime Minister Dini, on a visit to Washington, explains his government's budget and pension reform goals to President Clinton.

4 As Buttiglione chooses Berlusconi, the division in the PPI between supporters of Prodi's candidacy and supporters of Berlusconi's leadership deepens.

5 Prodi envisions a "team" including Walter Veltroni and Antonio Di Pietro. Buttiglione invites those siding with Prodi to leave the PPI.

7 The Left asks the executive of the PPI for a special congress, but Secretary Buttiglione's line prevails: "no" to Prodi's candidacy, agreements with *Forza Italia*, CCD, and UCD, but no accord with *Alleanza Nazionale*.
Bossi expels from the *Lega* parliamentarians who did not vote for the confidence motion in the Dini goverment and those who proposed a no-confidence vote against him from within the *Lega*.

8 The Dini government declares that regional elections will definitely be held on April 23 and that the reform of the electoral system for the regions will have to be passed before this date.

11 At the congress of the *Lega*, the ex-Minister of the Interior Roberto Maroni abandons the party and annouces his resignation from the Chamber of Deputies because he favors an accord with the *Polo*. Meanwhile, PDS's Massimo D'Alema, speaking at the *Lega*'s congress, proposes an electoral alliance with the party.

13 Romano Prodi announces that the symbol of the Center-Left will be an olive tree.

14 Arguments within the *Polo* on regional elections. Berlusconi wants them in autumn after parliamentary elections which, in his opinion, should be held in June; Fini, like the *Progressisti*, the *Lega* and the *Popolari*, asks that the April 23 date be kept.

15 The Budget is at risk. *Polo* threatens not to vote for it because it is against new taxes.

16 Storm over the lira; state bonds and stock exchange in difficulty.

17 The cabinet approves a bill on *par condicio* (mandating equity in the distribution of media time for party propaganda). The ombudsman for the media will be able to require replies and corrections; negative advertisements will be prohibited and opinion polls limited.
The lira falls farther and the *Banca d'Italia* is forced to intervene.

19 PDS head Massimo D'Alema, speaking at the Congress of the *Cristiano Sociali*, proposes a federalist reform of the state and suggests a new political alliance composed of all the forces of the Left and the Center.

20 The supplementary budget will be 20,000 billion lire, of which 15,000 will come from new taxes and 5,000 in spending cuts. The unions are worried by the effect this may have on inflation. Dini tries to involve the various social groups, before the final drafting.
Industrial production rises again; in December it had reached an historic high with a 5.5 percent increase over November's figures.

21 Inflation takes off; the *Banca d'Italia* raises the discount rate. The lira sinks, penalized by the weakness of the dollar and by the news of the increase in inflation.

22 Berlusconi asks that the parliamentary elections be held in May in conjunction with the regional elections and leaves open the possibility that *Polo*'s members might abandon Parliament. He also makes it known that he may abstain on the budget.

23 The budget of over 20,000 billion lire is launched. It could cost 500,000 lire per family per year, but frees 3,000 billion for the South.
PDS, PPI and *Lega* will support the budget in Parliament; *Polo* remains critical and postpones its decision on the vote until after the debate in the Chamber of Deputies.

24 Serious clash between *Polo* and the President of the Republic. Berlusconi demands elections as soon as possible and accuses the president of trampling the country's interests.
The date for the regional elections is fixed for April 23.

25 The balance of payments is in the red for the first month of 1995.
   Polo prepares a no-confidence motion against the Dini government.

26 From Prague, Scalfaro declares that on his return he will meet representatives of *Polo* and attempt to cool the tone of the debate with the ex-majority on the date of the vote.

27 Umpteenth financial storm and further fall of the lira.
   The President of the Senate, appealing to the parliamentary groups' sense of responsibility, urges approval of the budget (by the Senate) at the earliest possible date. The IMF judges the budget positively.

28 Dini also appeals to the Senate to approve the budget as soon as possible in order to overcome the dramatic financial emergency.
   The *Banca d'Italia* gives a positive assesment of the government's budget.

March

1 The parties in the *Polo* alliance say "yes" to the budget.

2 Former Prime Minister Giulio Andreotti is bound over for trial on the charge of association with the Mafia. The trial date is set for September 26, in Palermo.

3 *Polo* announces that it will vote against the budget, after Dini refuses to launch social security reform by himself and continues discussions with social organizations about reform.
   Polo's "no" to the budget provokes a new fall in the value of the lira.

4 Dini says that the social security reform proposal will be presented by March 15.
   The Budget Minister warns that the financial storm which is affecting the lira has already "burned" 4,000 billion lire and could cause Italians' savings to go up in smoke.

6 Domenico Buscetta, grandson of Mafia informant Tommaso Buscetta, is killed. He is the eighth Mafia victim in Palermo in ten days.

7 The budget is approved by the Senate, with the *Progressisti, Lega* and *Popolari* voting for it, and *Forza Italia*, CCD, AN and *Rifondazione comunista* voting against it.

8 Buttiglione forms an alliance with *Polo* for the regional elections on April 23: a single list and symbol for the forces of the Center and an agreement with AN for the proportional vote. This provokes a violent reaction from the Left of the PPI.

9 Open warfare in the PPI. The national assembly is likely to be the forum for the showdown between the Left and the party leader.
   The President of Confindustria proposes limiting old age pensions in the future to people over age 60. Industrialists ask the House of Deputies to reject the Senate amendment on unemployment benefits.

11 Rocco Buttiglione is defeated at the PPI national council, which rejects the proposed deal with *Polo* and AN. Controversy breaks out over the voting: the exclusion from the vote of four councillors under investigation is contested.

12 The PPI leader refuses to resign despite the fact that his political line has been rejected by the national committee. He refuses to appear before the committee.

13 Outline agreement on the first part of the social security reform between government and unions: separation of assistance and social security insurance. New accounting measures for INPS.
   The lira loses ground against all the European currencies, particularly the mark which is valued at 1,200 lire.

14 The PPI arbiters accept Buttiglione's appeal against the national committee which had thrown out the deal with *Polo*. The Left rejects the decision and announces the election of a new secretary.

15 Dini links a confidence vote to approval of the budget to avoid its rejection. This announcement by the Prime Minister does not reassure the markets.

16 The Dini government wins the confidence vote in the Chamber of Deputies, with *Polo* and a part of *Rifondazione Comunista* against it and the *Progressisti, Lega,* PPI and *Rifondazione* dissidents voting in favour.

21 The Senate votes confidence in the Dini government with a large majority. The budget is now law.
   Further recovery of the lira and stock exchange.

22 Public finance for '95 goes well, even exceeding targets for the net balance.

23 Gerardo Bianco elected secretary by the PPI national committee. The judge rejects Bianco's appeal and confirms Buttiglione as the legitimate secretary; however, the committee's vote rejecting the secretary's political line is judged to be valid.

26 The Left of the PPI confirms Bianco as secretary.

27 The Prime Minister announces his plan to proceed rapidly with privatizations. The timetable is already set for the privatization of five state entities by the end of the year.

28 Two former cabinet ministers are placed under house arrest for *Tangentopoli* investigations in Bari.

29 The date for the referendum on the twelve questions accepted by the Constitutional Court is set for June 11. Parliament has seventy days in which to pass legislation to avoid them.
According to ISTAT data, employment levels have fallen by 1.6 percent since a year ago; with 332,000 fewer jobs.
The unions present their pension reform plan to the Prime Minister: a mixed system with the eighteenth year of paid-up contributions as the dividing line between contribution and payout.

April

3 Antonio Di Pietro leaves the magistrature, announcing his departure at a convention on the *Mani pulite* ("Clean hands") investigation. Meanwhile, General Cerciello of the Financial Police accuses Di Pietro of having induced some police functionaries to implicate him; the General also makes harsh accusations against the entire "pool" in Milan, specifically accusing it of having pressured witnesses to mention Berlusconi's name during the investigations.

4 According to ISTAT data, inflation is near 5 percent and rising.

5 Dini announces that the pension reform will be launched by April 23; the postponement is aimed at avoiding electoral exploitation.

6 The government report on the state of the economy in '94 confirms the marked rise in production, helped by an increase in exports and family consumption. This growth, however, does not help employment figures.

9 In Padova's election for its vacant seat in the Chamber of Deputies, the Center-Left candidate beats the *Polo* candidate alarming *Polo*.

12 Agreement between the government and unions on supplementary pensions, which will be optional.
The Labor Minister, Tiziano Treu, presents the unions with an "employment package" containing part-time work, extension of short-term contracts, division of full-time posts. The proposal seeks to render the relationship between supply and demand more fluid.

13 During a television transmission, Berlusconi states that Di Pietro told him in a private meeting that Di Pietro was not convinced there was a basis

for the notice of investigation sent to Berlusconi by the Milan pool of prosecutors.

14 After Berlusconi's declaration, the chief of Milan's Public Prosecutor's office, Borrelli, accuses Di Pietro of "guilty silence".
Foiled attempt on the life of the Deputy Prosecutor of Milan Gerardo D'Ambrosio.

19 Industrial production on the rise. In February, the ISTAT index shows an increase of 7.3 percent over the same month of the previous year.

21 Inflation increases again, and in April reaches 5.3 percent, but the lira and the Stock exchange are unaffected.

22 The Justice Minister, Filippo Mancuso, accuses Di Pietro of having interfered with the Bolognese Prosecutor during the investigations of the *Uno bianca* case when Di Pietro was consultant to a parliamentary commission on terrorist atrocities. The presidents of both Chambers reply that the Commissions of Inquiry have the same powers as judicial authorities.

24 The Center-Left wins the administrative elections, contrary to the forecasts of the exit polls. The PDS (24.9 percent), overtaking *Forza Italia* (21.4 percent), becomes the most popular party, AN grows less than expected. The Center-Left wins in nine regions, *Polo* six.
A large number of blank or invalid ballots are cast and challenges and appeals are expected.

25 The government issues a decree to jump start the residential housing market. 1,400 billion lire are set aside to fund the plan.

26 Division in *Polo*: Fini does not go to the summit organized by Berlusconi and states that elections in June will be impossibile.

27 Outline agreement between government and unions on pensions: in 2012, welfare benefits will be calculated on contributions paid and will not be connected to salary, providing a disincentive to those deciding to go into retirement between age 55 and 61.

May

4 The Justice Minister seeks disciplinary action against the *Mani pulite* pool and orders another investigation to determine if there have been abuses of powers of imprisonment.

5 Final meeting between government and unions on pensions postponed; this delay allows the introduction of measures against tax evasion.
After the pension negotiation, the lira has a record rebound.

7 In local and provincial elections, the Center-Left wins, and elects the majority of provincial presidents and mayors.

8 Agreement reached on pensions between government and unions. The accord is not signed by Confindustria, which judges it to be insufficient.

10 The Constitutional Court declares illegal the part of the *par condicio* which prohibits advertisments in the thirty days before the referendum.
ENI (holding company for oil and natural gas industry) moves towards privatization with record profits, the largest in its history.

12 The pension reform bill arrives in Parliament.

14 Dini summons Justice Minister Mancuso, seeking to avert a government crisis caused by the recent acts of the Justice Minister.

15 The Ombudsman for the press and broadcasting sets rules and timetables for the transmission of electoral publicity before the referendum; times, spaces and prices must be the same for both sides. The parties are not satisfied with the solution.

16 The Chamber of Deputies approves the framework of the law on contracts for public workers. Many new features, the controlling Authority remains; the law should have a smooth passage in the Senate.

19 According to ISTAT data, industrial production is still growing: in March it was up 0.9 percent with respect to the previous month and up 8.7 percent with respect to the same month in '94.

20 The Prosecutor's Office of Milan charges Silvio Berlusconi with corruption and abetting the suspected payment of bribes to the Guardia di Finanza during fiscal checks at Videotime, Mondadori, Mediolanum and Telepiù. The Milan Prosecutor's Office receives a notice of accusation from the Prosecutor General of the Court of Cassation as a result of Minister Mancuso's charges against pool magistrates.

22 Inflation returns to 1992 levels, with consumer prices increasing to 5.5 percent from 5.2 percent in April and 4.1 percent in May '94.

24 Government intervention is no help in getting the parties to agree on the referendum questions regarding television; a split remains over the number of networks controllable by one individual and the definition of such networks.

26 Marcello Dell'Utri, head of Publitalia, is arrested on the request of the Torin Prosecutor's Office, accused of issuing false invoices and fraud.
The governor of the *Banca d'Italia*, faced with the risk of a rise in inflation, decides to raise the offical discount rate to 9 percent.

28 At the federal assembly of the *Lega Nord*, Bossi proposes three parliaments: one each in the North and in the South to control the third central
   Parliament on choices regarding the two different parts of the country; the
   leader of the *Lega* maintains that a "break with legality" might be resorted
   to in order to introduce federalism.

29 Ministerial workers will have to work from Monday to Friday, both
   morning and afternoon; state workers react negatively to the new work
   schedules established by the Ministry of Public Administration.

30 Lamberto Dini explains the path to "latching onto" Maastricht within
   three years: the 1996 budget will be 32,000 billion lire and will be followed by two more decreasing budgets.
   The government approves the three-year objectives for public sector finances: inflation is high on the agenda. From the 4.7 percent average of
   this year it should decrease to 3.5 percent in '96.
   The Broadcasting Ombudsman Santaniello warns the Fininvest group's
   channels not to repeat its violations of the rules fixed for the referendum
   period.

31 For the Governor of the *Banca d'Italia*, the enemy to be beaten is inflation.
   To block it, he is ready to further raise discount rates. Fazio criticizes the
   excessive graduality of the pension reform.

June

1 Berlusconi denies rumors that he is about to leave politics, and instead
  confirms his leadership.
  The Constitutional Court puts a stop to decisions which increase public
  debt; if the national budget will not permit the extension of privileged
  treatment for all those who have a right to it, the privilege must be
  cancelled for all.

2 From Brescia, news leaks report that Di Pietro is under investigation for
  a second time.
  After approval by the government and Head of State, the economic program for 1996-98, is ready to be examined by the House of Deputies. Its
  objective is to reduce the public debt from the current 130,000 billion to
  63,100 billion in 1998.

3 Di Pietro formally requests that the Brescia Prosecutor's Office inquire
  into the source of the information which promoted magistrates to inves-
  tigate him.
  The media Ombudsman again admonishes the Fininvest group after
  having ordered it to transmit, free of charge, thirteen advertisements for
  the committee for a "yes" on the referendum questions relating to the

television system. Fininvest declares its intent not to broadcast the ads, and the Ombudsman threatens to close the networks.

5   In Brescia the investigation into the Di Pietro case continues. After meeting with the Milan Prosecutor, Francesco Saverio Borrelli, the Brescia magistrates have acquired new documents on Giancarlo Gorrini, the businessman and ex-owner of insurance companies who reported having lent one hundred million lire to the ex-prosecutor.
    The President of Confindustria, Abete, states that by the end of autumn the Italian economy must reach three objectives: an increase in the value of the lira, containment of inflation and the reduction of interest rates. The state deficit drops by 13,000 billion in the first five months of '95, with respect to the same period in '94.

6   The ex-Interior Minister, Antonio Gava, is arrested in connection with an investigation into bribes paid to Sorrento businessmen. The ex-Under Secretary Francesco Patriarca and the Vice President of the Naples Industrial Union, Corsicato, also end up in prison with Gava.

7   The Interior Minister Brancaccio resigns due to bad health. Justice Minister Mancuso tells the terrorism commission that he has been the victim of death threats.
    The TAR (administrative court) in Lombardy suspends the Media Ombudsman's order requiring Fininvest to transmit thirteen free advertisements for the "yes" coalition in order to restore the *par condicio*; the Administrative court will decide.

8   On June 16 the tax amnesty signed by Augusto Fantozzi will begin. Objective: assure the coffers of the State 11,500 billion this year and 4,000 in '96. Eight milion taxpayers will be affected.
    Giovanni Coronas, police chief during the years of terrorism, is named Interior Minister by Lamberto Dini, filling the post left vacant by Brancaccio.

9   A decree and two bills have been drafted by Labor Minister Treu to address the unemployment emergency. The decree postpones discussions on unemployment benefits until July 31 and refinances *contratti di solidarietà* (part-time contracts made to avoid lay-offs).

11 Italians vote on twelve referendum questions. The "no" win on the question on the television system. The "yes" vote wins on the question regarding privatization of RAI. The double round electoral system in local elections is approved.
    The lira and stock exchange are in difficulty following the referendum results.

14 Dini announces in the Senate that, even if parliamentary elections are held in October, his government will prepare the budget for 1996.

19 Talks between government and pilots' unions break down. A strike is confirmed for June 23 despite the order which prohibits strike activity before June 24.

20 Summit meeting of the Center-Left alliance with its candidate for premier: the task of proposing the packet of rules to be approved before the vote is entrusted to Veltroni and Prodi himself: antitrust law, *par condicio,* double-round electoral law, guarantees with respect to art. 138 of the Constitution; the proposal will then be compared with that of the *Polo.*

22 In Brescia, rumors of the arrest of Di Pietro and a notice of investigation are immediately denied by the Prosecutor Salomone.

24 Leoluca Bagarella, probable successor to Totò Riina as the head of the Sicilian Mafia, is arrested in a joint operation conducted by the police and DIA, the special anti-Mafia police force.

25 Rupert Murdoch proposes a "share exchange" under which Murdoch would buy 51 percent of Mediaset, the company which controls the Fininvest group and Berlusconi would join Murdoch's News Corporation.

26 Tension mounts between the President of the Republic and Justice Minister Mancuso. After President Scalfaro comments on a possible attempt by Mancuso to destroy the work of magistrates from the Milan pool, the Justice Minister sends an official message to the President, in which he asserts that ministerial inspections and the re-opening of the Cagliari case fall within his duties as Justice Minister.

27 ISTAT data show unemployment in April up by 313,000 over January.

28 There is now open warfare on the Mancuso case, with the majority supporting the government seeking his resignation. Mancuso replies that he will go only if the whole cabinet resigns.

29 The pension reform bill arrives in Parliament, in a climate of bitter political dispute. The head of the *Progressisti* in the House of Deputies accuses the Right of endangering the approval of the reform.

July

1 The Prosecuting Magistrate of Milan De Pasquale, who was the head of the investigations of Gabriele Cagliari, is under investigation by the Prosecutor's Office of Brescia. After the Justice Minister handed over the files from the ministerial investigation completed in July '93, an investigation by the Prosecutor of Brescia was obligatory.

2 Antonio Di Pietro is interrogated for seventeen hours by Brescia magistrates and investigated for extortion and abuse of office.

3 On presenting the bill on social security to the Chamber of Deputies, Dini asks the parliamentary groups to withdraw all the amendments because they will slow down the approval of the reform.

4 The government is ready to resort to a confidence motion on the social security reform; probable agreement between Center-Left and *Forza Italia*. *Polo* and Center-Left meet to discuss rules. There is near agreement on the guarantees for the opposition, while the issue of the *par condicio* and the antitrust law are far from resolution; there is a dispute over the electoral law.

5 Lull in the reform of social security. The resignation of the *Lega*'s leader in the House of Deputies feeds rumors of an attempt to postpone approval of the reform until September.

6 The Center-Left and *Forza Italia* reach an agreement on the adjustments to be made to supplementary pensions. There is a preliminary accord on equal opportunity for banks and insurance companies in the management of funds.
   "Making Italy a normal country" is the theme articulated by Massimo D'Alema at the PDS congress, where party strategy will be decided. On the question of anticipated elections, D'Alema maintains that after Dini, there can only be a new executive if the *Polo* is in agreement. For the first time Gianfranco Fini, President of AN, is a guest at the PDS congress.

7 Speaking at the PDS conference, Silvio Berlusconi declares that he does not recognize Prodi's leadership of the Center-Left.

8 D'Alema answers Berlusconi in his concluding speech at the congress by officially nominating Prodi.

9 In Pontida, Umberto Bossi organizes a new political group to oppose both *Polo* and *Ulivo*. It is to be called the *Polo del guerriero* (the warrior's "pole").

11 In the Chamber of Deputies Minister Treu presents a maxi-amendment to the social security reform bill, which incorporates the eleven articles of the original text as well as the safety-valve clause repeatedly requested by *Forza Italia*. Dini may resort to a confidence motion to get the maxi-amendment through.
   An international warrant is issued for the arrest of Bettino Craxi.

12 The government goes to a confidence vote over the maxi-amendment. The Treasury confirms the improvement in the public Fisc for '95.

The government wins the confidence vote in the Chamber of Deputies. To speed things up, it presents two more maxi-amendments. In this case too, the executive will have to resort to a "technical confidence vote".

14 With the confidence vote won on the two maxi-amendments, the Chamber of Deputies passes the social security reform, which then arrives in the Senate.

17 The Senate extends the amnesty for minor breaches of building regulations until December 31.

18 Large-scale privatizations of public services begin again, thanks to an agreement of between the forces supporting the government, plus *Forza Italia* and CCD, who vote for the maxi-amendment.

20 Berlusconi give up 20 percent of Mediaset. Leo Kirch, Johann Rupert and Al Waleed Bin Talal are the new partners in the sub-holding company which control the three Fininvest television channels and Publitalia. A second part of Mediaset is to be sold to another, as yet unassembled group of investors.

23 The congress of Buttiglione's *Popolari* ends in Rome, giving rise to a new party, the CDU (*Cristiani Democratici Uniti*).

29 The secretary of the *Lega Nord*, Umberto Bossi, is investigated by the Prosecutor's Office of Mantova for his "attack on the unity of the State," after his statements on the subject of secession.

30 An ambulance packed with explosives was to have been detonated inside the courthouse in Palermo, with Chief Prosecutor Caselli and his deputy Scarpinato as the probable targets. The plan is revealed by a Mafia informer.

31 The hypotheses on the contents of the budget for '96 include more flexibility for local governments to determine housing taxes and more income for the regions from taxes on energy.

August

1 Tax revenues rise in the first five months of '95.
At the summit between Dini and finance ministers, discussions are held on the basic budget guidelines for '96. These include amalgamation of some ministries, cuts in revenue transfers to local bodies, cuts in the health service without the introduction of higher contributions by the public.

2 In the debate in the Chamber of Deputies on institutional reform, Silvio Berlusconi insists on a presidential form of government and maintains that the reform of the State will have to be the subject of the next Parliament.

In his speech, the secretary of the PDS D'Alema rejects any presidential solution and expresses his preference for a head of state indicated by a vote of citizens but actually elected by Parliament.

Accepting the suggestions of the Antitrust Commission and the European Union, the government approves a decree which regulates "closed groups" in telecommunications, making it possible for anyone to supply different companies or sectors with a private telephone system.

3 New law on preventive detention. Imprisonment will only be possibile when there is a risk of tampering with evidence, danger of escape, or danger to the public. The suspect will be interogated first by a judge for preliminary investigations and only later by the prosecutor. Preventive detention will be shorter.

4 Pension reform definitively approved in a single bill which, in contrast to the prior system, calculates pensions based not on wages, but on contributions paid during employment.

7 The annual Mediobanca survey confirms that Italian public industry is back in the black and has made greater profits than private industry.

9 Over 61,000 billion lire, almost entirely provided by the state, European Union and private investors for investment in infrastructure, will soon be unblocked by the government; this could mean the creation of 160,000 jobs.

11 Pushed by the dollar and the interventions made by *Banca d'Italia*, the lira recovers strongly against the mark and reaches 1,108, its highest level in six months.

The real economy grows too. In June production has grown by 5 percent with respect to the same month in '94.

The Prosecutors of Bergamo and Treviso begin an investigation into the *Lega*, following the publication of one of Craxi's diaries in which he talks of insurrectionist preparations made in '93.

13 After rumors about a meeting in Sardinia between Dini and Berlusconi, in which the leader of *Forza Italia* is reported to have offered the leadership of *Polo* to the Prime Minister, Dini denies all, stating that he does not want to take sides.

15 During the annual visit to the police force, Interior Minister, Giovanni Coronas states that Mafia informers are in grave danger and are already targeted by organized crime.

21 The Prime Minister calls a cabinet meeting to discuss the budget. The unions mount a serious campaign against tax evasion and oppose the proposed health service cuts.
A new tax decree, providing for greater discounts and possible payment in installments, goes into effect.

22 A decision by the Constitutional Court criticizes the Italian tax system for penalizing single income families and asks for a law to eliminate these inequalities.

23 With the new norms on preventive detention posing stricter requirement for arrest and modifying the balance of power between prosecution and defense, thousands of requests for release from prison have already been filed with judges all over Italy.

24 The 1996 budget will provide 2,000 billion lire of aid for single-income families and payments for dependent spouses and family checks will be increased.

25 After an investigation made by *Il Giornale*, Labor Minister Treu makes public the list of tenants of reduced rent apartments managed by social service agencies. Includes names of members of Parliament, ministers and union leaders. The Rome Prosecutor's Office begins an investigation into the possibility of abuse of office.

27 Marco Pannella is arrested while distributing hashish openly in public as a means of generating debate on the liberalization of light drugs and of attracting attention for the eighteen referendum questions for which Club Pannella is collecting signatures.

28 In just one day, the lira loses almost all the gains made during the previous six months.
Because of new contracts, paychecks gain on inflation showing, on an annual basis, the highest increase in the last two years.

31 At the meeting between the government and unions on the budget, the unions ask that when public contracts are renewed, salaries reflect a full recovery of the difference between real and planned inflation.

September

1 SuperGemina, an immense financial empire which will control 30 percent of Montedison, is unveiled. Reducing their share in the group operated by Gemina to 8 percent, FIAT and Mediobanca will join the French Paribas as coinvestors.

2 In Cernobbio, Berlusconi reveals his goals to industrialists: he seeks direct election of the head of State, and immediately declares his candidacy for the office.
Antonio Di Pietro also speaks in Cernobbio, expressing his desire to mobilize the public against any attempt to throw in the towel and provide amnesty for corrupt politicians and businessmen. His speech causes rumors of his possible political ambitions.

3 President Scalfaro explains that a prerequisite for elections will be the establishment of both broadcasting fairness rules and political guarantees for the losers. Elections seem less likely.

4 With the 1996 budget, the government intends to transfer to the Regions a part of the taxes collected on natural gas, gasoline, electric energy, and refuse disposal. This operation is to be accompanied by an equivalent cut in direct contributions to the Regions.

5 In the new budget, the government considers abolishing value added tax on medicines and increasing the taxes on tobacco and hard liquor. Meanwhile, in a meeting with industrialists, Dini reiterates his wish to extend the property taxes on businesses, refining them in some points.

6 The announcement of *Forza Italia*'s vote in favor of the budget and declarations of a rapid re-entry of the lira to the European Monetary System push its value up.
The budget will provide three thousand billion lire in 1996, three thousand in 1997 and four thousand in 1998 as additional funding to finance infrastructure in the South; there will also be incentives for employment. President Baldassarre of the Constitutional Court, announces a decision holding that the prosecutors and judges are not "equal" under the Constitution. Therefore those conducting investigation do not enjoy the same protections as those judging.

7 Finance Minister Fantozzi approves fiscal amnesty.
Vincenzo Caianello replaces Antonio Baldassarre as President of the Costitutional Court.
The secretary of the PDS, D'Alema, proposes to the leader of *Alleanza Nazionale* a pact to dissolve Parliament and hold elections in June. Fini replies that he would prefer to vote in February.

13 The EU Commissioner delivers an ultimatum to Italy to restore competition in the mobile telephone market.
The leaders of *Polo* restate their opposition to the liberalization of light drugs, and seek elections after the approval of the budget.
Fini and Veltroni meet at the national *Festa dell'Unità* in Reggio Emilia.

14 The Venice Prosecutor's Office sends a notice of investigation to Occhetto and D'Alema on charges of illegal party financing and illegal receipt of funds. Another notice goes to the President of the Veneto League of Co-operatives, Bernardini.

18 After a month and a half of investigations, the European Commission concludes that the recent fluctuations in the value of the lira have not distorted competition on the internal market, but Italy is not yet seen as ready to reenter the European Monetary System.

19 The group leaders of the Center-Left in the Senate meet the Prime Minister and obtain his agreement not to include heavy new taxes on health in the budget. *Polo* is against transferring a part of the tax on gasoline to the Regions.
Head of the Court of Cassation requests that the accusations that the judges of Milan intimidated the inspectors of the Justice Ministry be dropped as unfounded. The Justice Minister replies that he will insist on his disciplinary action.

20 Minister Mancuso defines as "supine" the attitude assumed by the Prime Minister's office regarding the motions of no-confidence individually made against him.

21 After the German Finance Minister suggests that the Italian deficit/GNP ratio may keep it out of the European Monetary Union, the lira falls heavily.
Agreements reached on rules for equal broadcasting time break down.
Fisticuffs in Parliament after the speaker of the Chamber of Deputies declares a vote on the reform of RAI to be null and void.

22 With lira still in free-fall, Chancellor Kohl intervenes, stating that no one will be excluded from Europe.

23 President Scalfaro talks of elections again, suggesting the date of June '96. Speaking at an assembly of young industrialists, D'Alema affirms that he would not recognize the legitimacy of a government led by a politician with unresolved conflicts of interest.

25 The governor of the Banca d'Italia advises against Italy's reentry into the European Monetary System unless all the conditions are fulfilled.

26 In Palermo, the trial of Giulio Andreotti, accused of association with the Mafia, begins. The first hearing closes with a request by the defense to move the trial to Rome. The Palermo prosecutor argues that Palermo is the appropriate venue. The decision is postponed until the next hearing.

27 Higher taxes in the 1996 budget. The Prime Minister defends the fairness and incisiveness of his budget of 109,000 billion lire. The unions react positively, while industrialists remain critical.

28 The budget is not popular with the financial markets, and the lira suffers against the mark.

29 During a trial for bribes paid in construction of the Milan metropolitan railway, Prosecutor Paolo Ielo denounces the behavior of Former Prime Minister Bettino Craxi as that of a "practiced criminal". Numerous phone taps demonstrate that Craxi still has a role in Italian political matters.

30 From Hammamet, Tunisia, Craxi attacks Ielo, accusing him of having instigated a Stalinist show trial.

October

1 Venetian magistrates investigating the "red co-operatives" refute suspicions of ties with Craxi, which seem to arise from the phone taps. A dispute ensues with the Milan Prosecutor's Office.

2 After the presentation of the budget, there is a flurry of meetings between Lamberto Dini and other political leaders. The Center-Left is satisfied but asks for a change in the measures for the South and local finance. *Polo* remains critical.

3 Dini presents the budget for '96 in the Senate, and asks for the vote of all political parties in order to avoid the risk of a crisis of governability.

4 Another fist fight in Parliament over a vote on a contested seat. A member of *Rifondazione Comunista*, Vendola, is re-confirmed by the Chamber of Deputies, contrary to the opinion expressed by the Electoral Committee.
Documents belonging to the Secret Service and seized in Craxi's Rome office are reported to contain files on Milan magistrates Colombo and Davigo as well as on some PCI members.

5 The Authorities bill, dealing with large privatizations, is unfrozen. After examination by the Lower House, the new bodies will take shape.
The pool in Milan asks that Berlusconi be tried for bribes of the *Guardia di Finanza*. Berlusconi replies that he is the victim of a plot.

6 Dini declares that a 10,000 billion lire budget adjustment suggested by the Bankitalia is unnecessary.

10 From Washington, Dini lists institutional reforms necessary to guarantee political and economic stability in Italy: a majoritarian electoral law, a reduction in duplicate powers of the two Chambers of Parliament, abolition of no-confidence motions without alternative majorities, reinforcement of the premier, stricter controls on budget-making, more responsibility for Parliament and the executive, more autonomy for local governments.

12 Berlusconi accuses the Milan Prosecutor, Borrelli, of having informed the head of state before himself of the notification of accusation addressed to him. Borrelli strongly denies the accusation.

18 The Chamber of Deputies approves the tax amnesty in its new version. The measure should bring 11,500 billion lire to the state's coffers.

19 The Senate approves the motion of no-confidence in the Justice Minister, Filippo Mancuso. In his speech, Mancuso accuses Dini and Scalfaro of having privately approved his inspections and publicly denounced them. During his reply to the Senate, Mancuso removes four already-leaked pages from his speech which are very critical of President Scalfaro.

20 *Polo* presents a no-confidence motion in the government and *Rifondazione* announces one of its own. Meanwhile, Lamberto Dini assumes Mancuso's position on an *ad interim* basis.

22 In a long communiqué, the President denies Mancuso's charges that he pressured the Commision investigating the Secret Services'slush funds to change its report.

26 *Polo*'s no-confidence motion is defeated, with 310 votes against and 291 in favor.
   The Olivetti group approves a recapitalization to finance the group's revival plan.

27 The Constitutional Court decides to hear Mancuso's petition against the Senate, the Prime Minister's office and the President's office for his re-moval as Justice Minister.
   In the Enimont trial, the Milan tribunal sentences Craxi to four years, Forlani to two years and four months, Martelli to one year and Bossi to eight months.

28 Businessmen meeting in Rimini call for the political forces to try to bring Italy into full participation in the European Union and invite them to respect the majoritarian electoral system.

November

1 The *Banca d'Italia Bulletin* confirms the difficulties experienced by busi-nesses in recruiting specialized personnel not only in the North but also in some areas of the South, where the unemployment level is around 20 percent.

2 The budget is approved by the budget commission of the Chamber of Deputies. The Budget Minister, Masera, announces that the rumored additional budget adjustments will not be necessary.

7 A Work Safety bill is approved with modifications.

8 The President of the Province of Palermo, lawyer Francesco Musotto, elected in the lists of *Forza Italia*, is arrested, accused of association with the Mafia and aiding the Mafia boss, Leoluca Bagarella.

9 The government presents a law on immigration; previously, the *Lega* had said it would not vote for the government amendments on the budget if the executive did not draft a law requiring the immediate expulsion of clandestine immigrants committing crimes.
After a very long delay in Parliament, the law on the *Authorities* is passed with a large majority.

10 The Court of Cassation decides that the bribery trial of the Fininvest group will stay in Milan, thus rejecting the defense request to transfer the trial to Brescia.

12 President Scalfaro announces that if the political stalemate continues after December 31 he will have to dissolve Parliament.

14 At a Milan meeting attended by Di Pietro, the FIAT's Administrator Romiti asks for an institutional pact to begin a great majoritarian reform leading to a two-party system.

15 In Parliament, Dini has harsh words for the Calabrian magistrates who have begun investigating deputies. Sgarbi and Maiolo for association with the Mafia. He announces that he has arranged for an inspection to be made of the Catanzaro Prosecutor's Office.

16 The decree on immigration is approved by the cabinet.

17 The immigration decree remains secret, while awaiting the signature of the President of the Republic. In Parliament approval of the budget in danger. The Senators of the *Lega* decide to walk out in protest.
The European Commission officially approves to the plan allowing 18,000 billion lire to be invested in the South.

18 From Mantova, Umberto Bossi announces that the *Lega* will remain in Parliament and will act responsibly regarding the budget. Meanwhile, the debate on immigration shows signs of being prolonged.

19 Elections are held in twenty-five localities with a population more than 15,000 and in 108 with a population of less than 15,000.

21 Inflation leaps ahead. The annual rise in consumer prices reaches 6 percent in November.
First "yes" to the budget at the Senate.

22 Berlusconi receives another notification of investigation, this time for false accounting and fiscal improprieties during the acquisition of the Medusa company. Meanwhile, a newspaper reports an agreement between the leader of *Forza Italia* and D'Alema to avoid elections, which is immediately denied.

23 According to the Milan Prosecutor, the 10 billion lire credited to a Swiss bank account at the disposal of Craxi came from the Fininvest group. Preventive detention orders are issued for Craxi, and for Giallombardo and Vanoni, managers of Fininvest. Harsh reaction by Berlusconi.
The Chamber of Deputies approves a special law in favor of local radio and television, which extends franchises until 1997.

24 Berlusconi receives an invitation to appear before the Milan Prosecutor to respond to questions regarding the illegal financing of political parties. The President of Confindustria proposes a contract which permits wages below the minimum rate in order to generate new businesses in the South. Negative reactions from unions.

25 The PDS declares its availability to discuss the proposal for a presidential-type institutional reform.
The President of the Republic says he will dissolve Parliament in January if there is no general agreement on reforms.

26 In Pontida, Umberto Bossi asks for a government to oversee institutional reform.

29 Antonio Di Pietro, being investigated for corruption and abuse of office, is interrogated for seven hours by prosecutors Salomone and Bonfigli.
The heads of RAI will no longer be nominated by the presidents of Chambers of Parliament. The parties reach an agreement which provides for their election by members of Parliament.

30 On the back of the dollar's recovery, the lira reaches the threshold of 1,100 against the mark.
The gross national product grows again, with an annual increase of 3.4 percent with respect to the same period in '94.

December

2 One hundred and fifty thousand people take part in a national demonstration organized by AN, in Rome, to demand new elections.

3 Massimo D'Alema proposes that all political forces should get together, in advance of the December 15 meeting of the European Commission, to determine if the Dini government should be extended through the upcoming semester in which Italy will preside over the European Union.

5 A blitz by police against the *Camorra* organized crime group in Campania; 148 arrest warrants are executed and, 1,500 billion lire seized.

7 The magistrature asks that Cesare Romiti, the FIAT group administrator, and the director general, Francesco Paolo Mattioli, be tried on charges dealing with the company's use of slush funds.
Romano Prodi presents an 88-point program for the Olive.

11 Gianni Agnelli announces that he will leave the presidency of FIAT, to be replaced by Romiti.

15 The government goes to a confidence vote in the Chamber of Deputies on two maxi-amendments on the budget. *Polo* and *Rifondazione* announce that they will vote against the government but, thanks to absences in the ranks of the Center-Right, the motion is passed.

19 The ex-secretary of the PDS, Achille Occhetto, attacks the policies pursued by his successor, D'Alema, and requests an extraordinary party congress. No one pays any attention.

20 The Brescia prosecutor's office asks that Antonio Di Pietro be tried, on charges of corruption and abuse of office.
Mario Valducci, vice-coordinator of *Forza Italia*, declares that Berlusconi personally "put 23-24 billion lire plus bank guarantees on the table," to cover the party's debts.

22 At the meeting of the PDS national executive, D'Alema says that he is in favor of a government which would oversee the passing of institutional reforms.

23 The Senate approves the budget.

30 Prime Minister Dini hands in his resignation to President Scalfaro, who rejects it and sends him back to Parliament.
The possibility of an agreement between Berlusconi and D'Alema is rumored for the creation of an institutional reform government or at least an accord to realize certain institutional reforms.

31 In his end-of-year message, President Scalfaro invites the political parties to a broad coalition government, which will "save" the semester of the Italian presidency of the EU, put off anticipated elections, and carry out institutional reforms.

Translated by Timothy Cooper and Susan Kertzer

1

Introduction:
The Stalled Transition

Mario Caciagli and David I. Kertzer

The entire year of 1995 passed, in Italian politics, under the government of Lamberto Dini. Having taken office in mid-January, the government that Dini presided over lasted exactly to the year's end (with Dini handing in his resignation on December 30). Taking office as the government of technicians, succeeding the Berlusconi government, the new executive was supposed to be short-lived. That is, it was supposed to have given way, in short order, either to a new government of politicians or, more likely, to new elections. This was supposed to have happened just as soon as it had accomplished a handful of tasks, albeit important and urgent ones.

Berlusconi and the Pole of the Center-Right had assigned the Dini government only the briefest of terms, until March. Having gone beyond that term, the deadline was moved first to June and then to the autumn. At the beginning of the fall, it appeared as though the government would not last to autumn's end, and elections were forecast for December. And so the year passed as a continuing ballet over the date of the emergency parliamentary elections, called for first by one, then by another of the major and minor political actors, although most insistently by Gianfranco Fini, head of the right-wing *Alleanza Nazionale*, and Silvio Berlusconi, leader of the Center-Right coalition and head of his own party, *Forza Italia*.

While the technicians were governing, Italian political life continued to be marked by moments and events of great significance. Among the most important of these, listed in chronological order, were the candidacy of Romano Prodi at the head of the Center-Left coalition, the schism in the Popular Party, the holding of regional and local elections, and the referenda, all taking place in the first half of the year. Among the developments that unfolded throughout the whole year, at least two are worth highlighting. The first consisted of the "adventures" of the judge of Mani *Pulite* fame, Antonio Di Pietro, from his resignation from the judiciary to the bringing of criminal charges against him, amidst continuing speculation over his possible entry into politics. The second was the dimming of Berlusconi's star, as he too was brought to trial, but above all, as his own popularity among the electors declined, and the harmony among his allies frayed.

All the political excitement of the year, a year not without its surprises, did not succeed in producing a step forward in the transition from the First to the Second Republic. The institutional structure was not altered, despite all the calls for doing so. No new reform of the rules was enacted, if one excludes the new regional electoral law that had the potential of triggering a change in the type of government of the regions. The advent of a new political generation, brought about by the political scandals of Tangentopoli and confirmed by the national elections of March 27, 1994, did not eliminate the vices of the old, at least insofar as the Byzantine style of politics and the tendency to fight to defend one's own particular group or individual interest rather than seek to serve the general interest were concerned. The party system was further complicated rather than simplified. Communication between the political class and the rest of society remained tenuous.

The question of when the Italian political transition began has already been discussed at length, and will continue to generate discussion. Perhaps it began with the anti-corruption offensive by the Milan judges in the spring of 1992, perhaps with the advent of the Ciampi government, the first government of technicians, in the spring of 1993. It might have ended with the elections of March 27, 1994 if the completely new national leader and the completely new team of ministers that emerged had been able to impose a decisively new imprint on it. Instead, there arose another government even more "technical" than Ciampi's, which succeeded in surviving for the entire year, but which did nothing, because it was in no position to do anything, to accelerate the transition.

For the Italian transition, then, 1995 was *un anno di stallo*, a year of treading water.[1]

The Year of the Technician

Having had his government toppled on Christmas eve, 1994, as a result of the departure of the Northern League (Lega) from his coalition, and following no confidence motions introduced by the Democratic Party of the Left (PDS), the *Lega*, and the Popular Party (PPI), Berlusconi immediately proposed that either he be returned to office or that emergency parliamentary elections be held. By the end of 1994, however, the first of a long series of battles took place pitting the *Forza Italia* leader against the President of the Republic, battles that were to continue throughout the following year, for the President was committed to doing everything possible to avoid dissolving Parliament.

The initial struggle between the two men lasted two weeks, but in the end President Scalfaro succeeded in trapping Berlusconi with a skillful and stealthy maneuver. After launching various attacks and as many about-faces, the Pole of the Center-Right accepted the solution of a government of technicians whose formation was to be undertaken, with Berlusconi's approval, by one of the minister's of his former government.

But despite his previous position and despite the fact that his ministers and undersecretaries were largely university professors and other experts from outside Parliament, Dini failed to get the votes of the Center-Right. Their Parliament members abstained from the vote of confidence, while Dini obtained instead practically all the votes of the Center-Left and the League.

Gianfranco Pasquino's chapter in this volume examines in detail the nature and the activities of the Dini government. Here we simply recall that the brief term that Dini himself agreed to at the time of taking office was linked to his accomplishment of just a few well defined programmatic tasks.

Realistically, it was difficult to accomplish all of these objectives in a few weeks time. It could not be done by March, as Berlusconi had claimed, nor even by June, as the Communist Refoundation Party demanded, with both forces pushing for immediate elections. As it turned out, in the time that the government of the technicians ended up having available, they were indeed able to accomplish almost all of the programmatic points they had promised. The government even succeeded, once its life had been sufficiently prolonged, to pass the budget bill for 1996, in what became its last task before finally leaving the scene at the year's end.

The Dini government's major accomplishment was probably the reform of the pension system, a plan that in the form proposed by Berlusconi and by the same Dini the previous fall had been strongly opposed by the unions and by the general population. As Onorato Castellino argues in his chapter, which reconstructs the various legislative proposals of recent years and shows how the new reform grew out of them, the system that was finally put in place may not have furnished the final solution for the key problem of the balance between contributions and expenditures. But it is important to point out that it was a government of technicians, with the support of a parliamentary majority from the Center-Left, that brought the reform to fruition, through a difficult path, a reform with long-term implications. Perhaps it was just because the government was composed of technicians that it succeeded in obtaining so much in its negotiations with the labor unions.

As for the unions, 1995 seems to have been the year in which they finally came out from their long period of crisis. After having contributed to the defeat of the Berlusconi government, recuperating some of their capacity for mobilization and consensus-building, the unions of the three national labor confederations responded favorably to the formation of a government of truce. They further felt encouraged by the major role they played in drafting the pension reform thanks to the recognition that the government accorded them as important interlocutors, a recognition that was confirmed months later during the preparation of the new budget bill. Michael Braun, in his chapter, after reconstructing the course of the decline of the Italian unions from the beginning of the 1980's, shows the union movement's surprising recovery of strength and image, which seems to guarantee it a renewed political weight.

And so it appears not only that the three labor confederations have saved themselves from the general crisis of the parties of the First Republic, to which, to different degrees, they were all tied, but that they have also succeeded in consolidating their position in the system of industrial relations and in their relations with the government, in the framework of a renewed collaboration that has led to some talk of "neo-corporatism". If all this was favored by the existence of a government of technicians, it is also true that the unions themselves reciprocated by supporting the government's survival.

The Dini government succeeded in reducing the size of the public deficit and it could trumpet a substantial increase in economic production, which reached a high level in 1995, but which lay outside the more restricted sphere of government action. The reduction in the public deficit was still entirely inadequate and the growth in the gross national product remained by itself insufficient to allow Italy to reach the parameters imposed by the Maastricht treaty. The growth in inflation and the fluctuation in the value of the lira during the year continued to keep Italy far from the threshold for entry into the European Monetary Union. To these objectively measurable difficulties must be added various controversies and declarations that, over the course of the year, as Pier Virgilio Dastoli emphasizes in his chapter on Italy as the "silent dinner guest" in Europe, made the path all the more difficult.

The Dini government would not have been able to survive for almost a year (an average term for a government of the First Republic, and, we now know, also for those in the transition toward the Second), had it not been for the support, with different degrees of conviction, but with tenacity to the end, of both the Center-Left and the League. Nor would it have survived had it not twice been saved by the votes of the Communist Refoundation deputies. The first time was in March, when some of them, at the cost of a painful secession, voted in favor of the vote of confidence in the government's economic plan, and a second time in October when, guided by party head Bertinotti, after receiving Dini's assurance that he would resign at the end of December, the RC deputies contributed to the defeat of the Pole's no confidence motion.

However, the Dini government failed to achieve one of the points of its program, that which was referred to generically as the *par condicio,* that is, regulation of equal access to the television networks for political propaganda, a question that in the end turns out to involve the entire extremely complicated question of regulation of the television system. The Pole's strong opposition resulted in putting off consideration even of the simplest questions of television access, so that the government limited itself to charging the relevant minister with designing a law, which however has yet to be voted on. It will take something more than a government of technicians to reorganize a system of information that has been extraordinarily disturbed by the entry into national politics of one of its principal protagonists, Silvio Berlusconi.

Return of the Parties, but How Many and What Kind?

One of the most commonly lamented defects of the Second Republic has been party fragmentation. The simplification of the party system was one of the goals of all the reformers, from the referenda champions to the constitutional engineers searching for years for the electoral system best designed to limit the number of parties.

Yet the transition to the Second Republic has instead resulted so far in a proliferation of parties, *partitini,* and assorted political groups. The fact that twenty-six different parliamentary groups were called, at the end of the Dini government, to climb the steps of the Quirinale Palace for consultations with the President of the Republic might be attributed to an excessive solicitude by the head of state or to an overly generous interpretation of the rules of the two parliamentary houses. But other events demonstrated the querulous and immodest presence of a plethora of political formations. These included the difficulties in preparing electoral coalitions and the equally arduous process of selecting candidates for regional and local elections, the rapid succession of various conventions and congresses, and the cross-cutting polemics and conflicts, one after the other, which the media covered with great relish.

As a result of the 1994 election campaign, which led to the formation of the two poles, it seemed that a concentration of the various political forces into more stable alliances might occur, with the possibility of creating a small number of large political forces, perhaps no longer organized as the widely criticized old political parties were, but into new kinds of groupings, more open and flexible. Instead, within each of the two alliances of 1994 various conflicts arose and the divisions grew. At the same time, no new organizational innovation came about.

The newest formation, *Forza Italia*, gave no sign of wanting or being able to give rise to a new type of organization, whatever that might have consisted of. In fact, as Marco Maraffi reminds us in his chapter, *Forza Italia* continued to be run from above in a manner more authoritarian than hierarchical. Is this to be the model for the future forms of organization of the political will of Italy's citizens? Meanwhile, FI's clubs atrophied, when they did not in fact die out entirely. Those whom it elected to office may not have yet had time to create solid bases in society. But the fact is that *Forza Italia* not only identifies with its leader, Silvio Berlusconi, but depends entirely on him.

Of quite a different sort is the lack of novelty found in the heir of the *Movimento Sociale Italiano*, the newly constituted *Alleanza Nazionale*. We refer here to the fact that beneath the new clothing of the AN the old body of the MSI remains very much alive. In January, 1995, the congress of Fiuggi decreed the dissolution of the MSI and the transformation of AN, established the previous year as an electoral coalition, into the new party of the Right. But what exactly is *Alleanza Nazionale*?

Alleanza Nazionale has a well known leader, but it is certainly not a leader-based party. Gianfranco Fini has done a great deal to change the MSI and to make it into a protagonist in the transition to the Second Republic, but the charisma he enjoys is essentially positional, that is, a charisma that derives from the office he held in the old party and not simply from his own personal qualities. Fini has to (and wants to) count on a structure that remains practically that of the dissolved MSI in its organizational characteristics (the old territorial sections remain in force and indeed are on the rise), its method of articulating its political goals, the number and the composition of its membership and, with but few exceptions, its leadership. All these are unchanged. As for its ideology, it is difficult to say if AN has truly become "laicized," that is, separated from its patrimony of nationalist and fascist ideas, despite the new contents of its programs and statements of principles.

What continued to change during 1995, after the profound changes of the preceding years, was the *Partito Democratico della Sinistra* (PDS). If its organization had still not changed (reflecting the inheritance, with its unresolved problems, of the old Italian Communist Party), certainly its position in the party system had, as had its ideology. As Mark Gilbert shows so well in his chapter, in attempting to keep up with the evolution of its allies of the Center-Left, the PDS continued to move toward the Center, to the point where, on the one hand, it proposed the construction of a "single large democratic force," and, on the other, declared, through its highest leaders—though more through second-in-command Walter Veltroni than from party secretary Massimo D'Alema— that it wanted to drastically reform its patrimony of ideas through the acceptance of liberal democratic principles and values.

All this was not enough to appease the PDS's smaller allies, concerned as they were about remaining too much in the shade of the PDS oak tree (the PDS symbol). Furthermore, the numerous little parties of the Center and the Center-Left were worried about the effects that Romano Prodi's candidacy might have on their own autonomy.

Gilbert's chapter provides an excellent analysis of Prodi's project, and the genesis of the "Olive Tree," that is, the grouping of Center and Left forces—from the PDS to the Popular Party—for whom Prodi would serve as leader. It was a difficult year for Prodi, and at year's end the exact nature of the coalition, its composition and its mode of operating, remained unclear. The point we would like to emphasize in this introduction, beyond the fragmentation of the Center-Left parties (the situation in the Center-Right being, however, not all that much better), is the nature of these parties. It may be that one can speak of a "rebirth of the parties," as Aldo Di Virgilio proposes in his analysis of the nature of the electoral competition in 1995, but one must ask just what kind of parties these are.

If the membership party, the successor to the mass party, is itself in eclipse (though this does not seem to be true for the PDS and the AN), what kind of party will come to characterize the Second Republic and, hence, take Italy into the new century?

With the new model that *Forza Italia* appeared to represent not having really taken off yet—indeed practically having already failed—small political formations having few of the characteristics of a party swarmed across the political scene. They have most in common with those political groups that in the wake of the fall of Franco sprouted like mushrooms in Spain and then all disappeared following the first elections in 1977, many joining the government party, the Unión de Centro Democratico. Hence, the name that was coined in Spain for these groups, the "party-taxi," referring to the fact that all their members could fit into a cab, might be resuscitated today in Italy, for the assorted progeny of ex-socialists, ex-socialdemocrats, ex-liberals, ex-republicans (notwithstanding the fact the Republican Party continues to exist), and even of ex-Christian Democrats who have given rise to the so-called "bushes" (*cespugli*) of the two poles.

Even the ex-Christian Democrats, survivors of the dominant party of the First Republic, have divided into many branches, despite the attempt to have a single unit, the Popular Party (PPI) succeed it in January, 1994. Even by that date, however, the followers of Pier Ferdinando Casini and Clemente Mastella defected, creating the Christian Democratic Center (CCD), while Social Christians (Pierre Carniti and Ermanno Gorrieri) had already decided to ally more closely with the PDS, and years earlier Orlando had already left to found the Network (*Rete*). The most profound split of the ex-Christian Democrats in the PPI, however, occurred with the schism of March 1995, and constituted one of the most important events of the year as far as the party system is concerned.

It is difficult to say how much the decision of the Left of the PPI to back the candidacy of Prodi for the Presidency of the Council (i.e., Prime Minister) pushed party Secretary Rocco Buttiglione to declare his support for Berlusconi's Pole, with which he had hardly begun discussions. One thing that is clear is that, in the tragicomic sequence of denunciations and attacks, of claims of ownership of the party symbol, headquarters, and name, the PPI ended up hemorrhaging leaders, activists, and voters, while Buttiglione's followers founded a new group (can we refer to it as a party?), calling it United Christian Democrats (CDU).

Following the creation of a Diaspora of this importance, even the Italian Church was forced to recognize that the political unity of Catholics was a thing of the past. Within the CEI, as Sandro Magister notes in his chapter, the conservatives hoped until the very end to save a single moderate Catholic party, capable of hegemonizing the Center-Right, but for those bishops most in touch with the changes taking place in Italian society, the end of the single Catholic party seems to have occasioned a sense of relief.

An Unstable Electorate

1995 was an electoral year. Indeed, it was yet another electoral year, following a long line: parliamentary elections in 1994; the referendum on the senatorial districts (leading to the change in the voting system) and the first local elections under the new electoral rules in 1993; and the last parliamentary elections of the First Republic in 1992. The repeated calls to the voting booth were an expression of the feverish pitch of the transition, and to some degree provide a measure of it.

The 1995 electoral results do not speak with a single voice. They reflected an electorate that was still unstable and uncertain, perched uncertainly between the two principal alliances and the different choices that they represented.

The regional elections, held under the new rules which had just been put into place, appeared to be a success for the Center-Left, both because the forecasts were against them and because the exit polls themselves— which predicted a victory for the Center-Right— were dramatically proven to be wrong. But, as Di Virgilio reminds us, not only was the Center-Left's margin of victory quite small in many regions, but the actual popular vote as a whole went in favor of the Center-Right, if only by 126,000 votes, about half a percent. The Center-Left was also apparently aided by an increase in abstentionism, as well as by various other factors, including, almost certainly, the presentation by Marco Pannella of his own autonomous electoral lists in at least two regions, which took votes from the Center-Right.[2]

The Center-Left's victory in the local and provincial elections, by contrast, was clear. A number of factors contributed to the success of the Center-Left's candidates, evident from the first round of balloting, to the Center-Left. These included the variable nature of the coalitions, the larger number of parties in the coalitions, the local infrastructure some of these parties had, and the capacity of many of the parties to put forward a sufficient number of highly visible and well regarded candidates. The Center-Left's success became a breakthrough by the second round of voting, confirming in this difficult historical moment that the two-ballot system is working in its favor. Furthermore, the Center-Left's candidates for mayor in 1995 received more votes than their colleagues had in 1993, because in almost all cases not only the Communist Refoundation supporters but those of the Northern League as well voted for them.

After the euphoria of April and May, the Center-Left parties soon suffered the negative results of the referenda results on the television system, the three most important of the twelve referendum questions for which Italians were again called to the polls. The alliances of the parties in the face of these three questions, as Pier Vincenzo Uleri and Roberto Fideli point out in their chapter, mirror the alliances put together in the aftermath of the fall of the Berlusconi government, with the Northern League joining Communist Refoundation and the Center-Left.

On the other referendum questions the alliances were more frayed and, depending on the particular question, the various parties, big and small, barely made their voices heard. The outcome of the referenda that mattered were favorable to Berlusconi, not only due to the victory of the "no" forces in the vote on the abrogation of the provisions of the Mammì law which favored Fininvest (Berlusconi's huge holding company), but because the no votes exceeded by far the votes cast in the previous elections for the parties of the Center-Right coalition. Many of the citizens who had voted for the Center-Left just a few weeks earlier had taken Berlusconi's side in defending his position on the television industry and his methods of employing television advertising.

The spring vote, then, revealed the existence of a rather large sector of the electorate that was quite mobile, liable to change its loyalty in just a short time, and voting differently depending on the type of vote involved and the particular issues at stake. The fluctuation in abstentionism, varying not only by the election, but also by geographical area, was but another sign of how uncertain the result of future elections would be. If the referenda demonstrated once more Berlusconi's capacity for mobilization on a terrain favorable to him, the local elections showed that the anti-Berlusconi forces had their strong point in their ability for form electoral alliances. But this same point of strength could quickly become transformed into a weakness, for it exposed the alliance to the cross-cutting demands of its various partners.

A Place for President Scalfaro Amidst the Comedy over Setting an Election Date

Among all of the problems that crowded the 1995 political agenda, one in particular, discussed repeatedly and insistently through the year, sometimes seemed to overwhelm all the others: the dissolving of Parliament and calling of parliamentary elections.

We have already mentioned some of the episodes in this "ballet of the date". In his chapter, Maraffi recalls when and how often Berlusconi demanded an immediate call to the polls, justified almost always by reference to the presumed betrayal of the "March 27 voters," who had been defrauded by the breakdown of the coalition of the *Polo delle Libertà* and the *Polo del Buon Governo*, and by the formation of a government that was supported by a different majority. But Maraffi also recounts how this demand gradually, over the course of the year, diminished in the light of increasingly unfavorable opinion polls for *Forza Italia* and in the face of the upcoming trials of its leader, the first of which began just before Christmas. Heard instead was the call to prolong the legislature in order to undertake institutional reforms.

The PDS itself wavered from time to time in its position on the holding of emergency elections. Once the Dini government was formed, the PDS and its allies preferred to see that the regularly scheduled regional and local elections were held, thus postponing the parliamentary elections that were so loudly being demanded by their antagonist.

The project behind the Prodi candidacy, however, seemed to require, after a minimum of time to get organized, a positive attitude toward the holding of elections. In this perspective, a date of June seemed realistic, and was made all the more appealing in the wake of the electoral successes of April and May. But the referenda results, followed by surveys that reported less encouraging figures than had been expected, and, above all, the difficulty in constructing an electoral alliance on the two borders of the Center-Left—that is with the League and with Communist Refoundation—made the prospect of elections less appetizing for the PDS. The final outcome of this was the interest, by year's end, of PDS leader D'Alema in Berlusconi's proposal to reopen the dialogue on institutional reform.

The other parties took less ambivalent stands on the holding of elections. The two extremes—National Alliance and Communist Refoundation—remained steadfast in their desire for elections, both seeking possible gains as a result. By contrast, the "bushes" both of the Center-Left and the Center-Right opposed the elections, fearing they would be swallowed up in a polarizing battle between the major contenders. The minor parties and the groups surrounding them sought the greatest possible postponement of the election date, hoping to be able to regroup their weakened membership, to build a higher profile, and, not least, to open a dialogue between the opposing sides.

Given this community of interests in opposing the dissolution of Parliament, those who had landed on opposite shores following the sinking of their ship with the demise of the First Republic soon took up their own dialogue once again. In their opposition to holding elections and in their openness to dialogue, the former Christian Democrats stood out for their well developed culture of mediation and compromise. The *Popolari* (members of the PPI), guided since June by Gerardo Bianco, and the CCD, founded by Pier Ferdinando Casini and Clemente Mastella, were notable for their efforts to call on their respective alliance partners for moderation and patience, arguing that holding elections soon would be harmful. But even Buttiglione's CDU, despite their close relations with *Forza Italia*, increasingly opposed the dissolution of Parliament.

The President of the Republic, Oscar Luigi Scalfaro, a former Christian Democrat himself, became something of an honorary member of this grouping of refugees from the Christian Democratic Diaspora who tenaciously opposed holding elections. Scalfaro, too, showed himself a worthy offspring of the culture of mediation and compromise that had marked the Christian Democratic tradition.

Without doubt, Scalfaro played an important part in the comedy over the setting of the election date, employing all the weight of his office. The President of the Republic gave strong support to the Dini government, aiding it as far as possible to prolong its life. He resisted all the pressures placed on him to exercise that power that only the president had, and dissolve the houses of Parliament. He used great astute-

ness in deflecting all of Berlusconi's outbursts and demands, right from
his initial reluctance to invest him a second time with the presidency of
the Council of Ministers following the crisis of December, 1994. He also
suffered the accusation of seeking, through his delaying tactics and other
maneuvers, some public and others not, to prepare the conditions for the
birth of a neo-centrist political grouping on the model of the old DC, to
serve as the axis of the entire party system.

For all these reasons, at various critical moments of the political year
Scalfaro became a direct antagonist of Berlusconi. The two engaged in
verbal duels at a distance, sometimes very heated, though Scalfaro always returned swiftly to his more accustomed bland tones, as displayed
in the paternalistic style that typified his official speeches.

If Berlusconi was disposed to engage in polemical reactions of indig-
nation and impatience against Scalfaro, the attacks by Fini and Marco
Pannella were harsher, though less personal because they were more
political. Fini succeeded in getting 150,000 people to attend a demonstration called against the President of the Republic in a Roman piazza.
Under the banner of the AN, though including many not of the AN, they
demonstrated in December to call for immediate elections. Pannella,
following a series of blistering attacks, indeed organized an impeach-
ment campaign aimed at the head of state, charging him with an assault
on the Constitution.

Antonio Di Pietro's Adventures
and the Judges' Accomplishments

David Nelken has a chapter in this volume dealing with the strange
and tortuous path of the judicial investigations into political corruption,
identified with the term *Tangentopoli*, that continued to affect the political
landscape. He touches there on another of the protagonists of 1995,
Antonio Di Pietro. As the best known investigating magistrate prosecuting corruption cases from 1992 through the end of 1994, Di Pietro remained in 1995 at the center of the political stage, even when he said—
as he often did—that he was staying out of politics.[3]

Removing his judge's robe in a dramatic gesture (in a scene that was
repeated constantly on television throughout the year) on December 6,
1994, the judicial symbol of *Mani pulite* was catapulted into the limelight
not only by his legion of admirers, but by his many friends. As a result,
one of the questions that kept coming up throughout 1995 was whether
Di Pietro would enter politics and, more importantly, with whom he
would ally. His noted sympathy for moderate, if not indeed conservative, causes, gave hope to the Right, but more to the AN—which had

from the beginning been a champion of *Mani pulite*—than *Forza Italia*, which was worried about its leader being a target of the investigations of Di Pietro's former colleagues. Above all, it was the parties of the Center who seemed most hopeful of attracting Di Pietro, seeing in him someone who might be able to bring together their all too scattered components. In the end, even the Left showed they were more than ready to welcome the ex-magistrate.

For all of them Di Pietro represented an extraordinary resource for gaining popular support, given his constant position at the top of all the surveys measuring the Italians' respect for public figures, and the mass of votes that experts estimated he could help attract. In the articles and the letters he regularly wrote for the newspapers, in the columns he prepared for the weeklies, in the interviews he gave following his university lectures, and his comments at a raft of conventions, and during his trips abroad, Di Pietro succeeded in keeping his interlocutors guessing as to which side he would ultimately choose. He even drafted a series of programmatic points, which were interpreted as providing the basis for negotiations with one or another political grouping, if not, indeed, as the basis for launching his own political party. Nor did he pass up holding various meetings—some public, others secret—with politicians of various stripes.

Everyone feared that Di Pietro would end up entering the political arena on the opposite side. But the man who feared the most was Berlusconi, who faced the prospect of a slew of upcoming corruption trials. It was a fear that was only compounded when it looked as though it was appointees of his own government who were behind the investigations being launched against Di Pietro himself.

It appeared as though Di Pietro would be able to show his innocence when he contested the accusations of having improperly served personal interests while in office in a period that predated *Tangentopoli*, accusations made against him in June by the investigating magistrates of Brescia. But despite his spirited defense he was subsequently ordered to trial, a development that not only made his legal situation more difficult, but which, above all, made his political situation more delicate, for he had long argued that it was improper for people to run for political office while they faced criminal trial. By the end of 1995 it seemed that Di Pietro's political plans, and those devised for him by his many and diverse suitors, were left on hold, with an uncertain future.

Di Pietro's difficulties received a great deal of attention, both for the fame he had in the past and for the popularity which he seemed to enjoy still as "the judge most loved by Italians". But his difficulties had more personal implications as well. Indeed, the difficulties encountered by the investigating magistrates, or at least those who had for years been on the front line of the fight against corruption and organized crime, had precise institutional and political implications.

The power of the magistrates and their political weight have been the subject of a great deal of discussion in recent years, and the decisive role that they played in bringing about the demise of the First Republic will no doubt continue be discussed for some time. Critical voices have been raised from a variety of pulpits over the years, accusing the judges of improper interference in the political sphere. In 1995 the strongest criticism of this sort came from Berlusconi's forces, some of whom went so far as to charge the magistrates with launching an actual strategic plan aimed at "persecuting" the head of *Forza Italia* and thus favoring, whether intentionally or not, his political adversaries. The Center-Right also took up the defense of Minister of Justice Filippo Mancuso, who had subject the work of the Milanese magistrates to censure, and strenuously defended him when the parliamentary majority forced him in November to step down from his post.

Whatever the ultimate result of the conflict between a part of the magistrates and a part of the new political class, it is worth recalling that in 1995 the Italian judges performed two sensational acts against the two major leaders of the old political class. Bettino Craxi was condemned, together with other politicians, by the courts of Milan for the secret funds of Enimont (one of Italy's largest holding companies). It was the first guilty verdict for the formerly all-powerful Socialist Party head and ex-Prime Minister, and other such verdicts were in the offing. And venerable Giulio Andreotti, at the summit of Italian politics for over forty-five years, and seven times President of the Council of Ministers, was brought to trial for his presumed ties with the Sicilian Mafia.

The magistrates' investigations of the Mafia and of its many accomplices stirred critical reactions in certain political sectors during the year. The charge that the magistrature had been "politicized," and hence was no longer impartial, would continue to be heard, as would the call, from more or less self-interested sources—to find a legislative solution to *Tangentopoli*, a problem discussed by David Nelken in his chapter.

A Slower Pace

It is likely that the judges will continue to be politically influential until such time as the Italian system has been able to establish new political and institutional structures. The distance traveled down this road during 1995 was minimal.

Institutional reforms were once again proposed with insistence at the end of the year by the same people who for the previous twelve months had called for nothing other than a return to the ballot box. Nor was the government in a position to take action, for institutional reforms could not be part of the tasks of a government of technicians, not only because of its nature, but because it had been assigned a well-defined mission both in terms of its program and its short time frame (although the latter ended up being extended).

In the absence of those reforms that were needed to give it dynamism and efficiency, the political system remained blocked. The worsening fragmentation of the party system only made matters worse. Those who had somehow thought that the wisdom derived from bitter past experience or, better yet, the beneficial effects of having introduced an electoral system with a majoritarian component would lead to a bipolar system remained disappointed. Virtually all the political protagonists and observers continued to call for the formation of two opposing blocs, with the possibility of alternation between them, and a consequent degree of executive stability. Thus far this has not happened.

The year of 1995 saw the formation of a Center-Left that, on paper at least, is broader than the alliance of Progressive that competed in the 1994 elections, but Communist Refoundation remains outside it. Nor is it any more solid, because the twelve different official coalition partners have thus far given little signs of cohesion or harmony. The "bushes" roiled the waters of the Center-Right as well, although they showed greater compactness around Berlusconi as their officially recognized leader. Finally, there is the Northern League, ready to use its potential for blackmail that it has enjoyed as the party providing the balance of power. In short, the party system, rather than experiencing a simplification, shows a degree of complexity that gives reason to fear for the stability of possible government alliances.

In the year of the government of technicians the Italian economy, by contrast, showed signs of considerable vitality, public revenues improved a bit, and the unions took a responsible attitude. But it is a paradox to argue that all this happened because the technicians did not do the damage that politicians normally do. The country must return to being governed by politicians who alone are able to lead it, in one direction or another, out of the transition. We cannot say that, in this sense, 1995 was a lost year, but certainly the pace of change had slowed down dramatically.

Notes

1. A satisfactory interpretation of the Italian transition will have to await its end, and the very lack of adequate theory proves a hindrance in offering an

analysis in mid-course. While a rich literature exists on the transitions from authoritarianism to democracy, with an adequate development of relevant theory, thanks to the rich empirical material furnished over the past three decades by changes of political system in southern Europe, Latin America, and East Europe, little or nothing exists on the transition from one kind of democracy to another, a fact attributable to the lack of historical cases suitable for study. The only case that readily comes to mind for a comparison with the Italian experience is the transition from the Fourth to the Fifth Republic in France, too slender a base for developing adequate interpretive schemas.

2. An initial, exhaustive analysis of the regional elections can be found in R. D'Alimonte, "La transizione italiana: il voto del 23 aprile", *Rivista italiana di scienza politica*, 1995, n. 3, pp. 515-59.

3. On Antonio **Di Pietro** and on the magistrates' anti-corruption activities, see, in the earlier volumes of *Italian Politics*, the chapter by V. Onida on "*Mani pulite*, Year III" in the volume edited by R.S. Katz and P. Ignazi subtitled *The Year of the Tycoon* (Boulder, Co: Westview Press, 1996), and D. Della Porta's chapter entitled "The Immoral Capital: Payoffs in Milan", in the volume edited by C. Mershon and G. Pasquino subtitled *Ending the First Republic* (Boulder, Co: Westview Press, 1994).

2

The Regional and Administrative Elections: Bipolarization with Reserve

Aldo Di Virgilio

The elections of April 23 and the May 7, 1995 were interesting for a series of reasons. In the first place, in all the regions and many of the local and provincial districts the voters completely changed the assemblies that had been elected in 1990.[1] The spring elections saw the remains of the ancien régime's ruling class, elected before the "revolution" of 1992-1994, swept away.[2] Seventy thousand municipal councillors were elected as well as over two thousand provincial councillors and roughly seven hundred councillors in the fifteen regions having regular status.

If this was the institutional outcome of the vote, it also had a more general political resonance. The local and regional elections were a chance to check up on changes in voting behavior, parties, and alliances a year after the general elections of 1994 (and after important political events such as the defection of the *Lega* from the Center-Right coalition and the split of the *Partito Popolare* - allied in the regional elections, not unsuccessfully as we shall see, with both the Right and the Left).

The vote was seen by the parties on the Center-Right as a kind of dress rehearsal for the general elections that *Forza Italia* and *Alleanza Nazionale* were clamoring for after Bossi's "betrayal" had led to the fall of the Berlusconi government. For the parties and *cespugli* (small satellite parties) of the Left and Center, however, the vote represented ideal terrain on which to review their alliance strategies and test out new political accords not only with a view to possible early general elections—which they were in no hurry to bring about—but also new parliamentary formations (which had already begun to take shape with the presentation of two noconfidence motions against the Berlusconi government and the creation of the Dini government).

A third more specific point of interest was the new regional electoral system which had been passed by Parliament two months before and which brought to an end the cycle of electoral reform begun five years before with the promotion of the first electoral referenda.

In view of the above the elections introduced a new stage in the transition of Italian politics.

The New Electoral Systems

The new regional electoral system (introduced by law no. 43 of February 23, 1995) is a mixed system like those adopted for parliamentary, local, and provincial elections. Yet despite this common characteristic, the systems are quite different both as regards the actual ballot-paper (its characteristics and the way the vote is cast) and the mechanism for allocating seats.

The regional electoral reform, then, completed the passage—more the result of external political developments and changing party fortunes than any carefully designed reform plan worked out round a table—from a situation where all the voting rules were homogeneous to one marked by differentiation. This passage seems to have cost the electorate a good deal of effort in learning the new complicated voting proceedures, as is demonstrated by the surprising number of invalid votes recorded in the elections of the April 23. The greater technical complexity of the new electoral systems and, above all, the contemporaneity of regional, provincial, and local elections in many areas of the country, helped raise the number of invalid votes to just under seven million (21 percent of the total votes cast) in the regional elections (proportional vote), to more than three million (nearly 10 percent of votes cast) in the regional elections (majority vote), and to over three and a half million votes in the provincial elections (approximately 12 percent of votes cast).

The new regional system envisages two votes in a single round and on a single ballot paper: one for the allocation of four-fifths of the seats, elected by proportional representation in districts coinciding with the territory covered by the provinces; the other for the assignment of the remaining 20 percent of the seats, via majority vote, in a single regional district. This latter share of seats, the most important and characteristic element of the new electoral law, represents a bonus awarded to the regional list which obtains the most votes. The party lists which compete for the assignment of proportional seats in the provincial districts must "link" themselves to one of the regional lists. Each regional list—identified on the ballot-sheet by the name of the *capolista* (the head of the list), designated by the list or inter-linked lists as candidate for the office of president of the regional council[3]—must be linked to a group of provincial lists present in not less than half of the provinces in the region. The voter can use the double vote available in one of three main ways: he or she may (a) choose one of the regional lists but not a provincial list and thus vote only by majority system; (b) vote for only one provincial list, and thus only by proportional representation (though this option is also counted as a vote in favor of the regional list linked to the provincial list pre-selected); (c) express a separate vote: for a given party in the proportional vote and for a different party or for a coalition not tied to it in the majority vote. In the proportional part, the voter may also express a (single) preference vote for one of the candidates on the list chosen; the regional list is, instead, a closed list. The allocation of proportional seats closely follows the previous voting system (using for example, as in the past, the HagenbachBischoff quotient or the "plus one" corrector). It introduces, however, a clause which bars the assignment of proportional seats to parties polling less than 3 percent of the valid votes expressed in the whole region or, alternatively, to parties linked to a regional list which has polled less than 5 percent of the valid votes. The threshold is, all in all, low; in the vote of April 23, however, it did work well enough as a filter to prevent over-fragmentation.[4] As for the majority system seats, as was mentioned, they are attributed to the most voted regional list. Since Parliament, via the majority system bonus, wanted to guarantee the winning party or coalition an absolute majority of seats on the council and hence governing control of the region, it was, as we shall see, a more variable bonus, not always corresponding to 20 percent of the seats at stake.[5]

The new regional election system has certain affinities to and many differences from the local and provincial electoral system (introduced with law no. 81 of March 25, 1993). In the latter case, too, we find ourselves faced with a duplication of arenas (the representative arena which is proportional; the executive arena which is majoritarian) and the casting of a double vote by the electorate (in large local councils and the provinces, but not in councils elected by majority vote only). What is different however is the degree of interdependence between the two arenas, the ways votes are cast and the mechanism for allocating the seats.

The most conspicuous change in the new local and provincial electoral system (which in April, 1995 saw its fifth concrete application) is the direct election of the mayor and of the president of the provincial council.

In the case of local councils, the voting methods, as in the past, vary according to demography. The use of the majoritarian principle, limited until 1993 to communities with fewer than 5,000 inhabitants, has been extended to include administrations with a population of up to 15,000 inhabitants (representing four-fifths of the 8,100 Italian local councils and 40 percent of the total population). In these *comuni*, each list of candidates for the council is linked to a candidate-mayor. The voter makes a double choice: for a mayor and for the list he is linked to. Within each such list, the voter may also indicate a (single) preference vote. The candidate for mayor who obtains the largest number of votes wins. The list he or she is linked to takes two-thirds of the seats. The remaining third is divided up proportionally among the other lists using a d'Hondt divider. Councillors are elected according to the order of preferences and then the list order, except for assignment of the first seat obtained by the opposition lists to the losing mayoral candidates.

In the largest centers—the 633 local Italian councils with over 15,000 inhabitants—the connection between candidate-mayor and candidate-councillor list may differ. The same candidate-mayor can be associated with several lists which, outside this convergence, still compete with one another for the council. The voters, for their part, dispose of a double vote which they may utilize in three main ways: they may (a) choose one of the candidates for the office of mayor without choosing any list; (b) vote only for a list without choosing a mayor, though this choice is counted as a vote in favor of the candidate-mayor linked to the list chosen; (c) cast a divided vote, i.e. for a candidate-mayor and a list which are not linked one with the other. The voter can also cast a (single) preference vote for one of the candidate-councillors on the list chosen.

In *comuni* with over 15,000 inhabitants, candidates polling the absolute majority of votes win. If one of the candidates does so, seats on the council are distributed in one of two ways: (a) the list or coalition of lists which supported the winning candidacy has also gained more than 50 percent of the valid votes, and thus is allocated (even when it has not earned it by its own electoral forces alone) 60 percent of the seats; (b) the list or coalition of lists which supported the winning candidate gains less than 50 percent of the valid votes, and thus the allocation of seats to the lists takes place, as in the past, on a proportional basis (using the d'Hondt divider).

If no candidate-mayor obtains an absolute majority of votes, there is a second round of "closed" balloting limited to the two bestplaced candidates (who are allowed, in the first of the two-weeks between the first and second rounds, to widen their base of support by tying themselves to lists whose mayoral candidates have been eliminated). As long as no other list or coalition of lists has received more than 50 percent of votes in the first round, 60 percent of the seats are allocated to the list or coalition linked to the candidate elected as mayor. The remaining 40 percent is allocated to the lists on a proportional basis (d'Hondt divider). The election of councillors follows the order of preferences and then the list order, except for assignment of the first seat obtained by the opposition lists or coalitions—in this latter not counted in the quota of the single components—to the losing mayoral candidates.

The new electoral systems are, all in all, rather complicated voting mechanisms put together in two distinct phases of the transition. More specifically, they are a "proportional electoral system with a variable majority bonus" in the case of the regions and a "variable formula electoral system: proportional with possible majority bonus" in the case of councils with over 15,000 inhabitants, and a "majority electoral system with proportional minority representation" in the case of councils with fewer than 15,000 inhabitants.[6]

These differences correspond to distinct demands and objectives and, above all, to the two different phases of the Italian transition in which the electoral systems were drafted. In the case of local electoral law, the break-up of the traditional party structure and the referenda outcomes helped shape voting rules which aimed at personalizing the contest, pushing the parties into the background and giving birth to a sort of municipal presidentialism. In the case of regional electoral law, on the other hand, the reformed—albeit precarious and unstable—party political equilibrium favored the adoption of voting rules which guarantee the stability of regional governments and meet the interests of the single players: for the *piccoli* (minor players) their survival, for the *grandi* (major) a coalition leadership which is less exposed to the risks of blackmail by minor allies than in the parliamentary electoral system.

The Offer: Two Coalitions, Many Parties

The mixed character of the electoral systems introduced in Italy between 1993 and 1995 has added to the traditional logic of competition on a party political basis a new logic of alliance building with the aim of "voting to elect a government".[7] The working out of electoral alliances (be it for the presentation of candidates in the single seat constituencies of the Chamber of Deputies and Senate, of candidates to the office of mayor and provincial president, or of lists in regional majoritarian seats) has thus become the main challenge for political players because of its key importance under the new rules. The politics of alliance-forming has transformed itself into the leit motif of the Italian transition, and has to date dictated the pace of the different phases of change. The aggregational force of the PDS and its ability to put together alliances were a decisive factor, in the absence of alternative alliances, in the left's success in the local elections of summer and autumn of 1993. The ability of Silvio Berlusconi to capture moderate votes by resorting to a geographical electoral map which saw *Forza Italia* allied in the North with the *Lega* and in the South with the MSI-AN allowed the Right to win the political elections in March 1994. The objective of winning Center votes, pursued by both the left-wing alliance and the right-wing *Polo*, as well as the readiness of the Center to renounce its own fragile identity as a way of circumventing its political and electoral decline, made the administrative elections of autumn 1994 a ground for experimenting new aggregations, most of them joining the Center and the Left.

From the point of view of the electoral coalitions, the regional elections pointed to some important new developments. The main innovation was undoubtedly simplification of the number of coalitions on offer. As typically happens in majoritarian systems, the four groupings of 1994 (the *Cartello dei Progressisti, Patto per l'Italia, Polo delle Libertà*, and *Polo del Buongoverno*) were cut back in 1995 to just two: Center-Left and Center-Right. This development is particularly worthy of note in that it took place in a highly disjointed electoral climate, "composed," that is, of fifteen synchronous but completely independent electoral areas.

A second innovation regards the make-up of the two coalitions. Unlike in 1994, the Center-Right did not on this occasion present significant geographical variations in that *Alleanza Nazionale* replaced the *Lega* even in Northern regions. It was instead the Center-Left coalition which varied, presenting a range of partners and a degree of political/ideological diversity. In eight regions out of fifteen (Piedmont, Lombardy, Veneto and Liguria; Emilia-Romagna and Toscana; Basilicata and Calabria) the Center-Left coalition was "closed" on the Left and did not include *Rifondazione Comunista*. In four cases (Lazio, Abruzzo, Molise, and Puglia) it stretched from *Popolari* on one side to neocommunists on the other. Aside from the PDS the coalition overall included *Verdi, Patto dei Democratici, Popolari,* Federation *Laburista*, PRI, PSDI, *Cristiano Sociali* and the *Rete*, variously assorted in different places. Only in Tuscany, in a region where it is particularly weak, did the Northern League ally itself with the Center-Left coalition.

A third aspect of note (important because it distorts the two-party framework just described) was the appearance of political players who adopted a proportionalist strategy outside the alliance-forming logic, taking part in the majoritarian contest *uti singoli*. Some of these aimed simply at highlighting their importance for their coalition partners and showing how they held the alliance's fate in their hands (this was the case of Pannella's *Riformatori* and, in seven regions out of fifteen, of

Rifondazione Comunista); others sought instead to distinguish themselves from the two new coalitions and play a waiting game (the case of the *Lega* and of the *Popolari* in Marche and Campania).

The different coalitions on offer for the local councils and provinces (supporting the mayoral candidates and provincial presidents) were more varied than those at the regional level.[8] The reasons for this can be found in a series of factors: the specificity of local political conditions; the personalization inherent in single-office elections; the mechanism of the double round, which promised to transform the eventual presence of a double coalition candidacy into a sort of primary area election. The agreements made by the parties at the regional level appear, however, to have "disciplined," at least in part, the municipal and provincial coalitional supply. These lower levels were for the most part respectful of choices made at a higher level.[9]

The innovations emerging from the three different types of consultation as regards the electoral alliances and their make-up were dependent, as can be seen by running down the list of parties taking part in the proportional contest, on an identity change of some of the single players.

The main transformations came in the Center. Just a few weeks before the vote, the PPI split. This crisis, which signalled the end—even if perhaps only momentary—of a central *Polo*, arose from rifts within the party as to which alliance and coalition partners the movement should look to. Rocco Buttiglione's opening towards *Forza Italia* and his readiness to find an accord with the Right led by Fini (described as "democratic" by the secretary of the PPI after the Congress in Fiuggi where AN finally took over from the MSI) encountered unsurmountable resistance from the Left of the party, which instead favored an agreement with the PDS. The clashes which followed triggered older and deeper internal disagreements, leading to a break-up. The *Popolari* of Buttiglione reached an understanding with *Forza Italia* to present common lists for the proportional vote and to stand with the Center-Right coalition (with CCD and AN) for the majority vote. The *Popolari* of Gerardo Bianco, who was elected by a somewhat controversial procedure as new secretary of the PPI, decided to run alone in the proportional vote, standing with the Center-Left alliance for the majority vote.[10]

One month before the vote, the *Patto dei democratici* was formed, encompassing *Patto Segni, Alleanza Democratica* and the *Socialisti Italiani*. The aim of the operation was to help the small parties of the Center-Left coalesce, a process that had already got under way in Parliament. In the proportional vote, finally, the CCD ran with its own list, hoping in this way to claim a more autonomous position within the Center-Right coalition.

The new coalitions and party political innovations that emerged allow us to point up two final, important aspects of the electoral forces present on April 23.

The first element is the inversion of the trend towards the "de-party-ization" at elections which had been a feature of the administrative elections of 1993 and 1994 when civic and municipal movements had predominated with their own lists in some large urban centers.[11] This phenomenon may simply indicate the impact of the regional elections, which had been made more political and national, on local ones. But we can also find evidence to support the idea of a "return of the parties" as described above with regard to the characteristics (and objectives) of the new regional electoral law.

The second conclusion which can be drawn from the electoral land-scape of April 23 is more specific and concerns the intra-coalition rela-tions among the parties of the two alliances. In this regard, the compo-sition of the regional majoritarian lists—and the selection of the heads of those lists, or rather the coalition candidates for the presidency of the regional council—offer some important indications. Thanks to the char-acteristics of the new regional election system, this point was not as crucial as the intra-coalition negotiations on the distribution of single seat constituencies for the Chamber of Deputies and Senate and on the selection of candidates in 1994.[12] Nevertheless, some points for analysis and comparison can be drawn from it.

In Table 2.1 (for the Center-Left) and Table 2.2 (for the Center-Right) the division of the candidates in the regional majoritarian lists is given by coalition party and region and is grouped by geopolitical area (the North without Emilia-Romagna, the "red zone," and the South including Lazio).

In the Center-Left coalition—which, as in 1994, selected its own can-didates at regional negotiating "tables," keeping the intervention of central offices to a minimum—there emerged alongside the PDS a strong presence of the *Popolari*, whose support was evidently recognized as being strategically important for the result. Though their electoral weight (proportionally) turned out to be around a quarter of that of the PDS, the *Popolari* of Bianco assured themselves a much-more-than-propor-tional number of candidates in the regional majority lists and the can-didacy to the presidency of five regions (against the four of the PDS), to which we must also add those of the RAI TV journalist Piero Badaloni and the former leftist DC sympathiser, Luigi Ferrara. Both were area list heads for the PPI, in Lazio and Puglia respectively. Less significant was the presence of the *Patto dei democratici* which, while securing leadership of the coalition in Lombardia (Masi for the *Patto Segni*) and in Molise (Veneziale for AD), was numerically less successful than AD and PSI had been in the progressive coalition of 1994.

TABLE 2.1 Regional Elections of the April 23, 1995. Center-Left Regional Candidates: Party Membership

Region	RC	PDS	Verdi	Rete	CS	Fed. lab.	PSDI	PRI	Demo-cratici	Popo-lari	Indep.	Tot.
Piedmont	no	4	1	-	-	-	-	-	3	3	1*	12
Lombardy	no	6	2	-	-	1	-	1	1*	5	-	16
Veneto	no	3	1	-	-	1	-	-	4	3*	-	12
Liguria	no	3	1	-	-	1	-	1	1	1*	-	8
North	no	16	5	-	-	3	-	2	9	12	1	48
%		33.3	10.5	-	-	6.25	-	4.2	18.7	25.0	2.1	100
EmiliaRomagna	no	4*	1	-	-	-	-	-	2	3	-	10
Tuscany	no	4*	1	-	-	1	-	-	3	1	-	10
Umbria	1	4*	-	-	-	-	-	-	-	1	-	6
Marche	1	2	2	-	-	-	-	1	1	no	1*	8
Red zone	2	14	4	-	-	1	-	1	6	5	1	34
%	5.9	41.2	11.8	-	-	2.9	-	2.9	17.7	14.7	2.9	100
Lazio	1	1	1	-	-	1	1	1	1	-	5*	12
Abruzzi	1	3	1	-	-	-	-	-	1	2*	-	8
Molise	-	-	-	-	-	-	-	-	1*	3	2	6
Campania	2	5*	1	1	-	1	-	-	2	-	-	12
Puglia	1	1	1	-	-	-	-	-	-	1	8*	12
Basilicata	no	1	-	-	1	1	-	-	1	2*	-	6
Calabria	no	3	-	-	2	-	no	no	1	2*	-	8
South	5	14	4	1	3	3	1	1	7	10	15	64
%	7.8	21.9	6.2	1.6	4.7	4.7	1.6	1.6	10.9	15.6	23.4	100
Italy	7	44	13	1	3	7	1	4	22	27	17	146
%	4.8	30.1	8.9	0.7	2.1	4.8	0.7	2.7	15.1	18.5	11.6	100
Candidates for president	-	4	-	-	-	-	-	-	2	5	4	15

Source: Our own elaboration of data supplied by the PDS and PPI.

Notes: The regions in which the Center-Left obtained the majority bonus and the government of the region are written in italics. An asterisk marks the party membership of candidates for regional president. The four candidates for regional president indicated as independent were loosely tied to the PPI in the case of Lazio and Puglia, to the Center-Left (*Ulivo*-PDS) in the case of Marche and with no definite ties in the case of Piedmont. As for the other independent candidates, in three cases these were left-wing independents linked to the PDS (two in Molise and one in Lazio), in nine cases were Catholic independents from the CISL-PPI area (three in Lazio and six in Puglia) and in one case was an independent with no definite ties (again in Puglia). Of the 22 democratic candidates, five were in the *Patto Segni*, eight from *Alleanza Democratica*, six were *Socialisti Italiani* and three were identified as from the *Patto dei Democratici*. A "no" indicates that the party was not part of a coalition and was present with its own regional list.

Though penalized by the policy of the Center-Left's "opening to the Center," which in many regions meant it was excluded from the coalition, RC (where it took part) repeated its showing of 1994, winning roughly 13 percent of available candidacies. In the end it was the PDS which saw its already "sacrificed" presence vis à vis 1994 cut back as it yielded space especially in Southern regions (except Campania) and mostly in favor of the *Popolari*. On this occasion, however, there were no serious repercussions for the PDS (either internally or in terms of seats) precisely because of the prevalently proportional nature of the electoral system which ensured it a dominant position in the coalition (even if conditioned by its numerous and, at times, noisy allies).

The ex-Christian Democratic component also played an influential role in the Center-Right coalition which, like the Center-Left, nominated its majoritarian candidacies in line with the criteria adopted in 1994, i.e. via regional negotiations guided by central party direction. The CCD drew particular advantage from this, doubling its presence within the coalition vis à vis the political elections of 1994. *Alleanza Nazionale* seems to have sacrificed itself to a small extent, playing once more the moderate card and leaving the initiative to *Forza Italia* to which it played a "support" role. The weight of Fini's party within the coalition fell with respect to 1994, even in the regions where it is most firmly rooted. In the South, from control of over half the single-seat candidacies in the *Polo del Buon Governo*, AN had to make do with fewer than a third of the candidacies in the regional majority lists of the Center-Right). Moreover, only one position as *capolista* was allocated the Right, in Campania. With the spring vote, however, AN extended its coalition influence across the whole of the national territory despite its obtaining no more than a quarter of coalition candidacies in Northern regions. It was *Forza Italia* which, at least on paper, posted the best results with more than a third of coalition candidates and a total of eight *capolista* positions. The persistent local inconsistencies of Berlusconi's movement, however, meant that such a presence was not always reliable or significant.

The Majoritarian Contest:
Light and Shade in the Center-Left's Success

The spring vote gave a mandate to the Center-Left to govern most regions, provinces, and councils in the coming years. The Center-Left did in fact win 9 regions out of 15, 56 provinces out of 76 and 205 councils with over 15,000 inhabitants out of 282 (including 31 of the 35 provincial capitals where elections were held).

Against this background, the biggest surprise was the results in the regional elections. On the eve of voting, not many people would have bet on the Center-Left to come through in a vote which had been billed as having general political importance. But to what extent, beyond the

TABLE 2.2 Regional Elections of April 23, 1995. Center-Right Regional Candidates: Party Membership

Region	Forza Italia	Popolari	CCD	AN	Others	Total
Piedmont	4*	2	2	3	1	12
Lombardy	8	1*	1	4	2	16
Veneto	6*	2	1	3	-	12
Liguria	3*	1	1	2	1	8
North	21	6	5	12	4	48
%	43.8	12.5	10.4	25.0	8.3	100
Emilia-Romagna	3	1	2*	3	1	10
Tuscany	2*	2	1	3	2	10
Umbria	2*	1	1	2	-	6
Marche	3	1*	1	3	-	8
Red zone	10	5	5	11	3	34
%	29.4	14.7	14.7	32.4	8.8	100
Lazio	3	2	2	4	1*	12
Abruzzi	3	1	1	2	1*	8
Molise	1*	1	1	2	1	6
Campania	5	1	3	3*	-	12
Puglia	3	3	3	3	2*	12
Basilicata	2*	1	1	2	-	6
Calabria	2*	2	1	3	-	8
South	19	11	10	19	5	64
%	29.7	17.2	15.6	29.7	7.8	100
Italy	50	22	20	42	12	146
%	34.2	15.1	13.7	28.8	8.2	100
Candidates for president	8	2	1	1	3	15

Source: Our own elaboration of data supplied by the Electoral office of *Alleanza Nazionale*, *Forza Italia*'s Territorial coordination office and the Organization office of the CDU.

Notes: The regions in which the Center-Right obtained the majority bonus and the government of the region are in italics. An asterix indicates the party membership of the candidate for the regional presidency.

unexpected number of regional governments won, can we talk of a real Center-Left success?

The verdict of the ballot box was, in reality, a lot less clearcut than it may seem at first sight. Not only was the destiny of three of the regions won by the Center-Left—Lazio, Abruzzo and Molise—decided by a total of just 15,204 votes in total, but, as can be seen from Table 2.3, the margin between the two coalitions in the majority vote was just 126,000 votes - equal to less than half a percentage point. And it was in point of fact the Center-Right which won that half point extra by coming out on top in the demographically larger regions.

This does not mean that the regional vote did not change the electoral alignments of March 1994 and reroute slightly the difficult Italian transition.[13] The accord between the Left and the Center (or rather, a large part of it) did in fact lead to a substantial shift in the equilibrium between the two (new) coalitions. Though somewhat crowded with twelve partners and politically and ideologically heterogeneous, the Center-Left alliance showed it was capable of winning majoritarian elections.

Two elements could, however, put this undeniable success of the Center-Left into a different perspective, throwing the whole argument about the shift in equilibrium between the coalitions into a different light and explaining the regional vote as nothing more than the unfolding of a more uncertain situation.

The first element is the comparison between majoritarian and proportional voting shown in Table 2.3 from which three important points emerge: in the proportional vote, the Center-Left obtained, overall, almost half a million votes more than the Center-Right; the Center-Right therefore, as in the parliamentary elections of 1994, would seem once again to have done better (comparatively) than the Center-Left in the majoritarian versus proportional vote.[14] On this occasion however, the point is, at least in part, controversial because of the consistent and surprising difference between the number of votes cast in the two systems (the three million ballots where the voter preferred to express only a majoritarian vote).[15] A second element also gives rise to reservations surrounding the showing of the Center-Left, notably certain specific conditions of the regional vote which for the winning coalition seem to translate into actual competitive advantages (significant, though not repeatable in a general election). The first of these advantages is the actual electoral system itself, which, being mostly proportional, helped temper conflict in the coalitions, more marked—as already confirmed by the experience of the progressive coalition in March, 1994—in the more crowded coalition. A second factor is the level of voter turnout. With respect to the parliamentary elections of 1994, the turnout at the ballot box went from 87.7 percent to 81.3 percent (equivalent to two and half million fewer voters: see Table 2.7 in the paragraph below). Being able to count on a higher overall number of candidates than the Center-Right and, perhaps, being able to draw greater advantage from a marked contrast between alternative coalitions, means it is plausible that the Center-Left mobilized its own electoral base more effectively than the

TABLE 2.3 Regional Elections of April 23, 1995. Comparison of Majority and Proportional Vote

	Majority			Proportional		
	Votes	*%*	*Seats*	*Votes*	*%*	*Seats*
Center-Right	12,226,172	41.6	72			
Forza Italia-						
Polo Popolare				5,875,260	22.3	150
AN				3,722,382	14.1	92
CCD				1,104,022	4.2	26
AN-U.Umbra-CPA				84,065	0.3	5
Total				10,785,729	40.9	273
Center-Left	12,100,240	41.2	68			
PDS				6,470,445	24.6	164
RC				885,066	3.4	24
Verdi				780,712	3.0	15
Progressisti				205,734	0.8	8
Popolari				1,308,895	5.0	33
Democratici				911,308	3.5	23
Popolari-Democratici				187,171	0.7	3
Popolari-Democratici-Liberali				135,895	0.5	2
PRI				130,005	0.5	3
Laburisti				94,222	0.4	3
PSDI-Laburisti-PRI				119,805	0.4	1
Lega North				15,049	-	-
Lega Italiana Federale				24,530	0.1	-
Total				11,268,837	42.9	279
Rifondazione comunista	1,632,809	5.6	-			
RC				1,319,838	5.0	25
Popolari	297,563	1.0	-			
Popolari				271,614	1.0	6
Lega North	1,932,053	6.6	-			
Lega North				1,672,150	6.4	29
Pannella-Riformatori	557,050	1.9	-			
Pannella-Riformatori				357,249	1.4	-
MS-Tricolore	151,940	0.5	-			
MS-Tricolore				107,201	0.4	-
Others	468,120	1.6	-			
Others				540,698	2.1	5
Total	29,365,947	100.0	140	26,323,316	100.0	617

Source: Calculated from data provided by Ministero dell'Interno - Direzione centrale per i servizi elettorali.

Center-Right. Thirdly, and finally, the holding of local and provincial elections contemporaneously most likely played in the Center-Left's favor, given that the Left has traditionally performed better in more local elections.

From this we may infer that, on the one hand, the voters who abstained are for the most part moderate voters, oriented probably more towards the Center-Right than to the Center-Left and, on the other, that in such conditions, breaking through the threshold of 40 percent of votes was a positive result for the Center-Right coalition (especially if one considers that the Center-Right did not boast any advantages and if anything was seriously handicapped by the tough rules regarding the use of TV and radio in electoral campaigning as laid down by the decree on the *par condicio*).

Before moving on to examine the vote for mayors and provincial presidents, it is useful to turn our attention once more to the regional majoritarian vote in order to analyze some of its characteristics with reference to single cases.

Table 2.4 shows the percentage of votes obtained by the two coalitions, the seats won, the margin separating them, and the percentage polled by the third-placed candidates. In all the regions, the Center-Left and Center-Right are the only lists capable of competing for the majority bonus. The high concentration of votes for the two coalitions is indicative of a basically bipolar pattern to the contest, a consequence of the centrifugal effect of the majoritarian component of the new electoral mechanism. In none of the fifteen cases did the "third lists" constitute a competitor to be feared at all by the two coalitions, even if in Lombardy (the only region where the total votes for the Center-Left and Center-Right remained under 70 percent of the votes cast), in Veneto (the only region where candidates won with under 40 percent of votes) and in Piedmont, the *Lega* succeeded in taking votes away from the two major coalitions. The third-placed candidates appeared furthermore to act as strategic players who could have tipped the balance in the contest between the two coalitions in as many as six regions—the *Lega* in Piedmont, Lombardy and Veneto; *Rifondazione Comunista* in Calabria; the *Lista Pannella Riformatori* in Lazio; the *Movimento Sociale Fiamma Tricolore* (Rauti's secessionist formation) in Abruzzo—where they could have overturned the result by allying themselves with the losing coalition (in four cases out of six favoring the Center-Left).

The Center-Right did not win once by an absolute majority. The Center-Left did so in six cases out of nine (and in five of them, the regions in the "red zone" plus Basilicata, with a margin between 12 and 22 points). In some regions this different way of winning triggered the mechanism which increased or reduced the bonus awarded by the electoral system. The Center-Right took most advantage of the former. In four out of six regions captured by the Center-Right coalition, the majority bonus of 20 percent was not, in fact, sufficient to guarantee the winning coalition the number of overall seats laid down by the electoral law (60 percent in Lombardy, Puglia and Calabria, where the Center-Right won with more than 40 percent of the votes; 55 percent in Veneto where it won with less than 40 percent). The mechanism reducing the majority bonus (by half) was, however, triggered, to the detriment of the Center-Left, in Umbria and Basilicata, where the winning coalition netted an absolute majority on the regional council with the proportional seats only.

At a local and provincial level, the good performance of the Center-Left in the majoritarian vote was clearer. While in the previous elections based on the new electoral system the Left had done conspicuously well in the contests for mayor and provincial president, on this occasion the Center-Left did even better.[16]

TABLE 2.4 Regional Elections of April 23, 1995. Majority Vote by Region (Percentage Values out of Valid Votes)

	Center-Right		Center-Left		Third-placed List		
	%	seats	%	seats	Δ	%	
Piedmont	39.7	12[+10]	35.2	-	4.5	11.1	[Lega]
Lombardy	41.6	26[+4]	27.6	-	14.0	17.7	[Lega]
Veneto	38.2	16	32.3	-	5.9	17.5	[Lega]
Liguria	38.0	-	42.4	13[+5]	4.4	8.6	[RC]
Emilia-Romagna	32.0	-	53.8	10	21.8	8.8	[RC]
Tuscany	36.1	-	50.1	10	14.0	12.4	[RC]
Umbria	39.0	-	59.9	3[-3]	20.9	1.1	[Lista Pannella]
Marche	38.9	-	51.6	8	12.7	6.4 [Popolari]	
Lazio	48.0	-	48.1	15[+3]	0.1	2.2	[Lista Pannella]
Abruzzo	47.2	-	48.2	8	1.0	2.5	[MS-Tricolore]
Molise	49.5	-	50.5	6	1.0	-	
Campania	47.9	12	39.3	-	8.6	8.1 [Popolari]	
Puglia	49.8	15[+3]	45.8	-	4.0	2.2[Lega d'az. meridionale]	
Basilicata	36.6	-	54.8	3[-3]	18.2	6.4	[RC]
Calabria	44.2	10[+2]	38.0	-	6.2	9.6	[RC]

Source: Calculated from data provided by Ministero dell'Interno - Direzione centrale per i servizi elettorali.

The new coalition succeeded, first of all, in having a significant number of candidates elected during the first round (see Table 2.5a). In the second place, the Center-Left's candidates performed well in the second round of voting. As can be seen in Table 2.5b, these were elected in over 85 percent of cases in the provinces and capital-town comuni and in just under 80 percent of cases in smaller centers, i.e. with a better performance rate than that of the left-wing candidates in the administrative elections of 1993 and 1994 (calculated, moreover, on a more modest number of cases). In the third place, the Center-Left coalitions supporting the candidacies in question presented a front which excluded for the main part *Rifondazione Comunista*. In cases where RC was an integral part of the coalition (from the first round or after joining the coalition between the first and the second round), the Center-Left performed slightly worse in the provinces and local councils (but apparently slightly better in the smaller centers). A fourth important aspect of the Center-Left's success in the majoritarian vote at a municipal and provincial level was its relative geographical homogeneity. Surprisingly, the candidates of the Center-Left did better in the provinces and local councils of the North than in those in the South, where they were defeated by the Center-Right candidates on only a few occasions.

The performance of the moderate party candidates in the provinces and *comuni* was therefore fairly mediocre. The Center-Right won eight out of 76 provinces, four out of 35 provincial capitals and 22 out of 247 smaller centres, concentrated mostly in tradition MSI strongholds in Lazio and Puglia.

How can we explain the result of the majoritarian vote in the provinces and local councils? It is possible to distinguish three main reasons for the Center-Left's success over and above the local factors which obviously played a crucial role in the elections.

The first reason is probably the quality of the candidates. The Center-Left knew how to make better use of this factor than the Center-Right, relying in some cases on the experience of tried and tested *uscenti* (outgoing councillors) and managing in others to put up—especially at a municipal level and in particular in the larger local councils—candidates rooted in city life who represented civil society more than they did the party apparatus. In this regard, the Center-Right proved to be less able, handicapped as it was by the limited number of local personalities it had at its disposal and by its recourse, in lieu of anything better, to members of the old parties (which was the case with MSI candidates, "professionalized" perhaps but generally exercising little appeal, or else with politicians from the old guard "recycled" via *Forza Italia-Polo Popolare* or the CCD).

The second reason is undoubtedly the different degree to which the two coalitions were territorially rooted. In this regard, the Center-Left enjoyed a clearly advantageous position thanks to the organizational resources of the PDS and the presence in its ranks of the PPI which, though much weakened vis à vis its Christian Democratic past, was nevertheless a far from negligible force. The Center-Right paid a price for the organizational evanescence of *Forza Italia*, the very limited geographical presence (certain areas of Campania and Puglia) of the CCD, and the problems experienced locally by AN in breaking into areas outside old MSI strongholds.

Finally, by way of a third explanation, there was the defection of the *Lega* from the Center-Right coalition. Although AN performed well in the North in the proportional vote and the *Lega* suffered a general decline, the new make-up of the alliances seemed to sensibly weaken the competitiveness of the Center-Right in Northern local councils and provinces. Despite the drop in votes for the *Lega*, it nevertheless captured the presidency of nine of the 27 provinces called to the ballot box in the North and won many of the few second round votes it was involved in by allying itself with the PPI and the other *cespugli* of the Center-Left (see Table 2.5b).

TABLE 2.5a Local and Provincial Elections of April 23, 1995. Provincial Presidents and Mayors Elected in the First Round

	Provinces	*Provincial Capitals*	*Local Councils (not Capitals)*
(no.)	(22)	(11)	(87)
Left			7
Center-Left (with RC)	6	2	21
Center-Left (without RC)	14	8	49
Center-Left Total	20	10	70
Lega/Center-Left (without RC)			1
Lega/Center-Left (without PDS)			1
Lega/Center-Left Total			2
Center			5
Center-Right	2	1	2
Civic Lists			1

Source: Calculated from data provided by Ministero dell'Interno - Direzione centrale per i servizi elettorali.

TABLE 2.5b Local and Provincial Elections of May 7, 1995. The "Field" of Candidates in Second-Round Balloting

	Provinces			Provincial Capitals			Local Councils (not Capitals)		
	2nd Round	Elected	%	2nd Round	Elected	%	2nd Round	Elected	%
(no.)		(54)			(24)			(160)	
Left							27	19	70.4
Center-Left (with RC)	14	11		7	6		26	21	
Center-Left (without RC)	28	25		16	14		75	58	
Center-Left Total	42	36	85.7	23	20	87.0	101	79	78.2
Lega/Center-Left (without RC)	1	1					1	1	
Lega/Center-Left (without PDS)	7	7		1	1		12	8	
Lega/Center-Left Total	8	8	100.0	1	1	100.0	13	9	69.2
Lega	1	1					7	6	
"Cespugli" (without PDS)							18	11	
Center				1	1		24	11	
Center Total	1	1	100.0	1	1	100.0	49	28	58.3
Center-Right	52	6		21	3		104	16	
Center-Right (without AN)	2	-		2	-		11	2	
AN-CCD							2	1	
AN							3	1	
Center-Right Total	54	6	11.1	23	3	13.0	120	20	16.6
Local/Civic Lists	3	3	100				10	5	50

Source: Calculated from data provided by Ministero dell'Interno - Direzione centrale per i servizi elettorali.

The Party Vote: Continuities and New Developments

The differences between the various types of election observed so far in reference to the majoritarian contest, are confirmed in the proportional vote, i.e. the vote cast by electors for the party lists in order to elect

TABLE 2.6 Regional and Local Elections of April 23, 1995. Party Vote in Regional, Provincial and Local Elections (Percentage Values out of Valid Votes)

	Regional	Provincial	Local (Capitals)	Local (not Capitals)	Local (majority system)
(no.)	(15)	(76)	(35)	(241)	(4.841)
RC	8.4	8.6	7.1	7.4	1.4
PDS	24.6	22.2	22.2	20.9	0.8
Verdi	3.0	2.8	2.8	2.1	
Popolari	6.0	6.2	4.5	3.5	2.0
"Cespugli"	6.0	5.7	4.9	3.9	0.1
Center-Left		0.4	6.7	8.3	31.1
Left	0.8	0.7	0.7	5.7	
(Center-Left)	(48.8)	(46.6)	(48.9)	(49.7)	(41.1)
FI-Polo Popolare	22.3	16.7	3.3	6.0	
AN	14.4	13.1	12.0	7.9	0.9
CCD	4.2	3.1	2.1	2.7	0.2
UDC		0.1		0.2	
Pannella-Riformatori	1.4	1.4	1.0	0.3	
Polo		2.8	11.0	6.8	0.6
Center-Right		0.4	4.6	4.7	12.2
Right				0.1	0.2
(Center-Right)	(42.3)	(37.6)	(34.0)	(28.7)	(14.1)
Lega	6.4	6.6	2.9	4.1	3.7
PPI		3.1	2.9	3.0	
Center		0.2	0.6	8.8	20.7
Other Leagues	0.6	1.5			
Civic Lists		0.8	7.2	4.9	20.4
Other Lists	1.9	3.6	0.9	0.8	

Source: Calculated from data provided by Ministero dell'Interno - Direzione centrale per i servizi elettorali.

regional, provincial and local councillors. Table 2.6 gives a breakdown of the situation. Some useful pointers can be drawn from these data even if the information is only partially comparable, based as it is on areas that are not homogeneous.

The Table 2.6 highlights, above all, the absence of large parties and the presence, instead, of medium and small-sized groups. Despite the trend towards bi-polarization in the majoritarian contest, the party system maintained a low profile owing to the peculiarities of the new electoral systems and the propensity of single political players to "proportionalize" the majority vote (the first two parties together polled less than 50 percent of the votes cast and the first four did not reach 70 percent). In this setting of two coalitions and many parties, the PDS was the most voted party in every kind of election (as well as being the majority party in 10 Regions out of 15 and in 40 of the 61 provinces in which it was present). It captured roughly two-thirds of the votes for the Center-Left alliance (half, in coalitions with *Rifondazione*) and provided the backbone for most of the coalition lists in the small local councils. Its (many) allies—the *cespugli* which had grown from the ashes of the traditional parties of government during the previous two years—were confirmed as being electorally very weak. They continued, however, to be decisive for the fate of the alliance, as much for their high coalition potential and the center-ground position of their electorate as for the fact that the new electoral law has helped ensure their institutional survival at a regional level.

On the opposing front, *Forza Italia* was head to head with the PDS, presenting lists together with Buttiglione's *Popolari* and netting 22.3 percent of the votes cast at the regional elections. The party's weak grass-roots structure, however, did not allow Berlusconi's movement to do so well in the provinces and it performed worse still in local councils.

The result obtained by AN in the Center-Right coalition was much less uneven. The party of Gianfranco Fini, remaining below the 15 percent mark, did however record a worse than expected result mainly because of the general drop in support in the South which almost entirely canceled out its gains in the North. The CCD, on the other hand, did well, managing to get more than 4 percent of the votes at the regional elections, a critical threshold in that it entitled the party to take part in the allocation of proportional seats in the Lower House - thus giving it a more autonomous position within the coalition.

In all the different kinds of election, finally, the proportional vote confirmed the overall supremacy of the Center-Left versus the Center-Right - with a margin which increases as the vote becomes more localized, a result which is in line with the trend already seen in the majoritarian vote.

Other indicators regarding changes in the balance of power between the political parties can be drawn from a comparison between the regional proportional vote of 1995 and the proportional vote for the Chamber of Deputies of 1994 as shown in Table 2.7. In this regard, it is useful to carefully consider absolute values as well as percentage values, allowing us to take account of the relative importance of abstentionism in the two elections. As on other occasions in the past, the abstentionism effect seems to be an advantage for parties that are better able to mobize supporters. This was the case with *Rifondazione Comunista*, which captured the same number of votes it had polled in 1994, with a consequent percentage rise of almost two points, and of the PDS, which lost only about 400,000 votes vis à vis 1994, compared to the more than a million votes lost by *Forza Italia*.[17]

The party that suffered the heaviest losses with respect to 1994 was the *Lega*, losing 45 percent of its 1994 proportional vote. Despite this, it remained a strategic player in many areas (and single-seat constituencies) of the North. There was also a sharp drop in support for the *cespugli*, which on the eve of the regional vote had promoted the formation of the Center-Left coalitions, proposing former IRI chairman Romano Prodi as possible coalition candidate for the office of Prime Minister. The parties gathered under the *Patto dei democratici*, for example, dropped from two and a half million to little more than a million votes.

TABLE 2.7 The Proportional Vote for the Parties: Comparison of Parliamentary Elections 1994 and Regional Elections 1995

	Chamber of Deputies 1994		*Regional Elections 1995*	
	votes	%	*votes*	%
RC	2,205,316	6.6	2,204,904	8.4
PDS	7,042,391	21.2	6,470,445	24.6
Verdi	938,047	2.8	780,712	3.0
Progressisti			205,734	0.8
Rete	375,534	1.1		
Rinascita Socialista	10,070			
Fed. Laburista			94,222	0.4
Labur.-PSDI-PRI			119,805	0.4
PSI	712,007	2.1		
AD	418,033	1.3		
Patto Segni	1,455,603	4.4		
Patto Democratici			911,308	3.5
Popolari	3,726,231	11.2	1,580,509	6.0
Popolari+Patto Dem.			187,171	0.7
Pop+Patto Dem.+Liberali			135,895	0.5
PRI			130,005	0.5
CCD			1,104,022	4.2
Forza Italia	6,632,834	20.0	5,875,260	22.3
Pannella-Riform.	1,191,221	3.6	357,429	1.4
Socialdemocrazia	155,722	0.5	20,892	0.1
PSR-Sin. Lib.			23,866	0.1
Lega	3,037,426	9.1	1,687,199	6.4
AN	4,500,454	13.6	3,722,382	14.1
AN-U.Umbria-CPA			84,065	0.3
MS-Fiamma tricolore			107,201	0.4
Other Leagues	330,771	1.0	162,385	0.6
Others	499,057	1.5	358,085	1.3
Valid Votes	33,230,717	93.0	26,323,316	79.1
Voters	35,721,717	87.7	33,275,391	81.3
Electors	40,754,183		40,950,831	

Source: Calculated from data provided by Ministero dell'Interno - Direzione centrale per i servizi elettorali.

The fall in support for the *Popolari* is of the same order of magnitude. The drop from the over three and a half million votes the PPI netted in 1994 to the million and a half won by Bianco's *Popolari* in 1995, however, merits further comment. In the first place, it should be remembered that a large part of the moderate vote which in the general elections of March 1994 had chosen the PPI had already moved across into the ranks of the Center-Right (and mostly of *Forza Italia*) by the time of the European elections of the following June. Second, if we compare 1994 and 1995 by referring to single regional cases, a rather differentiated picture emerges. In five Regions (Veneto, Liguria, Molise, Basilicata and Calabria) the share of votes obtained in the regional elections of 1995 is only slightly less (by a few points) than that garnered in the 1994 parliamentary elections (instead of by half as in the national average). In four of these regions—in two of which the Center-Left then won the regional government—the PPI also held the leadership of the coalition and obtained more than 10 percent of the proportional seats. For Bianco's party this was, all things considered, not such a negative result as it might at first seem. The PPI managed to consolidate an organized peripheral presence which was also confirmed by the results obtained in the provincial and local elections.

It is less straightforward to work out the support obtained by Buttiglione's *Popolari* which in the proportional vote did not present their own lists, but, as in a renewed *Patto Gentiloni*, inserted their candidates in the lists of *Forza Italia*.[18] Table 2.8 presents a picture of the party affiliations of candidates and those elected in *Forza Italia-Popolari* lists by proportional vote for each region. While it is not possible to resolve the question of the electoral strength of the two parties, significant conclusions can be drawn regarding their political relations. Using the preference vote to their own advantage (by mobilizing pre-existing support) Buttiglione's *Popolari* managed to win a far-from-negligible number of seats—more than proportional, one might say, to their actual share of votes. In fact, by lending their own peripheral organizational network to *Forza Italia*, they ended up colonizing its lists—at least in part. Thanks to a success rate of over 40 percent (in Lombardy they had nine candidates out of nine elected, in Veneto seven out of seven, in Molise four out of five and in almost every case as the first-placed among those elected), Buttiglione's *Popolari* won almost 35 percent of the coalition seats, though with little more than 20 percent of the candidates (see Table 2.8). This represents almost 9 percent of the proportional seats and over 8 percent of the total number of seats, or between ten and fifteen seats more than those won by the *Popolari* of Bianco.

TABLE 2.8 Regional elections of April 23, 1995, proportional vote. Candidates presented and elected members in *Forza Italia-Polo popolare* lists - by component

	Popolari (Buttiglione)			Forza Italia			Others		
	presented	elected	%	presented	elected	%	presented	elected	%
Piedmont	8	3		30	10		10	1	
Lombardy	9	9		50	18		5	1	
Veneto	7	7		38	9		1	-	
Liguria	5	2		18	7		8	1	
NORTH	29	21	72.4	136	44	32.4	24	3	12.5
Emilia-Romagna	5	2		26	4		9	1	
Tuscany	11	4		23	3		5	-	
Umbria	6	4		16	3		2	-	
Marche	11	3		17	2		4	1	10.0
RED ZONE	33	3	39.3	82	12	17.6	20	2	
Lazio	10	1		34	9		4	9	
Abruzzi	12	1		19	5		1	1	
Molise	5	4		17	1		2	-	
Campania	10	3		35	7		3	-	
Puglia	10	5		24	6		14	-	
Basilicata	7	3		13	2		4	-	
Calabria	9	3		19	3		4	1	
SOUTH	63	20	31.7	161	33	20.5	3211	34.4	
ITALY	125	54	43.2	379	89	23.5	76	16	21.1
%	21.6	33.9		65.3	56.0		13.1	10.1	

Source: Our own elaboration of official data and data supplied by *Forza Italia* and *Cristiani Democratici Uniti.*

Conclusions: Another Stage in the Transition

From what has emerged above we have seen that the local and regional vote of April-May, 1995 represents a new stage in the Italian transition.

As in all the elections of recent years, on this occasion too there was an enormous turnover of the political class. At the regional level, for example, the new councillors elected accounted for 74.5 percent of the total, a turnover higher than that recorded among deputies and senators elected in 1994.[19] In the Region with the highest turnover (Abruzzo), new councillors represented over 90 percent of the total (from the old council only three councillors out of 40 survived), in the Region with the highest degree of continuity (Tuscany) the percentage was 58 percent. Only three incumbent regional presidents were reelected (in Liguria, Emilia-Romagna and Tuscany). On the party political front, of the 193 reelected councillors, a third were from the PDS and another third were ex-Christian Democrats divided equally between the *Popolari* of Bianco and Buttiglione.

The new regional electoral system, on its first application, "manufactured" new majorities, ensuring governmental stability for the Italian regions. The same can be said for the provinces and local councils which were called to the ballot box and where new presidents and mayors were elected. The majoritarian electoral system (regional and local) shunted party politics and the interplay between the political players towards bipolarization. On the eve of the vote, the heirs of the old political Center surrendered to this logic and ended up by splitting over the question of what position to take in the new political landscape. The vote triggered a contest between Center-Left and Center-Right that was rich in political implications, both general and national.

The Center-Left managed to capture the great majority of positions at stake, though not without causing a certain amount of surprise. Its supremacy was most evident where the vote was more localized (in the municipal and provincial elections), being more modest regionally. This phenomenon confirms, on the one hand, the hypothesis that the electorate was more sensitized to what was on offer politically and the stakes being played for in the single electoral constituencies; on the other, it seems to point up a fundamental fact: the different performances of the two coalitions nationally and locally. As we have seen, two main factors are at play in this relation: the level of electoral turnout and the differing degrees to which the parties in the two coalitions are rooted territorially. If, then, the accord between the Left and a part of the Center reshaped, at least partially, the balance of power between the coalitions, we must keep in mind that the new Center-Left coalition—a little like the Left in the administrative elections of 1993—enjoyed certain advantageous conditions which, in large part, are not easily repeatable (especially in general elections).

The bipolarism that emerged from the majoritarian contest, made "imperfect" by the presence of forces that rejected the binary logic of the vote—for example the Northern League, which however came out of the elections in worse shape—was accompanied by the survival of a fairly well articulated party-political pluralism. This is a second, more noticeable "imperfection" in the new twoparty order and one that risks undermining the cohesion of the two coalitions and in particular that of the most crowded and ideologically composite, i.e. the Center-Left. In the future, it is likely that the two coalitions will continue to alternate periods of relative disunity with moments of cohesion in response to different kinds of conditions, from the electoral calendar to the climate in Parliament, from the strategic plans of single coalition members to the choices of those who, from institutional privilege or political weight, will be able to outlast the rest.

Translated by Timothy Cooper and Stephen Jewks

Notes

1. At the end of 1995, only the provincial councillors of Caserta and the councillors of roughly 300 (mostly smaller) local councils elected via the old electoral system remained in office. To these we may add the deputies from the Sicilian Regional Assembly elected in 1991. For the provinces and local councils, the elections of April, 1995 were less "general" than usual. Votes were cast in 77 provinces and 5,119 local councils (4,841 with under 15,000 inhabitants; 278, of which 35 provincial capitals, with over 15,000 inhabitants), while in 1990, 87 provinces and 6,367 local councils were called to the ballot box. The difference is due to the period of ingovernability of local and provincial administrations which forced the holding of numerous by-elections at the beginning of the Nineties.

2. It is useful to recall these and their results in the regional elections of 1990: DC (33.4 percent and 272 seats), PCI (24.0 percent and 182 seats), PSI (15.3 percent and 113 seats), MSI-DN (3.9 percent and 25 seats), PRI (3.6 percent and 21 seats), PSDI (2.8 percent and 21 seats), PLI (2.0 percent and 13 seats), *Lega Lombarda* (4.8 percent—equal to 18.9 percent in Lombardia, the only region where it was present—and 21 seats), other territorial leagues (1.2 percent, 6 seats), *Verdi* (5 percent and 28 seats, as a sum of the result obtained by *Liste verdi*, *Verdi arcobaleno* and *Liste verdi-Verdi arcobaleno*), *Democrazia Proletaria* (1.0 percent 4 seats), *Lista antiproibizionismo droga* (1.0 percent and 6 seats), *Caccia pesca e ambiente* (0.7 and 4 seats), *Partito dei pensionati* (0.5 percent and 3 seats).

3. The indication of the list head on the ballot paper is equivalent to a political commitment which the party or the parties tied to the regional list assume with the voters. However, this does not comport any connection of a formal or legal nature, since, according to article 122 of the Constitution, the election of the president (and members) of the regional council is the council's responsibility.

4. Not having passed the 3 percent barrier excluded the *Pannella-Riformatori* lists and *Movimento Sociale-Fiamma tricolore*, as well as many local lists, from the allocation of the district seats. Among the lists which failed to obtain 3 percent of the valid votes but which were able to gain some proportional representation thanks to their tie with a regional list which received more than 5 percent of the valid votes, were, in many regions, the CCD and the *Verdi*. There were also cases where district lists were excluded from power, even though tied to regional lists with more than 5 percent of the votes because they did not have the necessary total district quota (as was the case of the CCD and the *Verdi in Umbria*, of the

Verdi in Molise, and of the *Federazione dei laburisti* in no fewer than seven regions).

5. The magnitude of the bonus depends on three factors: the number of proportional seats delivered by the provincial lists tied to the winning regional list; the percentage of votes obtained by the winning regional list; the percentage of seats obtained overall by the winning regional list and by the provincial lists tied to it. More specifically: (a) if the provincial lists tied to the winning regional list deliver by themselves, or rather with the proportional seats alone, the absolute majority of seats on the regional council, then the bonus is halved and only 10 percent of the quota of majority seats are allocated to the winning regional list; (b) if the provincial lists tied to the winning regional list do not deliver the absolute majority of the seats on the regional council then the whole bonus, equal to 20 percent of the seats, is given to the regional list; (c) if with this bonus the party or parties tied to the winning regional list do not reach at least 55 percent of the seats on the council, the bonus is increased via the allocation of "extra seats," until 55 percent of the total number of seats on the council is reached (if the winning regional list does not exceed 40 percent of the valid votes) or 60 percent (if the winning regional list does exceed 40 percent of the valid votes).

6. The first definition is drawn from R. D'Alimonte, "La transizione italiana: il voto regionale del 23 Aprile", in *Rivista italiana di scienza politica*, 3, 1995, pp. 515-558. The others are my own. A still different type of electoral system is the one used for the election of president of the province and the provincial council which is intermediate between the system used in small local councils and in larger centers.

7. In this regard, when talking of the differences between the regional and parliamentary electoral systems, Roberto D'Alimonte reveals that, paradoxically, "a system where 80 percent of the seats are proportional is more majoritarian than one where 75 percent of the seats are majoritarian." *La transizione italiana: il voto regionale del 23 April*, cit., p. 531.

8. For example, in the North, An was isolated and presented its own candidates for the office of mayor or president of the province, or the *Lega* and *Popolari* made common cause in the name of a new central *polo*. In some administrations of the "red zone," instead, the *cespugli* presented their own candidates in competion with the PDS. In the South, it happened on more than one occasion that the *Polo*, especially in the zones most traditionally MSI or Christian Democratic, presented two or more candidacies, against the tendency of AN and the CCD to make common cause, or to each run on their own against the *Forza Italia-Polo Popolare* candidate.

9. The clearest example of this is the reproduction at local and provincial level of the position adopted by the center-left with regard to *Rifondazione Comunista* in the regions of the "red zone:" exclusion from the coalition in Tuscany and Emilia-Romagna; inclusion in the coalition in Umbria and Marche. This regularity is particularly evident in provincial capitals, less so in smaller centers.

10. The organizational break-up provoked by a division which took place just before the electoral test rendered the peripheral behavior of the *Popolari* not

always in agreement with the line adopted at a central level. Throughout the period of definition of the alliances, selection of candidates, and gathering of signatures necessary for candidacies, hypothesizing about the destiny of the PPI was really just guesswork.

11. For the data relative to the "departyization" of supply in the two administrative elections in 1993, cfr. A. Di Virgilio, "Elezioni locali e destrutturazione partitica. La nuova legge alla prova", in *Rivista italiana di scienza politica*, 1, 1994, pp. 107-165 (pp. 124-131).

12. The relative data may be found in A. Di Virgilio, "Dai partiti ai poli: la politica delle alleanze", in S. Bartolini e R. D'Alimonte, eds., *Maggioritario ma non troppo. Le elezioni politiche del 1994*, (Bologna: Il Mulino, 1995), pp. 177-232. See, also, O. Massari, "La selezione dei candidati", in G. Pasquino, ed., *L'alternanza inattesa. Le elezioni del 27 marzo 1994*, (Soveria Mannelli: Rubbettino), pp. 21-48.

13. The most significant change is without a doubt the passage from a majoritarian tripartite contest to a majoritarian bipartite one and the ability demonstrated by the center-left, at least on this occasion, in taking advantage of this fact.

14. The varying yield of the coalitions in the two arenas is examined by S. Bartolini e R. D'Alimonte, "La competizione maggioritaria: le origini elettorali del parlamento diviso", in S. Bartolini e R. D'Alimonte, eds., cit., pp. 317-372 in reference to the political elections of 1994, and by R. D'Alimonte, *La transizione italiana: il voto regionale del 23 April*, cit. in reference to the regional elections of 1995. The two authors explain this phenomenon by the difficulty that the Left (in 1994) and the Center-Left (in 1995) experienced in "summing" electorates which were ideologically distant and composite. In the case of the regional elections, the question is different since, because of the large difference between majoritarian and proportional votes, both coalitions have a positive balance in terms of majority votes.

15. The phenomenon is attributed by Roberto D'Alimonte to two main factors: "the fear of making a mistake," which induced many voters to simplify their vote, and the personalization induced by the majoritarian vote. See *La transizione italiana: il voto regionale del 23 April*, cit., p. 548.

16. For the data relative to the administrative elections of June and November, 1993 and June and November, 1994, see, respectively, A. Di Virgilio "Elezioni locali e destrutturazione partitica. La nuova legge alla prova", cit. and A. Di Virgilio, "Elezioni in Italia", in *Quaderni dell'Osservatorio elettorale*, 33, June 1995.

17. In the calculation of the differences, we must remember that in 1995 the PDS ran in Calabria together with the *Verdi* in the *Progressisti* list (which won little more than 200,000 votes, attributable in very large measure to D'Alema's party) and that in 1994 *Forza Italia* did not run in Puglia (where in 1995 Berlusconi's movement won more than 400,000 votes).

18. The question of the importance of the *Popolare* component in the moderate *polo* and of the relevance of its "slice" in terms of votes was the subject of a brief post-electoral skirmish among the allies. Disappointed by the vote, Giuliano Ferrara, ex-minister of the Berlusconi government, had commented: "Rocco [Buttiglione] brought us his vote and that of Formigoni and his relatives." Buttiglione, replying, maintained that he and his *Popolari* represented 10 per-

68 Aldo Di Virgilio

cent of the electorate (and therefore more than Bianco's *Popolari*). See *Corriere della Sera*, April 25 and 26, 1995.

19. For a correct evaluation of these data we must keep two facts in mind. In the first place, the number of councillors went from 720 to 757 and this increases the percentage of newly-elected councillors by almost 5 percent. During the 1990-1995 legislature, however, a certain amount of change had taken place for which some of the councillors re-elected in 1995 may be considered as "new." The infra-legislational change was also more significant than usual because for the first time, in the interval between one regional election and another, two national political elections were held and this, due to the unusual nature of the political circumstances, favored the promotion of some councillors elected in 1990 to parliamentary level.

3

Referenda Don't Fall from the Sky:
The June Initiatives

Pier Vincenzo Uleri and Roberto Fideli

On, June 11, 1995, the Italian electorate was called to the ballot box to answer "yes" or "no" to twelve referendum questions. This was the eleventh referendum in the history of the Italian Republic, including the institutional referendum of June 2, 1946, and the advisory referendum of June 18, 1989. The referendum phenomenon thus continues and its frequency seems to be increasing with the passing of the years: three questions were put to the public vote in the 1970s, eleven in the 1980s and twenty-four in the first years of the 1990s. The number of calls to the ballot box has also increased, from twice to three times in the first two decades and to four times at the beginning of the present decade (see Table 3.1).

The Frequency of Referendum Votes in Italy

In the twenty-five years between the passage of Law No. 352 on May 25, 1970, and June 11, 1995, Italian voters were called to the ballot box nine times to vote on thirty-eight questions raised either by official petitions signed by at least 500,000 citizens or by at least five regional councils. On three of these occasions, in particular in 1974, 1985, and

TABLE 3.1 Referenda Held from 1970-95 as per art. 75 of the Constitution and the Number of Questions on Abrogation Voted in Each Consultation

	1974	1978	1981	1985	1987	1990	1991	1993	1995	Total
Questions	1	2	5	1	5	3	1	8	12	38

1991, only one question was asked of the electors, while in the remaining six cases, the number of questions varied from two in 1978 to the three questions in 1990, to five questions in 1981 and 1987, to the eight in 1993 and finally the twelve questions of 1995.

The phenomenon is the subject of differing and conflicting interpretations and evaluations. On the one hand, there are those who fear the emergence of a new referendum democracy, the fruit of either an out-and-out "plebiscite drift"[1] or a blocked representative democracy[2]; on the other, there are those who emphasize the positive role played up to now by referenda.[3]

Thus, occurring in an already richly varied context, the referendum of June 11, 1995, shed light on many facets of the issue because of both the quantity and variety of subjects put before the electorate. The twelve questions themselves represented a third of all referendum questions voted on since 1970. This fact provoked argument about the capacity of the voters to provide a considered and informed vote when faced with such a large number of questions; thus, regular as clockwork, the proposal to increase the number of signatures necessary to generate a referendum was renewed.

What is the origin of such a large number of referendum questions? The most obvious response, but, we fear, the most simplistic, is to attribute the phenomenon to a "distorted use" or to an "abuse" of the referendum as a political instrument. Without excluding that possibility, which, however, requires some serious conceptual and empirical clarifications if we wish to avoid short-sighted partisan polemics, it seems to us that in the Italian experience, there are at least three principal explanatory factors involved in the phenomenon. The first factor, in descending order of importance, is the presence of votes of the initiative type (those, that is, generated on the request of a certain number of voters); the second is the presence of a referendum party (i.e. a political movement which makes the referendum its preferred tool of political mobilization); the third, and final, is a blocked democracy in crisis.

In the context of Western democracies, the referendum phenomenon occurs with a wide variety of forms and features.[4] The main discriminating factor may be viewed in terms of what we may identify as control of the "power of initiative." If we exclude referenda which take place obligatorily, as required by the constitution for consultations which are the result of an optional decision, in the vast majority of European democracies and also in some democracies outside Europe, the "power of initiative" is under the control of the executive and Parliament. The two most significant exceptions to this rule are Switzerland, which boasts an experience of over two centuries in this regard, and Italy, which, instead, has an experience of just a quarter of a century. The exception consists in the fact that in these two countries, citizens may call for referendum votes by signing appropriate requests, those we have proposed calling "initiative" in order to distinguish them from "referendum."[5] Switzerland and Italy are the two European democracies in which the greatest number of questions have been put to the public vote; they are followed by France, Ireland and Denmark (see Table 3.2). Since it is in Switzerland and Italy that we find the presence of initiatives and the high frequency of the referendum phenomenon, it is difficult to believe that there is not a simple correlation between the presence of initiative-type referenda type and the high frequency of the referendum phenomenon.

TABLE 3.2   Referenda (Both Referendum and Initiative Type) in 18 Western European Countries as of December, 1995

	Before 1945	*1945-69*	*1970-95*	*Total*
Austria	1	0	2	3
Belgium	0	1	0	1
Denmark	3	8	6	17
Finland	1	0	1	2
France	10	9	3	22
Germany	6	0	0	6
Greece	5	2	2	9
Iceland	4	0	0	4
Ireland	1	3	14	18
Italy	2	1	39	42
Luxembourg	3	0	0	3
Holland	0	0	0	0
Norway	4	0	2	6
Portugal	1	0	0	1
Spain	0	2	3	5
Sweden	1	2	2	5
Switzerland	139	83	215	437
United Kingdom	0	0	1	1
Total	181	111	290	582
Total excluding Switzerland	42	28	75	145

Source: M. Gallagher, *Conclusion*, in *The Referendum Experience in Europe*, cit., p. 231.

Three "Packets" of Initiatives

The twelve questions which appeared in the referendum vote of 1995 were the fruit of a rather mixed group of initiatives which took shape during a period of troubled political events. The questions were proposed by a number of committees which, at different times between the spring of 1993 and spring 1994, mounted campaigns to collect signatures on three groups of repeal initiatives.

The "Social Referenda": Trade Union Representation and the Decrees of the Amato Government

The first initiative that ended up making it onto the ballot in 1995 dealt with three questions regarding trade union representation. Two of the questions concerned article 19 of the Worker's Statute, proposing either "maximal" or "minimal" repeal of the the law then in force.[6] The third item concerned trade union representation for public sector workers.[7] The declared aim of the proponents of the vote was to break the so-called "trade union representation monopoly" held by the three largest labor confederations, the CGIL, CISL and UIL.

This initiative seems to us to be the result of the divisions and lack of agreement on the problem of the unions' right to represent all workers, and not simply their members, which has marked the organizations and the trade union movement for over twenty years.[8] In particular, in 1981, two initiatives effectively signalled the beginning of the recourse to the referendum as an instrument for deciding conflicts both between parties and groups of the extreme Left and between organizations and groups from the trade union movement. The first of these raised the question of living allowances (particularly, of their exclusion from the calculation of severance payments), while the second initiative sought the repeal of certain articles of the Worker's Statute (arts. 28, 35, and 37) and foreshadowed the problem of entitlement to represent all workers.[9] Shortly after, in February, 1984, a much harsher conflict would explode regarding the so-called "St. Valentine's Day Decree" on the cost-of-living adjustment which was then to become the subject of the referendum voted on in 1985.[10] Finally, in 1990, a new initiative was proposed regarding a section of article 35 of the Worker's Statute which permitted the termination "without just cause of workers of companies with fewer than fifteen employees."[11]

The 1990s thus opened with the question of trade union representation of the non-union members still unanswered. Over the course of several legislatives sessions, the Parliament and the government had still not been able to intervene efficiently on the subject—as testified to by the numerous bills left on the drawing-board. The lack of an agreement between the three confederations on the reform of the Worker's Statute relative to the problem of delegation actually hindered an autonomous parliamentary decision on the subject. Nevertheless, the debate was not exclusively an internal conflict of the labor organizations. In fact, in good measure, this matter was also the result of an internal conflict among the political forces of the Left and, in particular, among those parties which had grown wholly or in part from the roots of the Italian Communist Party: the *Partito Democratico della Sinistra* (PDS) and the *Partito della Rifondazione Comunista*. The initiative thus expressed not so much a clash between trade union groups and organizations but a competition between two political organizations which have in the working class—both workers and pensioners—their social and electoral base. It was a conflict between a left-wing party and trade union alliance which seeks to govern a society having a capitalist, market-based economic system and a left-wing political group which aims to "go beyond" that system.[12]

The final phase of the search for a compromise among some of the forces involved and the formulation of a referendum question was troubled and, in the end, fruitless, resulting in the presentation on December 18, 1992, of two distinct questions concerning the maximal and the minimal repeal of the art. 19 of the Worker's Statute. The item regarding art. 47 of the decree on public sector employees was presented on February 24, 1993.

The *Essere sindacato* ("Being a union") component of CGIL, *Cobas, Rifondazione Comunista, La Rete* (the Network) and the *Verdi* (Greens) joined forces with the sponsoring committee organized by the *Movimento dei consigli unitari* (Movement for unitary councils). Within this conglomeration of political and union forces supporting the referendum initiative, it is possible to distinguish various components reflecting different positions on the reform of trade union representation of non-union members. The most radical and intransigent position (expressed by *Rifondazione Comunista, Cobas, Consigli autorganizzati* [self-organized committees] and *Essere sindacato*) sought total repeal of art. 19, while the mainstream position (expressed by the majority of the PDS, by *Movimento dei consigli unitari* and by directors and groups linked to the majority in the CGIL) sought only a partial abrogation. The CGIL majority did not support the initiative, instead promoting a collection of signatures on a popular initiative bill for the reform of union representation of non-union members.

The campaign for the collection of signatures began on April 2 and ended on June 30, 1993. Seven hundred seventy thousand signatures were gathered for the maximal proposal and 670,000 for the minimal;

740,000 signatures were collected on the question regarding art. 47 of the law on public sector workers.

That the initiative on the theme of union representation of non-union members had a broader political meaning for a significant part of its promoters was demonstrated by the fact that the "packet" of referendum questions for which signatures were gathered contained six questions. In fact, the questions on three decrees made by the Amato government were placed alongside the three on union representation of non-union workers: the legislative decree on the reorganization of social security benefits for public and private workers, the decree on the reorganization of the health service, and the decree on the transformation of public economic bodies and the sale of public shares and state landholdings. The initiative thus had three aspects: as a political struggle within the trade union movement; as a competition among left-wing parties; and lastly, but no less importantly, as the political struggle of an alliance of left-wing parties and groups tied to the Communist Party (PDS and *Rifondazione Comunista*), left-wing populists (the movement headed by Leoluca Orlando, *La Rete*) and environmental groups (the Greens) against the Amato government. In the statements put out by some of the proponent groups, the initiative was seen as the nucleus of a political conglomeration called the "Left for an alternative."

"Strange Bedfellows:" The Initiative Packet of the Radicals and the Northern League

In June and November of 1993, the first two administrative elections took place under the new electoral laws.[13] They resulted in victory for the candidates and political groups on the Left. These elections, and the devastating effects of the investigations conducted by the prosecutors in Milan and other cities into the parties which had made up the Christian Democratic-based governments and majorities, seemed to suggest favorable prospects for a left-wing electoral victory. It was in this context that the Radical Party's Marco Pannella, with his movement of Clubs, and the Northern League put together two distinct "packets" of referendum questions which, at least in part, seemed to take for granted the probable electoral victory of the Left.

The primary declared objective of the Radicals' initiative was to change the recently approved electoral laws concerning election to both houses of Parliament, and to the governments of cities with more than 15,000 inhabitants. Continuing his campaign for a one-round, English-type majority system, Pannella, to that end, proposed three abrogative questions to make appropriate changes to the laws just approved by Parliament.

Other questions were added to these on subjects which, in the view of the radical leader, should be requirements for a liberal program of government. These questions proposed the abolition or modification of: withholding tax for employees; the direct deduction of union dues from worker's salaries; unemployment benefits; the commercial regulation concerning commercial licenses; the commercial regulation on shop hours; and the requirement of participating in the national health service. A further objective of the Radical referendum initiative was to press for the constitution of a democratic party.

Lega's referendum package included two questions on RAI, the state television network, addressing the public nature of the entity and publicity. The packet's other three questions dealt with internal exile of persons being investigated for association with the Mafia and organized crime, withholding tax, and participation in the national health service.

In November, the Club Pannella and the *Lega Nord* converged to propose a single referendum package composed of thirteen questions, of which eight bear the Radical stamp, three embody the *Lega*'s desires (the two questions on RAI and the item regarding internal exile), and two questions of common interest (withholding tax and freedom of choice regarding participation in the national health service).[14]

The Initiatives on the "Mammì Law:" The Failed Revenge of the Left

The packet which was third in chronological order but that which would be at the center of the clash in the June, 1995 campaign, contained three questions on the so-called Mammì law.[15] This is an extremely complex subject, which has occupied a notable amount of space on the Italian political agenda for over twenty years.[16] Since 1960, the Constitutional Court had confirmed the compatibility between a state broadcasting monopoly and constitutional principles in many of its decisions.[17] Parliament, especially in the 1990s, responded to the Court's decisions with an avalanche of legislation.[18] Beginning with law no. 103 of April 14, 1975, it passed at least ten decrees on the topic, including reiterations. Meanwhile, in mid-December 1994, the House of Deputies announced the formation of a special commission to discuss proposed bills for the reorganization of the broadcasting system.

The target of the referendum initiative proponents was the dominant position in the private sector acquired during the 1980s by the Fininvest television networks owned by Silvio Berlusconi and later ratified by some of the provisions of the Mammì law. The announcement of the filing of an appeal in the *Corte di Cassazione* was made on April 14, 1994, a little more than two weeks after the electoral victory of the political alliance led by Berlusconi. Given the identity of the promoting committee, one might suspect a reaction by the defeated groups aimed at revenge for what, in their judgment, was the principal instrument of victory in the hands of the Center-Right formation.

The idea of a referendum initiative on the Mammì law had, in fact, been circulating within the PDS and in other sectors close to it for some time. For example, in August, 1992, the hypothesis of such a referendum was formulated by Vincenzo Vita, the head of the PDS information department, for whom the "infamous agreement between the *pentapartito* (the five-party coalition government of the First Republic) and Fininvest, resulting in the Mammì law, is the offspring of another political era ... It is absurd that information remains a sort of last bastion of the old system of the majority parties."[19] According to Vita and Gloria Buffo, another director of the PDS, responsible for private publishers, the Amato government's August 13, 1992 decree on the matter of "concessions for television broadcasting on a national level" was "the rubber stamping of an old power pact dating back to the era of the *pentapartito*, which sought to safeguard the Fininvest empire...an attempt to change the material constitution of an essential chapter of democratic life."[20]

In 1993, the idea of an abrogative initiative on the Mammì law was continuously debated in left-wing circles orbiting around the PDS, *Rifondazione Comunista*, and *La Rete*; and the left-wing weekly *Avvenimenti* acted as their spokesperson. Within the PDS, different positions were distinguishable, with the left-wing minority of the *Comunisti democratici* more set on pursuing a referendum vote while the majority supporting the party leadership seemed more inclined to use the referendum initiative to put pressure on Parliament. In November, 1993, the PDS secretary, Achille Occhetto, stated that the Mammì law had to be altered and that "if we can't manage to change it then it must be abrogated via a referendum." In December, 1993 the idea became increasingly firm with the hypothesis of Silvio Berlusconi's entrance into politics. An early formulation of the referendum project was presented to the so-called *Gruppo di Fiesole*, receiving huge support.[21] By the middle of January, 1994, the referendum initiative began to take concrete form and was presented in a press conference held by ACLI, ARCI, and the *Gruppo di Fiesole*.[22]

It may be, then, that the electoral defeat suffered by the Left in the parliamentary vote on March 27, 1994, was the last straw causing their decision to proceed with the referendum initiative. In fact, Silvio Berlusconi's conflict of interest, as both the owner of the Fininvest television networks and the leader of the Center-Right electoral alliance, had been a central theme of that electoral campaign. Nevertheless, the decision for the referendum initiative was not simply a reaction to the electoral defeat. The political forces which had been defeated in Parliament on the occasion of the passing of the Mammì law—primarily the PCI and the Christian Democratic Left—had never really laid down their arms.

The Judgments of Admissibility Made
by the Constitutional Court

The Constitutional Court plays a crucial role in the referendum process. In fact, under art. 2 of the constitutional law of March 11, 1953, the court must judge the admissibility of referendum questions promoted in accordance with art. 75 of the constitution.[23] Throughout 1995, a total of seventy-five referendum questions were presented to the court for a judgment of admissibility: seventy were of the "initiative" type (brought forward by the collection of voters' signatures) and five were proposed by regional councils. The court judged forty-six questions to be admissible and rejected twenty-nine (see Table 3.3). Of the forty-six admissible questions, only thirty-eight were actually voted on because Parliament intervened eight times, repealing the texts of the laws in questions and, at least in part, adopted the positions of the promoters with new provisions of law. On the two occasions which we are particularly interested in, the court examined a total of twenty-two questions, accepting twelve and dismissing ten.

The twelve questions voted on in June, 1995 were thus the result of two judgments, handed down in January, 1994 and January, 1995. In January, 1994, the court examined six referendum questions proposed the previous spring: the three questions regarding trade union representation were accepted while the three questions on the social security system, the health service and the sale of state landholdings were rejected. The three accepted questions were to have been voted on in the

TABLE. 3.3 Judgments of Admissibility Made by the Constitutional Court on Abrogative Referendum Questions, 1971-1995

Questions proposed	1972	1975	1978	1981	1982	1985	1987	1990	1991	1993	1994	1995	*Total*
Accepted	1	1	4	6	1	1	5	4	1	10	3	9	46
Refused	0	0	4	6	1	0	3	0	2	3	3	7	29
Total questions judged	1	1	8	12	2	1	8	4	3	13	6	16	75

spring of 1994 but the early dissolution of Parliament meant that they were postponed until spring 1995.

In January, 1995, the court pronounced judgement on the other sixteen referendum questions—those promoted by the radicals and the Northern League and those on the Mammì law. Nine were declared admissible: authorizations for commerce, shop hours, privatization of RAI, internal exile, the electoral law for local councils, direct deductions of union dues and, lastly, the three questions on the Mammì law dealing with anti-trust laws, advertising breaks during television programs, and limitations on the number of publicity agencies. The seven referendum questions held inadmissible were relating to: regulation of publicity in RAI transmissions; obligatory participation in the national health service; the electoral law for the Chamber of Deputies; the electoral law for the Senate, supplementary unemployment benefits; the withholding tax and, lastly, the single treasury.[24]

Judgments on admissibility have always caused lively discussion among the players interested in referendum matters, especially the proponents of referendum questions. On this occasion, too, the Radicals had a strong reaction against the court for the judgments of non-admissibility regarding the questions central to their referendum initiative, those on the electoral laws regarding the Chamber of Deputies and Senate.[25]

Party Alliances and the Referendum Vote:
Berlusconi Wins Again

The months preceding the June 11 referendum were extremely turbulent, distinguished in particular by the polemics surrounding the decision of the Northern League to abandon the government coalition headed by Berlusconi. The June 11 vote thus took place in a climate of great uncertainty with, on the one hand, the possibility of the early dissolution of Parliament, which would certainly have required postponement of the vote, and, on the other, the attempts made to reach an agreement in Parliament on some of the referendum questions, thus avoiding the referendum vote. Of course, at the center of all the discussion were the questions on the Mammì law directly regarding the fate of the Fininvest television networks, which were, at the time, also the subject of negotiations with possible foreign buyers. Around the middle of May, it seemed that an agreement had been found until opposition by the *Lega Nord* and the referendum initiative committee forced the parties to make a U-turn.

Thus, the parties' and other interested groups' recommendations to vote for "yes" or "no" were the result of a complex stategy involving decisions of differing importance depending on the players in the game: the final outcome came from a complicated process whose logic was not always readily visible. To a large extent, uncertainty reigned supreme until three or four weeks before the vote and certainly renders the task of illustrating the different arguments and positions articulated in response to the twelve referendum questions much more difficult. Political and union forces feared that the vote on the three questions regarding the Mammì law (items 10, 11 and 12) would affect the vote on the remaining questions. Thus, on both sides there were those who suggested giving the voters a single recommendation on how they should vote: 12 "yes" or 12 "no". In the end, however, only the group of *Popolari* headed by Buttiglione announced a recommendation for twelve nos, while Pannella urged a vote of "yes" for the first nine questions and "no" for the last three; all the other political groups recommended a mixture of "yes" and "no" votes (see Table 3.4).

Although the political parties remained the principal players structuring the referendum campaign, they were not the only ones on the

TABLE 3.4 Voting Recommendations Made by the Parties on the 12 Referendum Questions in the Consultation of June 11, 1995

Ref.	RC	PDS	Verdi	Lab.	Dem.	Pop. Bianco	PRI	Lega Nord	Lega fed.	Pan-nella	Pop. Buttigl.	CCD	AN	FI
1.	yes	no	yes	no	no	no	no	yes	yes	yes	no	- [a]	yes	yes
2.	yes	yes	yes	no	no	no	no	yes	yes	yes	no	-	yes	yes
3.	yes	yes	yes	yes	no	no	no	yes	yes	yes	no	-	yes	yes
4.	yes	-	yes	yes	yes	yes	yes	yes	yes	yes	no	yes	yes	yes
5.	no	yes	no	no	yes	yes	yes	yes	yes	yes	no	no	no	yes
6.	no	no	no	no	-	no	yes	no	no	yes	no	no	no	no
7.	-	no	no	no	no	no	no	-	yes	yes	no	-	yes	yes
8.	no	no	no	no	no	no	no	no	yes	yes	no	yes	yes	yes
9.	no	no	no	no	-	no	yes	no	no	yes	no	no	no	no
10.	yes	yes	yes	yes	yes	yes	yes	yes	no	no	no	no	no	no
11.	yes	yes	yes	yes	yes	yes	yes	yes	no	no	no	no	no	no
12.	yes	yes	yes	yes	yes	yes	yes	yes	no	no	no	no	no	no

Key: 1. Union representation (maximal); 2. Union representation (minimal); 3. Union representation in public sector; 4. Internal exile; 5. Privatization of the RAI; 6. Commercial licenses; 7. Union dues; 8. Local council electoral law; 9. Shop opening hours; 10. National television concessions; 11. Advertising breaks; 12. Publicity grouping.

[a] The hyphen indicates that the party left the vote free.

Source: *Corriere della Sera*, June 10, 1995.

scene. Many newspapers and periodicals took more or less explicit lines regarding a "yes" or a "no" vote, in some cases becoming actual advocates for the referendum campaign. Needless to say, on this occasion, too, as in the elections of 1994, the roles played by RAI and particularly by the Fininvest television networks and the television ombudsman's attempts to discipline their actions were at the center of attention and political argument. The polemics obviously hinged on the networks' disparate treatment of the positions expressed by the various political forces and on the influence of broadcast information on the electorate's voting patterns. While reasonably reliable data seemed to indicate that more time slots were assigned to *Forza Italia* and Berlusconi than to the PDS and D'Alema, the debate on the actual influence exerted by broadcast information and propaganda must remain open.[26]

Besides the parties, businessmen also entered the arena, strongly supporting a "no" vote on the two questions (nos. 6 and 9) which directly affected them. The positions taken by the vast majority of parties and groups aligned with the "no," from the extreme Right to the extreme Left, may be considered—beyond the official reasons adopted—as a sign of the strength of these interests. It should also be mentioned that the Episcopal conference had also declared itself contrary to the liberalization of shopping hours, which would have brought with it the opening of commercial activities on Sundays and other religious holidays.

The party line-ups on the three questions regarding the Mammì law were the only ones to faithfully reflect the party alliances which characterized Italian politics between the March, 1994 elections and the June, 1995 referendum vote. The forces of the Center-Left joined with the *Lega Nord* and *Rifondazione Comunista* for a "yes" vote, just as the Center-Right *Polo* plus Pannella's radicals lined up for a "no." Except for the PDS's general efforts for all its recommendations, and its particular efforts on questions 1 and 8, the two groups of political parties described above were really the only ones to have entered the fray. In fact, apart from giving voting recommendations, on the other questions there was no real battle by all contenders, in the sense of any undertaking by the parties to support all twelve of their voting recommendations with equal organizational and propaganda resources. Thus, on many different fronts, polemics were rife regarding the paltry commitment of propaganda in support of the recommendations.

Voter turn-out in the June 1995 referenda was approximately 58 percent, the lowest after the referendum of 1990, in which the constitutional quorum level of 50 percent was not reached (see Table 3.5). With respect to the vote of 1993, there was a drop in turn-out of roughly twenty percentage points. This fact was interpreted as a sign of voter weariness and disorientation due to an excessive number of both referenda and questions. It should be remembered, however, that although the number of questions simultaneously placed before the voters in 1993 (8) was already high, the voter turn-out had nevertheless been significantly higher than in previous referenda. It is also necessary to underline the fact that the 1995 referenda were the first in which the voting was concluded in just one day. Through the 1994 elections, both electoral and referendum voting had taken place over a day and a half. In the political elections of 1994, the turn-out on the first day of voting was 57.3 percent, while the final turn-out was of 86.1 percent. When compared with the regional elections of 1990, the regional elections of April, 1995, with a turn-out of 81.3 percent, registered a significant six point drop in voter participation.

TABLE 3.5 Participation and Results of Voting (Percentage Values)

Referendum question	Voters	Valid votes	Blank ballots	Null ballots	"Yes"	"No"
1 Union rep. (maximal)	56.9	88.9	8.8	2.3	49.97	50.03
2 Union rep. (minimal)	56.9	87.9	9.7	2.4	62.1	37.9
3 Public sector contracts	56.9	87.6	10.1	2.3	64.7	35.3
4 Internal exile	57	87.1	10.3	2.6	63.7	36.3
5 RAI privatization	57.2	90.2	7.9	1.9	54.9	45.1
6 Commercial licences	57.1	88.5	9.3	2.2	35.6	64.4
7 Union dues	57.1	89.3	8.7	2.0	56.2	43.8
8 Local council electoral law	57.1	88.6	9.3	2.1	49.4	50.6
9 Shop hours	57.1	90.2	7.8	2.0	37.5	62.5
10 Television concessions	57.9	95.8	2.9	1.3	43.0	57.0
11 Advertising breaks	57.9	96.1	2.8	1.1	44.3	55.7
12 Publicity grouping	57.8	95.6	3.0	1.3	43.6	56.4

Source: Ministero dell'Interno. Direzione centrale per i servizi elettorali.

Let us now take a look at the results of the vote. Five abrogative initiatives obtained a majority of "yes" votes. They were questions 2 and 3 on union representation, question 4 on internal exile, question 5 on the privatization of RAI, and question 7 on direct deduction of union dues. The affirmative majority varied from 54.9 percent on the privatization of RAI to 64.7 percent on union representation of public employees.

The remaining seven initiatives were rejected. In addition to the three questions on the Mammì law—10, 11 and 12—these included question 1 on union representation (maximal hypothesis), question 6 on commercial licenses, question 8 on the local council electoral law, and question 9 on shop opening hours. The negative majority varied from 50.03 percent on the union question to 64.4 percent on question 6 relative to commercial licenses.

In two cases, the margin between the two options hit an all-time minimum: on question 1 the 50.03 percent majority was won with a margin of just 13,721 votes. On question 8 on the electoral law for local councils, the majority for the "no" was also very thin, with just 50.57 percent of the votes.

In general, commentators were fairly unanimous in interpreting the outcome of the vote as a victory for Berlusconi, since the three questions on the Mammì law had been at the center of the campaign. Some saw the results on these three questions as a confirmation of the role of the Fininvest television networks. On June 12, the PDS daily newspaper l'Unità ran the front page headline title "The 'no' Telewin it." Based on the outcome of the 1994 elections, the alliance which had favored abrogation of the Mammì law could have counted on a majority of about 55 percent, with the alliance against repeal expected to have less than 40 percent of the votes (see Table 3.6). Instead, the three questions were rejected by a clear margin, which varied between twelve and fourteen percentage points.

The referenda results were also interpreted as a severe blow to the three main labor confederations, mitigated only in part by the negative vote on question 1, which was, however, largely attributable to opposition to the question expressed by the PDS. The Lega Nord "cashed in," especially on the votes favoring the abrogation of the internal exile law and the privatization of RAI, even though it had shown more interest during the campaign in the questions on the Mammì law, where it suffered defeat together with the Center-Left alliance. The radical movement was victorious on question 7 (union dues), but was defeated on questions 6 and 9 (commercial licenses and shop hours) and above all on question 8 dealing with local council electoral law which was, without a doubt, the most important of those questions which had survived the court's judgement on admissibility.

TABLE 3.6 Electoral Weight of Parties in the Political Elections of 1994 and Referendum Vote Result (Percentage Values)

Ref.	"Yes"			"No"			Free vote
	Alliance consistency 1994 elections (%)[a]	Referendum result 1995 (%)	Difference	Alliance consistency 1994 elections (%)[a]	Referendum result 1995 (%)	Difference	Alliance consistency 1994 elections (%)[a]
1.	55.2	40.97	-5.2	38.2	50.03	11.8	-
2.	75.5	62.1	-13.4	17.9	37.9	20.0	-
3.	77.7	64.7	-13.0	15.7	35.3	19.6	-
4.	73.1	63.7	-9.4	0.0[b]	36.3	36.3	20.3
5.	69.0	54.9	-14.1	24.4	45.1	20.7	-
6.	3.5	35.6	32.1	85.3	64.4	-20.9	4.6
7.	38.0	56.2	18.2	40.9	43.8	2.9	14.4
8.	38.0	49.4	11.4	55.4	50.6	-4.8	-
9.	3.5	37.5	34.0	85.3	62.5	-22.8	4.6
10.	55.4	43.0	-12.4	38.0	57.0	19.0	-
11.	55.4	44.3	-11.1	38.0	55.7	17.7	-
12.	55.4	43.6	-11.8	38.0	56.4	18.4	-

[a] The sum of electoral weights in 1994 of the different alliances is always inferior to 100. We have excluded the votes obtained by smaller lists and parties which did not express an official position on the referenda (see Table 3.4).

[b] Only Buttiglione's party, which recommended a "no" vote on all the referendum questions, was in favor of the anti-abrogationist alternative (see Table 3.4). In the cases in which the two parties which the *Partito Popolare* was divided into took different positions (questions 4, 5, 10, 11 and 12) we have attributed the votes of the *Popolari* in the 1994 political elections to the *Partito Popolare* led by Gerardo Bianco on the basis of the results of the regional elections in 1995.

Source: Our own elaboration of data supplied by Ministero dell'Interno - Direzione centrale per i servizi elettorali.

Voter Turn-out: The Persistence of the North-South Divide

The referenda of June marked a strong decline in political participation. In the referendum with the highest percentage of voters (that dealing with television concessions) only 57.9 percent of the electorate took part. The discontinuity with respect to previous electoral and referendum experiences should not, however, be overemphasized. In fact, just as electoral abstentionism has grown steadily since the political elections of 1979, so too has that regarding referendum turn-out, if we exclude the inversion of the trend represented by the referendum of 1993 (see Table 3.7).

Elements of continuity with the past are even more evident if we examine the territorial distribution of abstentionism. The percentage of voters was, in fact, much higher in the Center-North provinces than in

TABLE 3.7 Voter Turn-out in Referenda from 1974 to 1995 (Percentage Values)

	Voters	Added abstensionism[a]	Eta-squared coefficient[b]
1974	87.7	5.1	.49
1978	81.2	12.2	.59
1981	79.4	11.2	.56
1985	77.9	11	.60
1987	65.1	23.5	.30
1990	43.4	44	c
1991	62.4	25	.06
1993	77.0	10.2	.63
1995	57.9	28.3	.42

[a] Percentage diffence between voters (out of electorate) in referenda and voters (out of electorate) in previous political elections.
[b] The eta-squared coefficient indicates the proportion of the variance of the cardinal variable (in this case additional abstensionism) which may be reproduced on the basis of the belonging of cases (the provinces) to one or the other types of category variable: Center-North (which comprises the 61 provinces of Valle d'Aosta, Piemonte, Lombardia, Trentino-Alto Adige, Veneto, Friuli-Venezia Giulia, Emilia-Romagna, Toscana, Umbria, Marche) and Center-South (which comprises the remaining 42 provinces). The coefficient assumes a value between 0 and 1. The higher its value, the more homogeneous the two areas are internally. and the more different they are the one from the other.
c Information not available.

Sources: For data on abstensionism and added abstensionism from 1974 to 1993: P. Corbetta. A. M. Parisi, "The Referendum on the Electoral Law for the Senate: Another Momentous April", in C. Mershon e G. Pasquino, eds., Italian Politics, Vol. 9 (Boulder: Westview Press, 1995), pp. 75-92. 148. For chi squared values from 1974 to 1993: R. Cartocci, "Fra Lega e Chiesa. L'Italia in cerca di integrazione", (Bologna: Il Mulino, 1994) p. 40.

those in the Center-South (respectively, 65.75 percent and 48.25 percent). A quorum was reached in all Center-North provinces, but only in thirteen of the forty-one provinces of the Center-South.

Everywhere the number of voters in the referenda was less than the number in the previous political elections (see Table 3.7). This phenomenon, called "additional abstentionism" by experts on Italian electoral behavior,[27] increased in the 1995 referenda, also reaching high levels in the northern half of the country (see Figure 3.1).

The map of additional abstentionism (see Figure 3.1) highlights the persistence of the differences between different parts of the country. In particular, the territorial fault-line separating the Center-North from the Center-South appears quite marked. Voter participation in the referenda continued to be more widespread not only in the provinces in the

Red Zone but also in some provinces, which have traditionally been placed in the White Zone.[28] Again, in terms of voter turnout, the Center-South half of the country was not as completely homogeneous. The map highlights the specificity of some Sicilian provinces compared to the other southern provinces. As previously noted there was an increase in additional abstentionism, in almost all the Italian provinces; on the contrary, the additional abstentionism figures in the Sicilian provinces did not change much from those recorded in the previous referenda.[29]

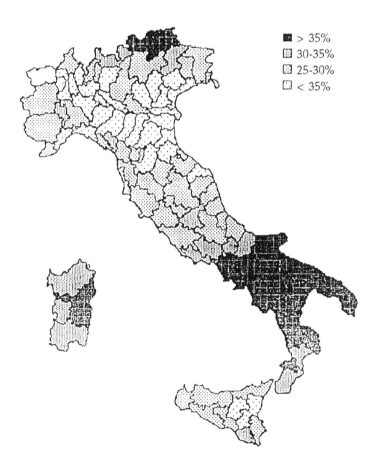

FIGURE 3.1 Difference between percentage of voters in the referendum of 1995 and percentage of voters in the political elections of 1994.

Source: Our own elaboration of data supplied by Ministero dell'Interno - Direzione centrale per i servizi elettorali.

In order to evaluate the degree of homogeneity of the two areas into which we have divided the Italian provinces, we have subjected the additional abstentionism figures to a variance analysis. The value of the eta-squared coefficient, although high (.42), was still less than that for the 1993 referenda (see Table 3.7). The Center-North and the Center-South were internally more heterogeneous than in the 1993 referenda. Moreover, the greater homogeneity of the two areas must almost exclusively be related to the smaller incidence of additional abstentionism in Sicily with respect to the rest of the South. If the Sicilian provinces are excluded, the eta-squared value (.58) was only slighly less than the value for the previous referenda (see Table 3.7).

"Yes" and "No" in Italy: Have the Electors Differentiated in Their Vote?

In Italian referenda, the electorate has, at times, been called upon to decide a large number of questions on the most diverse subjects. On these occasions, a portion of the voters expressed a preference on only some of the questions. Table 3.8 highlights the difference between the percentage of blank ballots in the referenda which had only one question (1974, 1985 and 1991) and those with a larger number of questions (two in 1978, five each in 1981 and 1987, three in 1990, eight in 1993 and twelve in 1995). Even if the relation is not linear, a growth in the (maximum) percentage of blank ballots seems to follow a rise in the number of questions.

TABLE 3.8   Blank Ballots from 1974 to 1995 (as Percentage of Total Voters)

	Number of questions	Maximum value	Minimum value[a]
1974	1	1.3	-
1978	2	3.3	3.2
1981	5	6.9	5.1
1985	1	1.4	-
1987	5	8.9	8
1990	3	3.2	2.5
1991	1	1.9	-
1993	8	4.1	3.3
1995	12	10.3	2.8

[a] In the referenda in which more than one question was presented.

Source: Our own elaboration of data supplied by Ministero dell'Interno - Direzione centrale per i servizi elettorali.

The data in the second column of Table 3.8 (maximum percentage of blank ballots) indicate that the tendency to split the vote between valid ballots and blanks was rather high in the June referenda. Moreover, a comparison between the data in the second and third columns suggests another interpretation. The clear difference in the percentages of blank ballots between the different referenda questions represent a novelty in Italian electoral behavior. In 1995, the percentage of blank ballots varied between 10.3 percent (in the internal exile question) and 2.8 percent (on the Mammì law question dealing with advertising breaks). When we examine Table 3.5, the clear difference between the three questions aimed at abolishing some parts of the Mammì law and all the others becomes evident—in the former there were not only far fewer blank ballots, but also fewer invalid ballots.

We may, therefore, hypothesize that a part of the electorate had focused its attention on the questions which dealt with the private television system. It is probable that many voters did not sufficiently understand the various questions which were the subject of the referenda, even though some of these (for example, the liberalization of commercial licenses and the opening hours of the shops) directly affected central aspects of the daily life of almost all citizens. Political debate and, especially, the attention of the mass-media had been concentrated on the questions regarding the television networks of the Fininvest group.

On the basis of aggregate data, it is not possible to analyze the choices made by individual voters; thus, we cannot calculate the percentage of voters who expressed a valid vote only on the three Mammì law questions. We can, however, calculate the difference between the percentage of valid votes on two different questions. The difference between valid votes (out of total votes) on the television concessions questions and on question on the privatization of RAI may be considered an indicator of the electorate's propensity to focus on referenda questions regarding the Fininvest group. The first question recorded the highest percentage of voters; the second obtained the highest percentage of voters of the questions which did not dealt with the private television system (see Table 3.5). The lower level of invalid votes on the television concessions question (which we will call "additional valid vote") was determined by three different voting patterns. The voter expressed a valid vote on television concessions, but on the question on the privatization of the RAI: a) did not request a ballot, b) deposited a blank ballot in the box; or c) deposited an invalid ballot.[30]

As Table 3.5 shows, the percentage of voters on the two questions presented quite consistent variations, but the phenomenon of the additional valid vote involved a much larger proportion of the electoral body. Comparing the percentage of blank ballots and invalid votes on the two questions (see Table 3.5), we may infer that the additional valid vote derived in large measure from the decision to place a blank ballot in the ballot box.

As with the territorial distribution of additional abstentionism, the distribution of the additional valid vote highlights the geographical divide between North and South (see Figure 3.2). The additional valid vote was less than 5 percent in 33 of the 62 provinces of the Center-North, and crossed the threshold of 7 percent in only three northern provinces (Pavia, Imperia and Massa Carrara). With the exception of two large metropolitan centers (Rome and Naples) and three of the four provinces of Sardegna (Cagliari, Nuoro and Sassari), the additional valid vote was, instead, higher than 7 percent in all the provinces of the Center-South. The threshold of 9 percent was breached in almost all the provinces of Sicily and Calabria; but at the top of the list we find a province of Puglia (Lecce), in which the additional valid vote came close to 14 percent.[31] A not insignificant part of the southern electorate had, thus, decided to vote only on the questions regarding the Fininvest television networks. And, it was exactly in the central-southern regions that the victory of the "no" in the three questions on the Mammì law was the most marked. The line-up for the "no" vote against abrogation reached more than 60 percent (and in some cases more than 70 percent) of the vote in all the provinces of Abruzzo, Molise, Puglia, Calabria and Sicily.

As previously mentioned, the worry that many voters were not sufficiently informed on the different questions had induced some scholars and commentators to hypothesize the possibility of a heavy "drag effect" of the Mammì law questions. It was thought that many voters might have chosen a certain option (and in particular a "no") based on their choice in the questions directly concerning the Fininvest group, rather than on the basis of a carefully thought-out evaluation of the different laws whose abrogation was in question.

In the absence of an analysis at the individual level, it is impossible to establish if there was a "drag effect." No trace of it is seen in the voting results and the data at an aggregate level; in seven cases the "no" vote prevailed and in five cases the "yes." Examining the difference between the percentage of votes obtained on a certain referendum alternative and the percentage of votes obtained in the previous political elections by all the parties which supported such an alternative (see Table 3.6), it is evident that there was no systematic increase in votes for the different anti-abrogation line-ups. In nine cases there was an advance of the "no" but in three cases the "no" front registered a retreat.

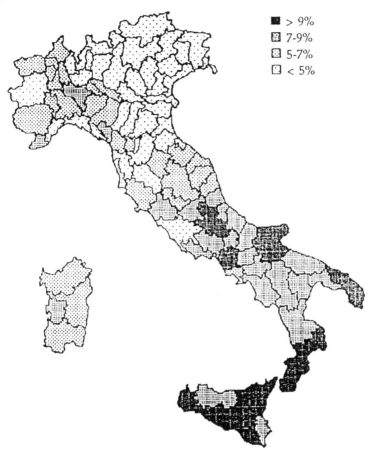

FIGURE 3.2 Difference between percentage (of total voting) in the question on television concessions and on the question on the privatization of RAI.

Source: Our own elaboration of data supplied by Ministero dell'Interno - Direzione centrale per i servizi elettorali.

Referenda and Party Mobilization Capabilities: The Case of the PDS

Contrary to first impression, the results obtained by the various alliances supporting a "no" vote on the four questions dealing with the labor movement (1, 2 , 3 and 7) were not wholly negative; on the three questions on union democracy, a positive balance can be seen (see Table 3.6). On the question aimed at the total liberalization of union representation, the "no" front actually succeeded in overturning the result which might have been foreseen on the two opposing alliances' electoral consistency (see Table 3.6). The outcome on this initiative was, moreover, determined by just a few thousand votes. Those in favor of abrogation obtained 12,297,033 votes, whereas 12,310,754 electors voted against abrogation (for the absolute values see the tables in the appendix at the end of the volume). This was not the only such case in this referendum; the margin between the "yes" and "no" votes was also extremely small (less than 37,000 votes) in the referendum seeking repeal of the double-round electoral system for local councils with a population of more than 15,000 inhabitants (see section 4). The two initiatives had been proposed by different groups and supported by party alliances composed of different political forces. In both cases the three major political forces took the same line: *Forza Italia* and *Alleanza Nazionale* supported abrogation while the PDS, instead, favored the anti-abrogation alternative which prevailed by just a few thousand votes.

To obtain a preliminary indication of the influence of the voting recommendations made by the PDS on the results of these two referenda, we have analyzed the territorial distribution of the vote in three large geographical areas: the North, the Red Zone and the Center-South.[32] As shown in Table 3.9, the success of the "no" vote on the two questions we are examining was determined, above all, by the result obtained by this side in the area where the electorate has traditionally been for the parties of the Left. On the question dealing with the local council electoral law, the lack of success of the anti-repeal option outside the Red Zone was not entirely predictable. In this case, the party alliance included not only the *Partito Popolare*, the *Patto dei Democratici* and all the progressive parties but also the *Lega Nord* (see Table 3.4). Moreover, the repeal vote also prevailed in northern regions (see Table 3.9).

As we have seen, the victory of the "no" on the question aimed at a total liberalization of union representation did not seem at all probable. The anti-abrogation alliance enjoyed an electoral base which was much smaller than that of the pro-abrogation side (see Table 3.6). In this case too, the analysis of the party alliances can provide us with useful

TABLE 3.9   "No" percentage (Out of Valid Votes) on 1995 Referendum Questions 1 and 8

	Italy	North	Red Zone	Center-South
Quest.1	50.03	48.6	57.5	48.7
Quest.2	50.6	48.1	58.8	49.1

Source: Calculated from data provided by Ministero dell'Interno - Direzione centrale per i servizi elettorali.

information. As shown in Table 3.4, except for the Democratic Party of the Left the parties reproposed the same voting recommendations on the two union democracy questions. The PDS sided against the total liberalization of union representation, but declared itself in favor of both partial liberalization of representation and the abrogation of the prime minister's powers with regard to public sector employees. On the first question, the percentage for the "no" vote was 50.03 percent; on the other two questions, this percentage was, instead, respectively 37.9 percent and 35.3 percent (see Table 3.5). We may thus consider the difference between the percentage of "no" votes on the two questions on the liberalization of union representation as an indicator of the PDS's mobilization ability.[33] In effect, the territorial distribution of the indicator appears to be strongly correlated with the electoral strength of the PDS: at the top (with values between 21,1 percent and 25,3 percent) we find the six provinces of the Red Zone (in order: Reggio Emilia, Bologna, Modena, Ravenna, Livorno, Siena) in which the PDS obtained the highest percentage of valid votes (over 34 percent) in the political elections of 1994.

The territorial distribution of this indicator highlights the PDS's rather weak mobilization capacity in the south of Italy (see Figure 3.3). In the Center-South, the indicator goes over the threshold of 5 percent in only three provinces of central Italy, Roma, Viterbo, and Teramo. This is a modest result, especially if we consider the results obtained by the PDS in the 1994 political elections and the 1995 administrative elections in some southern regions (in particular Basilicata and Calabria). The case of Crotone is emblematic. In southern Italy, the PDS obtained the best electoral results in this province (19 percent of the valid vote in the political elections of 1994). The difference between the percentage of "no" did not exceed 2 percent of the voters, a result which is analogous with the one obtained in the northern provinces in which the percentage of PDS voters is the lowest in the country: Bolzano and Sondrio (respectively, 2.9 percent, and 5.1 percent of the valid votes in the last political elections).

The PDS's mobilization capacity is instead very strong in the provinces in the Red Zone. The map (see Figure 3.3) allows us to distinguish a central nucleus with a surrounding belt in this area. The central nucleus contains the provinces with values over 15 percent (and in some cases 20 percent) and is made up of five Tuscan provinces (Firenze, Prato, Siena, Pisa, Livorno), two provinces of Romagna (Forlì and Ravenna) and three provinces in Emilia (Bologna, Modena, Reggio Emilia). Around this nucleus there is a peripheral area made up of 12 provinces (belonging to six different regions) in which the indicator value runs between 10 percent and 15 percent: Pistoia, Grosseto, Arezzo, Perugia, Ancona, Pesaro, Rimini, Ferrara, Mantova, Parma, La Spezia and Genova.

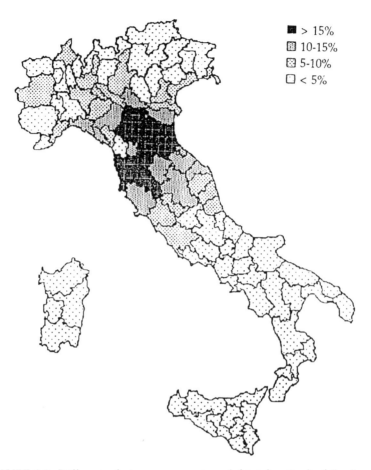

> 15%
10-15%
5-10%
< 5%

FIGURE 3.3 Difference between percentage (of total voting) of "no" votes on
the maximal union representation question and percentage of "no" votes on the
minimal union representation question.

Source: Our own elaboration of data supplied by Ministero dell'Interno - Direzione centrale
per i servizi elettorali.

The map (see Figure 3.3) confirms the well-known specificity of the
electoral behaviour of two Tuscan provinces: Lucca, an area which is
traditionally tied to the Catholic political subculture and Massa Carrara,
where for a long time the anarchic and republican movements enjoyed
a wide following. On the other hand, in the last political elections, the

PDS obtained an electoral result in these two provinces (respectively, 14 percent and 17.4 percent of the valid votes) which was clearly inferior to their results in the other Tuscan provinces.

To conclude, the results obtained on the referenda supported by the PDS underline the party's mobilization capacity in the Red Zone. We may thus hypothesize that, at least in the areas where the PDS vote is more widespread, a large part of PDS voters faithfully followed the directions given by the party. This did not impede the success of the alliance which supported the "no" vote on abrogation of some parts of the Mammì law, even in some provinces of the Red Zone, specifically, Grosseto, Perugia and Terni.

Conclusion

The decade opened in 1990 with referenda which left little trace, since the participation of the electorate was below the quorum level required by the Constitution. Many politicians, commentators and academics announced—a little incautiously and with scarcely concealed satisfaction—the beginning of the end for the referendum institution as such. The experiences of 1991 and 1993 showed that this announcement was premature. The referendum initiatives on the subject of the electoral laws represented an important stage in the crisis of Italian democracy. In the history of Italian referenda, the 1990s could come to be considered as the decade of the "referenda for the reform of the institutions."[34] The successive parliamentary decisions on the subject of electoral laws, especially those regarding the Chamber of Deputies and the regions, show just how strong resistance still is to institutional change. Moreover, from many sides, not only the prospect of institutional reform, but also the constitutional legitimacy of the use made of the referenda as a tool to this end, have been contested.

The 1995 referenda mark a lull in use of the initiative to implement institutional change; the constitutional court's judgment of inadmissibility on the referenda questions pertaining to the electoral laws offered Parliament more time to find a solution which, until now, it has demonstrated that it does not want or is not capable of finding. As was the case in 1991, postponement does not assure that Parliament will decide. At the end of 1995, it is not even possible to guess where the fate of electoral laws and institutional reforms will be decided. It is instead possible, however, that at the beginning of 1996 Pannella and his radical movement will present twenty referenda requests to the *Corte di Cassazione*. Mario Segni hopes for the reconstitution of the referendum movement and looks forward to a referendum vote on the subject of a presidential form of government for Italy. In this case, some will agree with political scientist Giovanni Sartori, according to whom the so-called plebiscite drift is the result of, among other things, "referendum obsession Pannella-style." Without undervaluing the importance of the "referendum party" factor, we, along with others, would instead highlight the fact that the presence of the referendum institution in its initiative form finds fertile terrain in the political context of a democratic crisis like Italy's.[35] Thus, referenda don't fall from the sky but are particularly favored by the combination of factors mentioned above.

Translated by Timothy Cooper and Susan Kertzer

Notes

This chapter is the result of a collaborative reflection. Sections 1- 4 and the conclusion were written by Pier Vincenzo Uleri, sections 5 - 7 by Roberto Fideli. The authors wish to thank Roberto Cartocci for his valuable suggestions and comments on the methodological approach for the data analysis; Lorenzo De Sio for his collaboration in construction of the data base; Tommaso Frosini for checking the data on the judgments of inadmissibility made by the Constitutional Court; Daniela Tauro for collecting the daily and weekly press; and finally hearty thanks go to the staff of **Ministero dell'Interno - Direzione centrale per i servizi elettorali e Servizio informatico per la documentazione fornita** and to the Florence office of the RAI TV who allowed us access to the ANSA press agency archives.

1. M. Calise, *Dopo la Partitocrazia: l'Italia tra modelli e realtà*, (Turin: Einaudi, 1994); M. Fedele, *Democrazia referendaria: l'Italia dal primato dei partiti al trionfo dell'opinione pubblica*, (Rome: Donzelli, 1994).

2. A. Pizzorno, "Democrazia della 'gente'? Scriviamola", in *Liberal*, n. 1, 1995, pp. 59-61.

3. G. Pasquino, "I referendum", in Gianfranco Pasquino, ed., *La Politica Italiana: dizionario critico 1945-95*, (Rome and Bari: Laterza, 1995), pp. 121-133.

4. V. Bogdanor, "Western Europe", in D. Butler and A. Ranney, eds., *Referendums around the World: The Growing Use of Direct Democracy*, (Basingstoke: Macmillan, 1994), pp. 24-97; M. Caciagli and P.V. Uleri, eds., *Democrazie e referendum*, (Rome and Bari: Laterza, 1994); M. Gallagher, "Conclusion", in *The Referendum Experience in Europe*, M. Gallagher and P.V. Uleri, eds., (Basingstoke: Macmillan, 1996), pp. 226-50; S. Möckli, *Direkte Demokratie: ein internationaler Vergleich*, (Bern, Stuttgart, Wien: Verlag Paul Haupt, 1994); W. Luthardt, *Direkte Demokratie: ein Vergleich in Westeuropa*, (Baden-Baden: Nomos Verlag, 1994); M. Suksi, *Bringing in the People: A Comparison of Constitutional Forms and Practices*

of the Referendum, (Dordrecht, Boston, London: Martinus Nijhoff Publishers, 1993).

5. On this point we refer to P.V. Uleri, "Le forme di consultazione popolare nelle democrazie: una tipologia", in *Rivista Italiana di Scienza Politica*, 1985, n. 2, pp. 205-254 e P.V. Uleri, "Introduction", in *The Referendum Experience in Europe*, see, pp. 1-19.

6. The law in question is that of May 20, 1970, n. 300, "Norms for the protection of workers' freedom and dignity, of union freedom and of union activity in the workplace and norms on employment" [Norme sulla tutela della libertà e dignità dei lavoratori, della libertà sindacale e dell'attività sindacale nei luoghi di lavoro e norme sul collocamento].

7. More precisely, article 47 (on union representation) of legislative decree n. 29, February 3, 1993, containing norms on the "Reorganization of public administration and revision of regulations with regard to public employment." On the methods and contents of the decree, see the comments of G. Bolaffi, "Il pubblico impiego privatizzato: una riforma per via sindacale", in *Il Mulino*, n. 3, 1993, pp. 546-552; and U. Romagnoli, "Pubblico impiego o pubblici impieghi: odissea di una riforma", in *Il Mulino*, n. 3, 1993, pp. 553-562.

8. The bibliography on this subject is very considerable. The following provide only a sampling but are sufficient for current purposes: M. Carrieri, *L'incerta rappresentanza. Sindacati e consenso negli anni '90*, (Bologna: Il Mulino, 1995); L. Bordogna, "Arcipelago Cobas: Frammentazione della rappresentanza e conflitti del lavoro", in P. Corbetta e R. Leonardi, eds., *Politica in Italia. I fatti dell'anno e le interpretazioni. Edizione 1988*, (Bologna: Il Mulino, 1989), pp. 257-292; I. Regalia, *Eletti e abbandonati. Stili e modelli di rappresentanza in fabbrica*, (Bologna: Il Mulino, 1984); S. Zan, *Organizzazioni e rappresentanza. Le associazioni imprenditoriali e sindacali*, (Rome: La Nuova Italia scientifica, 1992).

9. The first request was accepted by the Constitutional Court and resolved by parliamentary decision (law May 29, 1981, n. 297), the second request was rejected.

10. On this issue see P. Lange, "La fine di un'era: il referendum sulla scala mobile", in P. Corbetta e R. Leonardi, eds., *Politica in Italia. I fatti dell'anno e le interpretazioni. Edizione 1986*, (Bologna: Il Mulino, 1987), pp. 127-150; P.V. Uleri, "The Deliberative Initiative of June 1985 in Italy", in *Electoral Studies*, n. 3, 1985, pp. 271-277; for the conclusion of the affair of the *scala mobile* see R.M. Locke, "L'abolizione della scala mobile", in C.A. Mershon and G. Pasquino (eds.) *Politica in Italia. I fatti dell'anno e le interpretazioni. Edizione 1994*, (Bologna: Il Mulino, 1994), pp. 233-245.

11. This time the court accepted the question and Parliament intervened, changing the law in the sense desired by the proponents of the request.

12. The detonator which set off what may be viewed as a charge primed well before may be seen in the crisis and internal conflicts of CGIL which took form during 1991 and solidified at the twelfth congress of the confederation, with the emergence of the component of the extreme Left group *Essere sindacato*, led by the confederation Secretary, Fausto Bertinotti. On this event see C.A. Mershon, "La crisi della CGIL: il XII congresso nazionale", in *Politica in Italia. I fatti dell'anno e le interpretazioni - Edizione 1992*, edited by S. Hellman e G. Pasquino, (Bologna:

Il Mulino, 1992), pp. 137-166. According to Mershon, the arguments of this labor group were aimed not at "providing or bettering liberal democracy but at overthrowing it." Two groups took advantage of these divisions and internal conflicts, on one side the so-called *Movimento dei Consigli Unitari*, which arose in Lombardy in September, 1992, and on the other the Cobas movement and the self-made factory councils. The referendum drive took definitive shape in the last months of 1992. The important agreement among the three labor confederations, business organizations, and the government, which was signed at the end of July, 1993, arrived too late, because at that point the referendum mechanism was already underway; it is doubtful, however, that this referendum could have been avoided even if agreement had been reached beforehand. For an analysis of these agreements see G. Ghezzi, "Considerazioni sull'accordo tra governo e parti sociali del 23 luglio 1993", in *Politica del Diritto*, n.1, 1994, pp. 3-21; see also R. M. Locke, *L'abolizione della scala mobile*, cit.

13. See A. Di Virgilio, "Le elezioni in Italia", in *Quaderni dell'Osservatorio Elettorale*, n. 30, 1993, pp. 167-196 and n. 31, 1994, pp. 185-205. On the new electoral laws for the Chamber of Deputies and Senate and on the methods of their approval, see respectively R. D'Alimonte e A. Chiaramonte, "Il nuovo sistema elettorale italiano: le opportunità e le scelte", in *Maggioritario ma non troppo. Le elezioni politiche del 1994*, edited by S. Bartolini e R. D'Alimonte, (Bologna: Il Mulino, 1995), pp. 37-81, and A. Pappalardo, "La nuova legge elettorale in parlamento: chi, come e perché", in *Maggioritario ma non troppo*, cit., pp. 13-36.

14. On Christmas Eve, Silvio Berlusconi, who at least officially had not yet entered the arena to form his *Forza Italia* movement, signed the referendum petitions, except for those on RAI and the regulation of commercial licenses and shop opening hours.

15. The law in question is that of August 6, 1990, n. 223, on "Regulation of the public and private broadcasting system." The three questions were respectively on: the number of licenses for national television broadcasting; advertising breaks during television transmission of films; and the limits on publicity companies in positions of control or linked with radio and television stations.

16. On this subject too, the bibliography is huge. See P. Barile, E. Cheli e R. Zaccaria, eds., *Radiotelevisione pubblica e privata in Italia*, (Bologna: Il Mulino, 1980); for a general overview, see F. Monteleone, *Storia della radio e della televisione in Italia. Società, politica, strategie, programmi, 1922-1922*, (Venice: Marsilio, 1992); Camera dei Deputati, *Il sistema dell'informazione in Italia: indagine conoscitiva della Commissione cultura (gennaio 1988-gennaio 1989)*, Roma, Camera dei Deputati, 2 vols., 1989. Interesting points of view by "participant observers" are expressed in P. Del Debbio, *Il mercante e l'inquisitore. Apologia della televisione commerciale*, (Milan: Il Sole 24 Ore Libri, 1991); D. Giacalone, *Antenna libera. La RAI, i privati, i partiti*, (Milan: Edizioni di Comunità, 1990); L. Radi, *La Grande maestra. La TV tra politica e società*, (Roma: Cinque Lune, 1991); W. Veltroni, *Io e Berlusconi (e la RAI)*, (Roma: Editori Riuniti, 1990). For some of the most recent events, see G. Mazzoleni, "La RAI tra ristrutturazione e risanamento", in *Politica in Italia. I fatti dell'anno e le interpretazioni. Edizione 1994*, edited by C. A. Mershon and G. Pasquino, Bologna, Il Mulino, pp. 247-260 and S. Gundle, "RAI e Fininvest

nell'anno di Berlusconi", in *Politica in Italia. I fatti dell'anno e le interpretazioni. Edizione 1995,* edited by P. Ignazi and S. Katz, Bologna, Il Mulino, pp. 229-253.

17. P. Barile, *Idee per il governo. Il sistema radiotelevisivo,* (Roma-Bari: Laterza, 1995); with contributions by, among others, F. Confalonieri, A. Curzi, C. Dematté e P. Murialdi. For a juridical profile, see P. Caretti, *Diritto pubblico dell'informazione,* (Bologna: Il Mulino, 1993); E. Roppo e R. Zaccaria, eds., *Il sistema radiotelevisivo pubblico e privato,* (Milan: Giuffrè, 1991).

18. The expression is P. Barile's, *Idee per il governo. Il sistema radiotelevisivo,* cit., p. 6.

19. ANSA, August 10, 1992.

20. The declaration went on as follows "...foreshadowing a possible line of institutional reform in the direction of a plebiscite democracy, an electronic Peronism, requiring a hyper-concentrated media system which is thus more easily controllable ... it is certain ...that these things are written in the Licio Gelli 'recovery plan'," ANSA, August 13, 1992.

21. Among the others were the ex-Minister of the left-wing of the DC, Fracanzani, the President of Acli, Giovanni Bianchi; Stefano Rodotà; PDS's director of information, Vincenzo Vita; Mauro Paissan, for the Greens; Gaspare Nuccio, for *La Rete*; and Pietro Ingrao.

22. A ten-point "Manifesto for clean information" was also presented. Supporting this program were such political exponents of the Left as: Luciana Castellina, Fausto Bertinotti, Leoluca Orlando, Nando dalla Chiesa, as well as PDS personalities from the culture and information fields, such as the director of Telemontercarlo News, Sandro Curzi (formerly director of Raitre TV News) and the director of Raitre, Angelo Guglielmi.

23. A. Cariola, *Referendum abrogativo e giudizio costituzionale. Contributo allo studio del potere sovrano nell'ordinamento pluralista,* (Milan: Giuffrè, 1994), pp. 267-334; A. Tempestini, "Le forche caudine dei referendum: la Corte costituzionale", in *Democrazie e referendum,* cit., pp. 316-330.

24. It is necessary to remember how the Constitutional Court also in effect took part in the process with two other decisions which invoced the subjects of the referendum examined here. In particular, the court determined unconstitutional of section 4 of art. 15 of the Mammì law, which established that the same person could not own more than 25 percent of the national networks foreseen by the frequency assignment plan and in any case three at most. The sentence of the court was favorably received by the proponents of the three abrogative questions on the Mammì law. The court's decision rejected other claims of unconstitutionality raised by the Tar of Lazio following an appeal by the Beta Television group which heads the group of Maria Lina Marcucci, the owner of Video Music, who was elected in the regional elections of 1995 to the Regional Council of Tuscany as a PDS candidate.

25. The court's judgments of admissibility have always been the object of analyses and interpretations by jurists. On the January decisions see, for example, the comments of G. Azzariti, "Referendum, leggi elettorali e Parlamento: la 'forza' delle decisioni referendarie nei sistemi di democrazia rappresentativa", in *Giurisprudenza costituzionale,* n. 1, 1995, pp. 88-103 e G.G. Floridia, "Partita a tre. La disciplina elettorale tra Corte, referendum e legislatore", in *Giurisprudenza*

Costituzionale, n. 1, 1995, pp. 103-119.

26. In general, see P. Mancini e G. Mazzoleni, eds., *I media scendono in campo*, (Turin: Nuova Eri, 1995). The data we refer to are those contained in G. Sani, "C'è un leader in video: la forza della telepolitica" in *Il Mulino*, n. 5, 1995, pp. 877-888. For different evaluations of the possibility of determining the final outcome of an electoral competition, see the analyses by L. Ricolfi, "Elezioni e mass media. Quanti voti ha spostato la Tv", in *Il Mulino*, n. 6, 1994, pp. 1031-1046, e P. Legrenzi, "Produzione di voti a mezzo di reti", in *Il Mulino*, n. 1, 1995, pp. 131-135.

27. Added abstensionism is used as an indicator of the diffusion of the exchange vote and membership vote by A. Parisi e M. Rossi, "La relazione elettori-partiti: quale lezione?", in *Il Mulino*, n. 4, 1978, pp. 503-47 and later by R. Cartocci, *Elettori in Italia. Riflessioni sulle vicende elettorali degli anni ottanta*, (Bologna: Il Mulino, 1990). For an analysis of territorial distribution of added abstensionism in the 1993 referendum, see R. Cartocci, *Fra Lega e Chiesa*, cit., pp. 34-41.

28. If we exclude Massa Carrara, in no province in the Red Zone (Emilia-Romagna, Toscana, Marche and Umbria) does added abstensionism go over 30 percent. With the exception of Belluno, added abstensionism does not exceed 25 percent in any province of Veneto.

29. Added abstensionism exceeded 30 percent in just one province in Sicily, Ragusa. In this respect the provinces of Catania and Enna appear similar to many provinces in Veneto, Emilia-Romagna and Toscana. We must also consider that in the 1994 political elections abstensionism in Sicily was very high. L. Ricolfi has noted the specificity of Sicilian electoral behavior in, "Il voto proporzionale e il nuovo spazio politico italiano", in *Maggioritario ma non troppo*, cit., pp. 273-316. For a discussion of voter turn-out for the 1991 referenda, see M. Morisi and P. Feltrin, "La scelta elettorale: le apparenze e le questioni", in *Far politica in Sicilia. Deferenza, consenso e protesta*, edited by M. Morisi, (Milan: Feltrinelli, 1993), pp. 15-83; R. D'Amico e F. Raniolo, "L'elettorato siciliano e il referendum sulla preferenza unica del 1991", in *Democrazie e referendum*, cit., pp. 372-89.

30. Naturally, since it is calculated from national totals, the additional valid vote represents an estimate; in contrast with the prevailing behavior, some voters may have decided to ask for a ballot or to express a valid vote only on the question of the privatization of RAI.

31. The map (see fig. 3.2) also highlights the specificity of some southern provinces: the percentage of additional valid votes was not as high in the three most important metropolitan areas: Naples (6.4 percent), Bari (7.7 percent) and Palermo (7.6 percent). The difference between the provinces that are the regional capitals and those that are not is noticeable not only in the Center-South but also in the Center-North. For example, Turin in Piedmont with 3.6 percent, and Milan in Lombardy with 3.4 percent are both last in their regional rankings. The different incidence of the additional valid vote in the capital provinces and in the less central provinces can be related to the degree of centrality or marginality of a given area with respect to the elements composing the information system.

32. The North comprises Valle d'Aosta, Piemonte, Lombardia, Veneto, Friuli-Venezia Giulia, Trentino-Alto Adige; the Red Zone comprises Emilia-Romagna, Toscana, Umbria and Marche; the Center-South comprises the remaining regions. On a demographic level, the three areas are not homogeneous; in the provinces which we have placed in the Red Zone, there are 8,395,061 voters (a little over 17 percent of the Italian electorate). Moreover, as we have seen, voter participation in these regions was much higher than in the Center-South half of the country: the voters from the Red Zone (5,488,308 on the union democracy question) represent almost 20 percent of the total.

33. It is difficult to believe that such a large difference is due simply to the presence of fluctuating voters. On the three questions proposed by the union committees, there was in effect a tendency towards an increase in the "no" vote, which was much less marked in the case of the question aimed at a total liberalization (see Table 3.6).

34. G. Pasquino, *I referendum,* cit., p. 132.

35. G. Sartori, *Corriere della Sera,* December 19, 1995.

4

The Oak Tree and the Olive Tree

Mark Gilbert

At the beginning of February, 1995, Romano Prodi announced his intention to pursue a political career and put himself forward as the Center-Left's candidate for the premiership once the Dini government had exhausted its mandate. His initiative at first sight appeared to have created the preconditions for the establishment in Italy of the bipolar party system that prevails in other advanced democracies. However, by the end of 1995, Prodi's experience as *primus inter pares* of a fractious coalition of centrist and left-wing parties had, if anything, illustrated just how distant Italy in general, and its progressive parties in particular, are from this goal.

Prodi's candidacy did not lead to either the formation of a unified "Democrat party", or even to the fusion of the gaggle of progressive Catholic, socialist, liberal and environmentalist mini-parties into a reformist center party able to deal with the PDS on equal terms. Instead, much of the year was wasted in interminable squabbles as the so-called *cespugli* ("bushes")—Mario Segni's Democratic Pact, Carlo Ripa Di Meana's Greens, Ottavio De Turco's Labouristes—strove to protect their own patches of turf beneath the spreading branches of the PDS oak tree.

A Professor in Politics

Prodi's decision to run for office was not an act of vainglory. His qualifications for the post were unimpeachable.

Born in the province of Reggio Emilia in 1939, Prodi can boast an enviable record of achievement as an academic, a businessman, and a politician. Unlike Silvio Berlusconi, whose personal empire was accrued by sharp dealing in the property market and shrewd exploitation of television regulations rigged on his behalf, Prodi is not a financial buccaneer. He is a technocrat whose studies in industrial organization as a young man earned him early promotion to a university chair, a series of prestigious publications both in Italy and abroad, and a visiting professorship at Harvard. In 1979, he had a brief, but unhappy, spell as minister for industry in the shortlived Andreotti IV administration. Above all, between 1982 and 1989, Prodi was President of the Institute for Industrial Reconstruction (IRI), a post which made him directly responsible for the Italian state's extensive holdings in manufacturing industry. When he took over the company, the firm was losing three trillion lire per year, and was in debt to the tune of 35 trillion lire. When he was forced out of his job in October, 1989, Prodi had managed to turn the group around. The company made a profit of over a trillion lire in 1989, though political obstruction had prevented him from privatizing IRI's numerous under-performing assets.

The dates of Prodi's spell at IRI—1982-1989—are of course significant. These years were the time of Ciriaco De Mita's ascendancy within the DC, and while Prodi has never been as closely associated with De Mita as Berlusconi was with Craxi, Andreotti and Forlani, he is unambiguously identified with the ex-DC's left-wing. Indeed, the final shove that he needed to propel him into his announcement was almost certainly the decision taken at the end of January by Rocco Buttiglione, the then-leader of the Italian Popular Party (PPI), to reverse his policy of cooperation with the PDS and to throw the somewhat reduced lot of Italian Christian Democracy with Berlusconi and Fini in the *Polo della Libertà*.

Prodi, in short, is a social progressive who has met a payroll, a fact which makes him the ideal "anti-Berlusconi." But the excitement that greeted Prodi's announcement—the former Christian Democrat leader Mino Martinazzoli described his initiative as "providential"[1]—was less due to his personal qualities and political opinions than to the prospect that his candidacy seemed to offer of simplifying the Italian party system. As Gianfranco Pasquino argued in *L'Unità* on February 3, the importance of Prodi's candidacy lays in the fact that he was a figure around whom a Center-Left alternative government could be created.

Prodi was initially supported by the leftist majority within the PPI, by Mario Segni and *Alleanza Democratica* (AD), but within days Massimo D'Alema, the leader of the PDS, added his approval as well, saying that Prodi was "the right choice" to lead a broadly defined progressive coalition into the next election. When D'Alema's open encouragement of Prodi's initiative was followed by the tragi-comic split of the PPI, and the noisy departure into the *Polo della Libertà* of Buttiglione and his cohort of ex-Andreottiani, matters seemed to have clarified still further. Prodi's move seemed to have rendered real what the overwhelming majority of Italian political scientists and constitutionalists had long regarded as a *sine qua non* for a substantive reform of the political system: a straightforward electoral choice between Right and Left.

Prodi's decision to enter the political arena, in short, appeared to be pushing Italy towards a party system akin to that of Spain, in which a moderate Left confronts a slighly less moderate Right, with the parliamentary fringe being composed of a neo-communist party, as well as regionalist movements of various political hues. Yet differences remained. Unlike Spain, where Center-Right and Center-Left opinion is concentrated into two coherent and reasonably cohesive political parties, Italy's new bipolarism within its party system was—and is—based upon two heterogeneous coalitions. In February, nobody was suggesting that the Center-Left coalition, in particular, could be welded into a single political party. In an interview with *La Repubblica* on February 8, Massimo D'Alema dismissed the notion of a "Democrat party" as an idea whose time was not ripe, one which would inevitably lead to an electoral defeat, since it would be all too easy for the Right to portray such a development as a communist takeover of the center. Opposition to Berlusconi and Fini, D'Alema contended, would be all the stronger if it was a common effort by "distinct subjects."[2]

On March 10, 1995, Prodi was consecrated as the Center-Left's official candidate for the premiership by no fewer than twelve such "distinct subjects."[3] Prodi could also count upon the support of a growing network of activist groups working on behalf of his candidacy. His decision to enter public life had sparked enormous interest and all over Italy committees "For Prodi President" were spontaneously forming, coordinated by his personal staff in Bologna. By April, over 2,000 of these committees were in existence, and by Prodi's own count, over 60 percent of their adherents were people who boasted no previous political affiliation. They were simply concerned citizens working for "the Italy We Want," as the movement was baptised.What these citizens wanted above all, Prodi explained, was a "reassuring alternative" to the "extraneous" right-wing extremism of Berlusconi and Fini, and an antidote to traditional party politics.[4]

To symbolize the authenticity and patriotism of his approach to politics, Prodi chose the *Ulivo*—olive tree—as the emblem of his candidacy. As he explained in his interview-book *La mia Italia*, the olive "is to be found from the Trentino to Sicily, is the outcome of hundreds of years of human labour, is contorted because it has the strength to resist even the most severe weather, not because it is feeble."[5] Prodi was determined to ensure that his candidacy should not be seen as a "Berlusconibis." The "Italy We Want" committees were to be self-financing, limited to thirty members, and unhierarchical in structure. They were, in short, to be a genuinely democratic grassroots movement, not a rootless marketing operation like *Forza Italia*, or a rigid old-style electoral machine. Prodi also ostentatiously condemned the glitzy, media-driven style of politics brought into fashion by Berlusconi. He was adamant that his brand of politics would consist in listening and learning from the electorate, not a Berlusconi-style hard sell of a carefully packaged product.

To this end, the Professor embarked upon a somewhat quixotic, but deeply impressive, 100-day coach tour of Italy. Between March 13 and June 3, 1995, Prodi visited nine separate regions (Apulia, Venetia, the Marches, the Trentino, Friuli, Tuscany, Sicily and Sardinia), was welcomed at dozens of towns and cities, attended literally dozens of conferences and receptions, and made many fact-finding visits to factories, voluntary service centres and research institutes. If nothing else, Prodi demonstrated that he had the stamina to be Prime Minister. To give just one example of the gruelling schedule he followed during his tour, during his two-day visit on April 11-12 to Italy's northernmost regions of Trentino-Alto Adige and Friuli, Prodi visited four factories or agricultural co-operatives; conducted two walkabouts in the town squares of Bolzano and Portogruaro; held a press conference in Bolzano; gave speeches to the townsfolk of Bolzano, Rovereto, Trento, Trieste and Udine, and travelled rather more than 1000 kilometres in two days.

The Elections of April 23

Prodi's visit to the Trentino and Friuli was the last stop on his tour before the regional elections of April 23, 1995. In the run-up to the elections the first voices dissenting from his position as leader of the Center-Left began to make themselves heard. Conditioned by Berlusconi's opinion pollsters, who forecast a substantial victory for the right-wing alliance, and preoccupied that the "For Prodi President" committees might be transformed into a party capable of eating away at their base of support, the *Ulivo*'s chieflings hinted that their support for Prodi was less than absolute. The Greens wondered aloud why Prodi had not submitted himself to a process of primaries before nominating himself as leader, and the secretary of the PPI, Gerardo Bianco, emphasized that Prodi was only one of a number of would-be candidates for the premiership who would be acceptable to the PPI.

The regional elections thus became a test of Prodi's political standing. They were also a test of Massimo D'Alema's strategic acumen. Would the PDS's decision to open to the Center be rewarded in terms of votes?

Instead of making shining promises, the PDS's campaign had emphasized that the regions administered by the PDS were the best governed
in Italy. Was this electoral strategy too low key a response to Berlusconi's
blaring rhetoric and slick self-promotion? In the event, the voters decided that D'Alema and Prodi's competence was worth voting for.
Anybody could see that Bologna had been a civic success story for
decades, and that Antonio Bassolino had given back Naples' pride in
just eighteen months of creative local government. The candidates backed
by the Center-Left, upsetting the outcome predicted by the exit polls
and ballyhooed by Berlusconi's television channels, came in first in nine
out of fifteen regions. In Umbria, Bruno Bracalente, the Center-Left's
nominee for the presidency of the regional giunta, scored a staggering
60 percent. The PDS, with over 25 percent of the vote, overtook *Forza
Italia* to become Italy's largest party. In the second round of balloting,
two weeks later, tactical voting by the *Lega Nord*'s electorate made the
Center-Left's victory more imposing still.

The response of progressive opinion to the victory in the regional
and local elections was euphoric. On April 25, *La Repubblica* called the
results "liberating;"[6] Walter Veltroni wrote a Churchillian editorial for
L'Unità which seemed to be comparing the successful Center-Left coalitions in the regional ballots to the great coalition of Christian Democrats, *azionisti* and communists who had led the resistance to fascism
and the German occupation. The time, Veltroni intoned, was now. Time
for what? Time to take an unprecedented step in Italian history and
unite into a single political alliance the "values and programmes" of all
Italy's democratic forces.[7]

Veltroni could be forgiven for his rhetoric. The day his article appeared, Prodi nominated him as vice Prime Minister in waiting and the
PDS announced that it would suborn its own oak tree symbol to Prodi's
Ulivo in all of the 475 single member constituencies that would be contested in the coming general elections. For Veltroni, a youthful forty-
year-old Roman who is one of Italy's leading experts on the life and
times of Robert Kennedy, the PDS's move was the culmination of his
own lengthy campaign to persuade the party to rid itself of its last ties
with its communist past and remake itself as the voice of Italian liberalism. Veltroni can fairly be compared with Tony Blair, whose successful reinvention of the Labour party has made a deep impression in Italy.
Like Blair, Veltroni exudes intelligence and well-dressed charm; is
telegenic (unlike the somewhat homely Prodi); is a politician who rel-
ishes ideas and can present them clearly. Unlike Blair, Veltroni does not
have the support of a John Prescott figure able to appeal to greengrocers,
janitors and brick layers in everyday language. It is worth pointing out
that this is a fault hardly limited to the editor of *L'Unità*. As a brief scan

down the list of the "regional coordinators" of the "Italy We Want" movement shows, the upper reaches of the *Ulivo* are dominated by mostly male upper middle class professionals and academics. Of the ninety-eight "coordinators" listed, only six are women, and only four have working or lower middle class jobs. By contrast, there are no fewer than nineteen university professors—some of them very distinguished figures—and similar numbers of lawyers and doctors (who for the most part are eminent surgeons, not young general practitioners). The *Ulivo*, in short, is unambiguously led by the *alta borghesia*. It will be interesting to see if the PDS's close identification with such a movement will inspire an electoral backlash among its manual working class voters.[8]

The PDS's march into the center certainly inspired an immediate backlash among the *Ulivo*'s princelings. At the end of April, the "Democratic Pact" (the loose confederal structure uniting Mario Segni's supporters with AD and the heirs of the former PSI) publicly dissented in intemperate terms from both Prodi's decision to allow the PDS on to the ballot with the *Ulivo* and from the way in which Prodi had taken the decision (the matter had been decided over lunch with D'Alema and Veltroni at a chic restaurant in Rome). Prodi's handling of the decision had unquestionably been tactless. But Prodi's allies were motivated by more than injured vanity. Prodi's embracing of the PDS, and his appointment of Veltroni, had brought to the boil an issue that had to be answered sooner or later. Was the *Ulivo* to be an all-encompassing federation of the liberal Left? Or an electoral alliance between the PDS and a federal union of center parties? Or an electoral pact between wholly separate Left-Center subjects? The first of these proposals—witness D'Alema's remarks in February—had hitherto seemed an impossibility. The second proposal had seemed to be the position Prodi preferred: it was also the one vocally espoused by Mario Segni, though Segni's efforts in this regard had hardly made much progress. The third proposal was the position of both the Greens and the PPI. Before the April poll, Gerardo Bianco had made his opposition to any cession of the PPI's sovereign identity perfectly plain. A few days before he went to lunch with D'Alema, Prodi had suggested that the Union for French Democracy (UDF) might be the ideal model for the *Ulivo*: a federation of centrist parties that retained their own identities but combined their efforts in support of a single presidential candidate. This proposal was a subtle attempt to marry Segni's position with the PPI's: what nobody had envisaged was that Prodi would invite the "communists" to join the party too. In an important article in *La Repubblica* on May 3, 1995, Segni was adamant that *"L'Ulivo non è il partito unico."*[9] The expression *partito unico* carries totalitarian overtones and made Segni's central point abundantly clear. What he called the "ample area" of lay and democratic Catholic opinion was not going to be dragooned into a grouping dominated by a political force that until recently was of a wholly different political culture.

Prodi had two courses of action open to him in the face of this overt criticism of his leadership. He could either turn the "Italy We Want" committees into a political party and essentially become a rival for the center parties' votes (in an extremely candid interview with *La Repubblica* on May 13, 1995, Prodi did not hide the fact that this was an option that he was considering). Alternatively, he could hope that the split would heal as a result of the Center-Left parties' common campaign for a "yes" vote in the June referenda on television ownership, and the PDS's intended adoption of a new "liberal" platform of values. Prodi unsurprisingly took this second option. Beginning on June 8, the twelve "branches" of the *Ulivo* began regular summit meetings to debate and decide the movement's strategy and tactics. Everybody—the quark-like Christian Socialists, the forlorn Republicans and Social Democrats, the microscopic Liberals, the self-righteous Labouristes—would sit around the same table as the PDS and have the same say.

A Normal Country

The decision of the PDS to continue its evolution away from communism by becoming a "liberal" party has to be evaluated in the context of this political division within the *Ulivo*. D'Alema announced in May that the PDS would be holding a *Congresso tematico* in early July to discuss the party's ideological direction, and on May 27, the National Council of the PDS approved a substantial and intriguing general statement of principles that would form the basis for discussion at the congress.

This document is actually more thought-provoking than the speeches at the congress itself. Its starting point—although it is never cited—is Prodi's own *manifesto, Governare l'Italia,* which was first published in article form in *Micromega* in December, 1994, and was reissued in April, 1995 by Donzelli as a paperback. In *Governare l'Italia,* Prodi outlines his own personal preference for "a lightweight state" in which the state's ownership role (and the role of the political parties as controllers of the state's patrimony) is sharply reduced to the levels prevailing in the rest of Western Europe.[10] At the same time, his pro-privatization, pro-market views are tempered by a strong commitment to a welfare state that protects the market's inevitable casualties, and a passionate belief in the power of education, "the basis of every kind of wealth."[11]

In the document approved by the National Council of the PDS, the somewhat memorandum-like tone of Prodi's *manifesto* is enlivened with a dash of ideological excitement. The PDS presents itself as a party that is trying to find a middle way between the harshness of free market capitalism and the self-evident failings of social democratic welfarism. The alternative to excessive reliance on the invisible hand of the market, and the Social Darwinism of the Thatchers and Gingriches of the world is not a bureaucratic, centralized, welfare-dispensing, inefficient super-state, but a rule-making "slim state;" a state that combats monopoly business and industrial oligarchies in the name of economic innovation; a state that treats welfare as a means to create opportunities, not as a set of programs to be administered by plodding career civil servants; a state that wants people to manage their own lives, to be volunteers in the communal project, and is willing to help such volunteers with its re-sources.

Perhaps most strikingly of all, the document finally dispenses with the last traces of the language of the class struggle. The expression "work-ing class" is not mentioned once in a document that is nearly 10,000 words long. Although the document does commit the party to improv-ing opportunities for those without work, to massive investment in in-frastructure and technology, and to ending the policy of "tears and blood" practised by Ciampi and Dini, it does not represent such measures in terms of working class interests. Rather, the need for such policies is presented as an imperative in terms of Italy's international and Euro-pean standing. To this extent, the PDS's views are consonant with Prodi's. In *La mia Italia*, Prodi worried that Italy, despite its thriving commercial and industrial sector, might reproduce the economic example of Argen-tina, the world's seventh largest economy in the 1930s, which declined as a result of its wasteful state, and a failure to adjust to changing eco-nomic conditions.[12] Both Prodi and the PDS are alarmed by Italy's fail-ure to develop a tertiary sector worthy of the name, and to match other major industrialized nations in the fields of research and technology.

The document also laid out the outline of the political strategy that the PDS intended to follow over the coming months. In the abstract language beloved of the old PCI, the PDS proposed the unification of the non-communist Italian Left by appealing to the representatives of "the tradition of Catholic solidarity," (*La Rete*, Christian Socialists) and "he today dispersed forces of Italian socialism" (Labouristes, PSDI, Ital-ian Socialists) to join with the PDS in a single party of the Democratic Left that would present a common symbol on the ballot slip for the proportional quota. Furthermore, the PDS suggested that the unifica-tion of the Left might be merely the first step of a wider process of "synthesis" whereby "the democratic cultures" of "religious, environ-mentalist and liberal inspiration" were incorporated into a "great demo-cratic force" of the Center-Left.

This project, the document insisted, was one that had concrete hopes of success. All over Italy, exponents of the Center-Left's diverse cultures were already cooperating in town halls and regional administrations; the same groups had sustained the parliamentary majority of Lamberto Dini, and the candidacy for the premiership of Romano Prodi. What was now necessary was a further step forward towards unity. At this point, in its final paragraphs, the document contained a hint of menace. It would be "serious," it warned, if the hardline logic of "sectarian closure" or "self-isolation" won out over the necessity for "reasonable agreement" between the parties of the Center-Left imposed by the majoritarian electoral system. A "compact coalition" with a single program would be capable of achieving greater coordination among the parties of the Center-Left and putting an end to "useless polemic." If some such coalition did not come into being, the PDS would be driven—against its will—to become "somewhat relevant on the Italian political scene."

The *Congresso tematico* was held in Rome on July 6-8, 1995. Anyone expecting programmatic flesh to be added to the doctrinal bones of the National Council's statement of principles was disappointed; the congress, as usual at such events, prized rhetoric over substance, and generalizations over concrete detail.

A few sceptics aside (Achille Occhetto, who did not attend, being the most prominent of these), the party swallowed D'Alema's liberal *svolta* without a qualm. By the end of the congress, even Berlusconi (who was invited to address the delegates) was hard-pressed to detect any traces of Leninist sulphur in the stated political line of the PDS. It would have been discourteous if he had. Berlusconi was self-consciously treated as the "leader of the opposition" and the major speakers were extraordinarily restrained in their comments on *Forza Italia*'s alarming and anti-democratic behaviour since Berlusconi's expulsion from government in December, 1994. This restraint was intended to make a political point. Both D'Alema and Veltroni were at pains to stress that they wished to turn Italy into a "normal" country, where the Right could meet with the Center-Left and hold a rational and serene dialogue, without resorting to the politics of insult, to quasi-totalitarian media coverage, and to the brazen distortion of their opponents' arguments.

The *Congresso tematico* of the PDS was—still is—potentially the most important development in the Italian party system since the collapse of the DC in the spring of 1993. By invading the center ground in what Lucio Colletti called an "almost imperious" way, the PDS robbed the "bushes" dwelling in its shade of any meaningful reason for continuing to persist in independent political activity. But this bold step was followed by a prolonged bout of dithering, as the PDS failed to draw the logical political consequences of its action and hesitated to give the *Ulivo* a clear programmatic or political lead. In the weeks following the congress, the "bushes" were allowed to act as if they had equal status with the PDS and to exercise an effective veto over Prodi's choices for his government in waiting. The result was that Prodi assembled at the beginning of August a Diniesque committee of the great and good rather than a potential government of unconfoundable progressive sympathies.[13]

The summer was also wasted in futile wrangling over strategy and tactics. Mario Segni, in particular, flirted aggressively with the *Polo della Libertà* by sympathizing with Berlusconi and Fini's decision to promote a presidentialist reform of the constitution in the event of an electoral victory by the parties of the Right. Most of the *Ulivo*'s members—despite their vociferous disclaimers—seemed to be working harder to create an all-embracing Center party, perhaps led by Lamberto Dini, than a coherent party of the Center-Left. This led to an embarrassing auction between *Forza Italia* and the *Ulivo* for Dini's (unoffered) services. Veltroni, presaging a similar later bid to Antonio Di Pietro, even offered Dini the vice-premiership. Quite what conservative figures such as Di Pietro and Dini, admirable and competent though they may be, have to do with the creation of a government of the Left remains unclear.

Electoral considerations were at the bottom of this maneuvering. The great fear of the Center parties (including those allied to Berlusconi and Fini) throughout 1995 has been a Machiavellian compromise between the leaders of the *Polo* and the leaders of the PDS to hold a quick poll and return to "political" government. Segni, the PPI, their counterparts within the *Polo* (the Christian Democratic Center and Rocco Buttiglione's newly formed CDU), not to mention Bossi's *Lega*, all had a vested interest in keeping the legislature elected in 1994 alive. A new election would have meant the obliteration of the *Lega*, and the reduction of the *cespugli* to the status of satellite parties to the three political forces that together command over 60 percent of the vote: the PDS, *Forza Italia* and the AN. By flirting with the presidentialism dear to the AN (Segni), or the idea of a Center party (everybody), or declaring northern independence on a weekly basis (the *Lega*), the leaders of the mini-parties were not so much advancing serious solutions to the nation's problems as reminding Prodi and D'Alema that the *Ulivo* could not take their support for granted. In the meantime, Italy—the country Veltroni and D'Alema wanted to normalize—continued to be the only major western country unable to meet the first and most important "procedural minimum condition" for a democracy: government by elected officials.[14]

Some on the Left—most prominently the "philosopher-mayor" of Venice, Massimo Cacciari (who would have been a splendid addition to

Prodi's committee of experts)—argued that the behavior of the "bushes" was "squalid" and openly appealed for a quick election, even if it meant losing.[15] More cautious counsels prevailed, however. D'Alema and Veltroni were presumably convinced that the Center-Left could not win an autumn election without the support of the "bushes" and were thus willing to appease the permanent procrastination of their centrist allies (as well as to cut an electoral deal with *Rifondazione Comunista* in August, and to wink at an outrageous anti-immigrant campaign by the *Lega* in the fall). By October, the papers were talking openly of a crisis within the Center-Left coalition. The movement launched by Romano Prodi seemed to have lost all impetus in just eight months.

The *Ulivo*'s Basic Law

The *Ulivo* may have been saved from itself by the traumatic events of October and November. Berlusconi's judicial troubles, his attacks on President Scalfaro, his attempt to overturn the Dini administration over the Mancuso question, the alleged Mafia links of leading members of Forza Italia such as Vittorio Sgarbi, and the revelations regarding Fininvest's huge payments to Bettino Craxi have, to put it mildly, weakened the Milanese entrepreneur as an electoral force. By December, the *Polo della Libertà* was hopelessly divided, with the AN taking an increasingly independent and ominous role, and with the right-wing alliance's own "bushes" in a state of revolt against Fini and Berlusconi's desire to force early elections in February, 1996. On December 7, 1995, the *Ulivo* was able to present its draft program to the electorate in an atmosphere of relative optimism; a few days later, Veltroni and Prodi presented the official symbol of the *Ulivo,* and the somewhat wordy slogan ("The Olive is growing to help the reawakening of our country") which will provide the theme of the Center-Left's electoral campaign. In early 1996, a major congress of more than 4,000 delegates from Italy's 475 constituencies was due to ratify the programme and transform it into the manifesto of the Center-Left coalition. Despite some instant quibbling over some of the draft programme's provisions by the PPI, among others, the *Ulivo,* for almost the first time since the regional elections of April-May, suddenly looked like the most logical and coherent choice for the government of Italy.

The draft program is an interesting document that provides a clear picture of the direction in which Prodi and his closest collaborators want to take the country. It outlines the ambitious fundamental reforms that the *Ulivo* proposes to undertake in the different areas of competence of Prodi's neo-ministerial team. Inevitably, the aspects of the program that have aroused most interest are the proposals concerning constitutional

and electoral reform. In these proposals (which would be put into legislative form by a bicameral commission of Parliament), Prodi and the
Ulivo promise nothing less than a "new state."[16]

This new state looks remarkably like Germany. Despite (or because
of) the often passionate advocacy of presidentialism this year, from Fini,
Berlusconi, Segni, and Giovanni Sartori, the *Ulivo* opted unambiguously
for a parliamentary form of government "centred upon the figure of the
Prime Minister."[17] The draft proposal, however, is anxious to ensure
that the people shall choose who the premier will be. The *Ulivo* ingen-
iously suggests that each coalition should list the name of its premier-
designate alongside the name of its candidate in each single member
constituency, thus conferring a moral obligation upon the elected deputy
to back a specific person for the Prime Minister's job. In this way, it is
hoped that the new Italian state, despite its multi-party character, will
be spared the post-election bargaining and cynical intra-party deal-
making that surrounded the choice of the premiership during the First
Republic.

The *Ulivo*'s program gives the premier additional protection. A "constitutional convention" would require an immediate election in the event
of the defection of a component part of the premier's majority. A premier
would be protected from a coup within his majority by the German
device of a "constructive vote of no-confidence." Would-be plotters
against a premier would have to nominate one of their number as an
alternative Prime Minister and subject his or her candidacy to a parliamentary vote of confidence.[18]

This almost invulnerable premier, moreover, would be the benefici-
ary of substantive powers to direct the activity of both the executive
branch and the legislature. The Prime Minister would coordinate the
legislative activity of the government via a powerful private office on the
German or British model. He would have the power to ensure the "timely
discussion of government proposals" by controlling the parliamentary
timetable. Most strikingly of all, he would have the power to veto any
legislative initiative or amendment that would increase public expenditure: the "line item veto" beloved of American presidents.[19]

The *Ulivo*, in short, came out in favor of "Chancellor Democracy." As
in Germany, the office of president is reduced to a purely ceremonial
post. The program insists that the president will be "guarantor of the
rules, and representative of the country and of the continuity of its democratic institutions," but this high-sounding statement of the head of
state's mission cannot disguise the fact that the president's current role
as a crisis-broker will have been taken from him. His powers to dissolve
Parliament and to nominate the Prime Minister will become a cipher if
the *Ulivo* has its way.

The German model is also evident in the *Ulivo*'s proposals for Italy's regions. Prodi and his advisors concede that national legislation "interferes" with local autonomy. The program commits itself to remedying this state of affairs by—in effect—transforming Italy's twenty regions into *Länder*. Among other powers given to them, Italy's regions will be able to legislate on all matters not expressly limited to the national Parliament; choose their own form of government, so long as it is in accord with the constitution; decide for themselves the modality of subregional government, and have a degree of representation in the institutions of the European Union.[20] They will also enjoy the benefits of "fiscal federalism" by which a substantial part of the taxes currently levied centrally will be devolved to the regions, with national legislation ensuring that, as in Germany, the richer areas subsidize the poorer regions to guarantee minimum levels of sanitation, education and health care throughout the nation.[21]

Taken together, these proposals represent a huge step towards the reorganization of Italy on federal lines. In recognition of this fact, the biggest single change to the national institutions of government will be the replacement of the existing Senate with a "Chamber of the Regions," which, like the *Bundesrat*, will be an indirectly elected assembly composed of representatives of the various regional governments. The new Chamber's powers will be more limited than the existing second chamber. Again like the *Bundesrat*, it will concern itself only with matters concerning the regions (though the experience of Germany shows that most laws can and will be construed by the Constitutional Court as affecting the regions), and will not be able to cast a vote of confidence in the national government. Regions will be awarded representatives roughly in accordance with population, with a "corrective" to assist relatively unpopulated areas such as Molise or the Val d'Aosta. The support of an actual majority of regions, not just of votes, will be needed for a measure to pass.[22]

The strengthening of the figure of the Prime Minister, the devolution of legislative and tributary power to the regions, and the transformation of the Senate into a "Chamber of Regions" imply a substantial reduction in the powers of Parliament. If all these proposals ever become law, Italy's legislature-dominated constitution will have been fundamentally changed. Other parts of the *Ulivo*'s program would "weaken" the legislature still further by introducing changes to the procedural rules of the Chamber of Deputies that would give backbenchers and factional bosses far less authority to hinder legislation with time-wasting amendments, to propose pork barrel legislation, and to block legislation in committee. At the same time, the opposition would be given guaranteed time for debate; time would be found for unannounced parliamentary questions, and the legislative sovereignty of the Chamber of Deputies would be reasserted by stricter limitations on the use of the referendum instrument. The Chamber of Deputies, in short, would pass "fewer laws, but better ones." Instead of devoting its time to micromanaging the affairs of Italy's regions, or arguing for months over new codices to replace legislation struck from the statute books by a frustrated citizenry, the Chamber of Deputies will become a forum for debate and scrutiny of the major legislative initiatives of "a government that governs." Deputies will be elected from single member constituencies by the dual ballot system used in France.[23]

Italy has been waiting for a "great reform" since the end of the 1970s. It cannot be disputed that the *Ulivo*'s proposals constitute an institutional refit of breathtaking proportions. Italy would, in effect, be scrapping the Constitution it adopted in the aftermath of World War Two and starting afresh. At long last the leadership of one of the country's two competing coalitions has nailed its colors to the mast and proclaimed what kind of country it would like Italy to be. This step in theory will compel Berlusconi and Fini to do the same: the now inevitable spring election might turn into a complex public debate over whether Italy should follow the "German" model of institutional and political organization, as the *Ulivo* prefers, or whether it should not look westwards, to semi-presidentialist France, for a model.

Then again, it might not. In a cutting essay written at the end of 1994, Gianfranco Pasquino commented that:

> The outcome of the Italian transition appears extremely uncertain since none of the political actors who count, both in government and in the opposition, know what objectives they should pursue. They reason, if this verb is not too flattering, with almost exclusive reference to their particular, conflicting, short-term ends.[24]

This remark remains almost as true in December, 1995 as it was in December, 1994. The *Ulivo*'s adventures this year have demonstrated that a two-party system will not be brought into being without a profound change in the political culture of the principal Italian parties, including the PDS. Without excessively romanticizing the form of government that exists in Britain, Germany and Spain (the United States is in a different category), it is fair to say that in those countries politics is mainly driven by programmatic and ideological considerations. The two main parties in such systems traditionally stand for certain values and policies, and, when political necessity demands an electoral or parliamentary deal with a third party such as the FDP, the Liberal Democrats or the Catalonian CIU, the deal is one that operates within fuzzy, but nonetheless real, limits of intellectual principle. To give an obvious example: in the event of there being a "hung Parliament" in Britain after the 1997 elections, the Conservatives will not try to buy themselves back into office by promising the Liberals fully proportional representation and a British commitment to a federal United States of Europe. Opposition to such policies is part of what British Conservatism is, and the Conservatives themselves (not to mention the country at large) would feel that they had lost their programmatic integrity by abandoning these policies for the sake of parliamentary advantage.

It is the absence of integrity in this sense (I do not mean to imply that Italian politicians are not sincere) which is thwarting Italy's transition to two-party politics. It is hard to point to a single party that has a single policy commitment, or traditional value, that cannot be traded for a fleeting political advantage. In the case of the right-wing parties—what was the Berlusconi government but an exercise in opportunism?—this is obvious. More subtly, the same is true of the PDS. The oak tree bloomed in strange colors this year, as the party reinvented itself as a "liberal" party whose objective, supposedly, was to unite the Democratic Left into a single formation. This was a courageous and probably necessary step, but inevitably one is left wondering how far the party's move was motivated by political expediency, and how deeply rooted the new principles are among the party's leadership and membership. The PDS, moreover, has been as guilty as anyone in Italian politics of the opportunistic pursuit of electoral advantage. Its pursuit of an outright conservative like Dini, its pandering to both *Rifondazione Comunista* and the *Lega Nord*, not to mention its year-long appeasement of the "bushes," inevitably lead observers to believe that electoral victory is all that matters to such a party's leadership. Is the PDS's support for the draft program of the *Ulivo* a lasting commitment to a particular vision of Italy's future? Or will even its core principles (not just details) be subject to negotiation if an eventual Prodi-Veltroni government needs the votes of the *Lega*, *Rifondazione*, or Mario Segni to win and stay in office? It is perhaps worth noting that Massimo D'Alema said as late as the middle of November that he was prepared to discuss the option of presidentialism.

The commitment of the *Ulivo*'s "bushes" to the program that Prodi and his team of experts have drafted is even less certain. Will these parties, if the *Ulivo* wins the election, quietly enact proposals which are aimed at reducing the power of party chieflings to condition the activity of government? Or a new wholly majoritarian electoral law that might lead to their extinction? A good test will be these parties' willingness to renounce their electoral symbol not only for the 75 percent of seats assigned by first-past-the-post, but in the ballot for the proportional redistribution too. The experience of this year gives reasonable grounds for believing that the Democratic Pact, the Greens and the PPI will place their own political survival ahead of the transformation of the *Ulivo* into a fully fledged political party. If Berlusconi and Fini were cynical enough to offer a return to proportional representation—Fini, after all, was loudly in favor of preserving the old proportional system as recently as April, 1993—an *Ulivo* majority in Parliament might unravel very quickly in 1996. Prediction is a dangerous game in Italian politics, but it is possible that Italy is at least one *crisi di governo* away from the lasting realignment of its party system that Prodi's entrance into politics promised to precipitate.

Notes

1. Quoted in Carlo and Norberto Valentini, eds., *Prodi. La mia Italia*, (Bologna: Carmenta, 1995), p.93.

2. *La Repubblica*, February 8, 1995.

3. Prodi's candidacy was endorsed by the PDS, the PPI, the *Patto Segni*, AD, *Socialisti Italiani*, PRI, *Rete, Verdi, Liberali, Laburisti*, PSDI, *Cristiano-Sociali*.

4. *La Stampa*, April 18,1995.

5. Carlo and Norberto Valentini, *Prodi. La mia Italia*, cit. p.40.

6. Giorgio Bocca, *La Repubblica*, April 26, 1995.

7. *L'Unità*, April 25, 1995.

8. *L'Italia che vogliamo*, home page: http://www.krenet.it/welcome1.html

9. *La Repubblica*, May 3, 1995.

10. R. Prodi, *Governare l'Italia*, (Roma: Donzelli-MicroMega, 1995), p.24.

11. Ibid., p.32.

12. Carlo e Norberto Valentini, *Prodi. La mia Italia*, cit., p.68.

13. His choices—Luigi Spaventa (finance and budget), Valerio Onida (constitutional reform), Giovanni Maria Flick (justice), Gianni Bonvicini (foreign affairs), Adriano Bompiani (health), Laura Marchetti (environment), Stefano Zamagni (human resources, education)—were all figures of indisputable professional expertise, but hardly sent a clear message to the electorate of what government by the Center-Left would signify.

14. R. Dahl, *Dilemmas of Plurality Democracy*, (New Haven: Yale University Press, 1982), p.11.

15. *La Repubblica*, August 22, 1995.

16. *Tesi per la definizione della piattaforma programmatica de l'Ulivo*, home page of L'Italia che vogliamo, cit.

17. Ibid., Tesi n.1.

18. Ibid., cit., Tesi n.1.

19. Ibid., Tesi n.9.

20. Ibid., Tesi n.3.

21. Ibid., Tesi n.37.

22. Ibid., Tesi n.4.

23. Ibid., Tesi n.7-9.

24. Gianfranco Pasquino, "Un sistema politico che cambia. Transizione o restaurazione?", in Gianfranco Pasquino, ed., *La Politica italiana. Dizionario critico 1945-95*, (Bari: Laterza, 1995), pp. VI-VII.

5

Forza Italia:
From Government to Opposition

Marco Maraffi

Forza Italia's success in the parliamentary elections of March 27, 1994 made it one of the key elements of the Italian political system. For eight months *Forza Italia* and its leader, Silvio Berlusconi, dominated the political and governmental arena. But in December '94, the *Lega Nord*, its most recalcitrant and intractable ally, provoked the fall of the government (the so-called *ribaltone*, or big upset), putting an end to the first phase in the history of *Forza Italia*. A year later, it can be said that the end of the Berlusconi government and the subsequent formation of a cabinet led by Lamberto Dini signalled the beginning of a second phase in the life of *Forza Italia*—a phase which has yet to be completed.

Forza Italia's exit from the government and passage into the opposition should have constituted just a brief interlude until the new parliamentary elections, which Berlusconi hoped would rapidly return him to Palazzo Chigi. The interlude, however, has lasted much longer than was either hoped for or foreseen. Lamberto Dini's "technical" government stayed in office for all of 1995, until his resignation on December 30. *Forza Italia*, therefore, spent the entire year in opposition: a drastic, unexpected and traumatic change for a party conceived for the purpose of governing.

After the lightning victory of the year before, 1995 was a year lived in the trenches. It is well known that there is a big difference between an offensive war and trench warfare. The second requires organizational structures and psychological resources very different from those required by the first. *Forza Italia*, which had shown itself more than adequate in offensive battles, turned out to be badly equipped for trench warfare. For this reason, 1995 could, in the long term, become a decisive year for the fate of the party.

Strategy and Tactics

The opposition to the government and its decisions, the attempt to bring it down, or in short, the continual confrontation with the new executive mark the sum total of *Forza Italia*'s political strategy and tactics in 1995. The party was divided, however, between support for a government thought to be moderate and therefore substantially wellaccepted by a large part of the electorate and the necessity of opposing it more for show than for substance. *Forza Italia* expressed this conflict, which generated great internal tensions in the party (for example, concerning its relationship with the other sectors of the Center-Right coalition), by giving the impression that it is politically uncertain and directionless. In actual fact, *Forza Italia*'s political strategy remained relatively linear and coherent throughout the whole year, if one takes account of the restrictions imposed on it by the respective strategies of its allies and political adversaries. Only near the end of the year, when *Forza Italia* seemed amenable to making an agreement with the PDS and postponing the elections was there a significant change of course.

For eleven and a half months, the pole star of *Forza Italia*'s political and parliamentary navigation was the demand for new elections. This was the strategy which determined its political and parliamentary tactics. The choices made on many crucial occasions in 1995 were aimed principally at having a certain election date, and *Forza Italia*'s support, or lack thereof, for the government's actions was the leverage used to reach this objective. The year's news may be summed up as a continuous repetition of requests made to Dini and Scalfaro to fix a date for new parliamentary elections. It should be underlined that, beyond the possible advantages for Berlusconi himself, returning to the government quickly would have achieved important objectives for the still weak and disorganized party, *Forza Italia*, including the broad possibilities of patronage, access to government resources, and stable prospects for those elected. A return to government was thus vital for the whole party, not only for its leader.

The "wound" inflicted on democracy by the "treason" of the *Lega*'s defection could only be healed in one way. "New elections now" was *Forza Italia*'s demand and was to be the leit motif of its political strategy for the first six months of 1995. This was a calculated political risk. Polls on voting intentions in the second week in January signalled a rise in approval ratings for the parties of the *Polo* (the Center-Right coalition whose main components were now, without the *Lega*, *Forza Italia*, *Alleanza Nazionale* and the Christian Democratic Center).[1] But the requests of *Forza Italia* and its Center-Right allies were not accepted by the Head of State, who instead conferred the task of forming a new government on

Lamberto Dini, the current Treasury Minister, who is still in office and presumed to be a super partes "technician."

Before the vote of confidence, Berlusconi announced that he was ready to support the new government in exchange for an undertaking to hold new elections by the spring. On January 25, the Dini government won the confidence motion in the Chamber of Deputies by a margin of 302 votes to 39, with 270 decisive abstentions. *Forza Italia* abstained *en masse*, despite the fact that in the days preceding the vote, the majority of *Forza Italia* deputies had demonstrated, in an unusually clear and decisive manner, their willingness to vote in favor of the appointee president.[2] The following week in the Senate, the *Forza Italia* delegates, together with those of AN and CCD, left the chamber during the vote. Thus, the hard line wanted by the party leadership prevailed. This was the first serious conflict between the leader and his party, with Berlusconi going so far as to declare: "Whoever is not with me should leave *Forza Italia*." On February 9, at the *Polo*'s first meeting following the installation of the government, Berlusconi urged that the next administrative elections be held in June together with new parliamentary elections.

The situation was repeated during negotiations on the budget, one of the four specific tasks to be accomplished by the new government. Dini's open solicitation of the support of *Forza Italia*, was again subordinated to elections in June: To those who ask of us a sense of responsibility, we ask the same of them. They must realize that only a swift return to the ballot box can give stability to the economy.[3] The party then went on to threaten a noconfidence motion. *Forza Italia*'s Senate leader, Enrico La Loggia, maintained, however, that the *Polo* was prepared to switch from abstention to support of the budget, which it did not even agree with, if Dini would explicitly agree to a swift end to his program and new elections.[4] Instead, the next day, after Dini's speech to the Senate, the same *Polo* leadership decided to force the situation by opposing the budget. In an interview, the leader of *Forza Italia* declared that

> democracy no longer exists in Italy. There is a dictatorship, the dictatorship of the minority which cannot last and cannot be accepted, otherwise everything will fall apart... If [the budget adjustment] is necessary, then let's put it with pension reform and the government program for 1996. And with the next Parliament. It's so easy: on Tuesday we vote, they have three days to examine their consciences and decide in the interests of the country. And not in the interests of the Left, who some would like to turn the country over to, since today the Left has already taken power. This we cannot allow.[5]

In order to pass the budget bills and overcome the parliamentary obstructionism of *Forza Italia* and its Center-Right allies, the government was forced to fall back on a confidence motion, which it wins on March 15 in the Chamber of Deputies and March 21 in the Senate, in both cases with a "no" vote by the delegates of *Forza Italia*, AN, and CCD (and *Rifondazione Comunista*, with some defections, which have their effect on the vote).[6]

After a disappointing showing in the administrative elections (see *infra*), the request for new elections was shifted to the autumn. To achieve this goal, the leader of *Forza Italia* announced that he would make sacrifices, such as accepting a compromise with the Center-Left parties on the *par condicio*. In airing his conviction that the budget could be passed "in the very near future," Berlusconi gave a preview of his constructive attitude, stating that "we can even overlook some of our convictions in order to give the country the parliamentary government it need.." The ex-Prime Minister was thus very firm in rebuffing the idea of a coalition government. "We are diametrically opposed to this position because Italians do not love muddles."[7]

During the summer, however, *Forza Italia* softened its intransigent position and adopted a more moderate approach in Parliament. In particular, after having reached an agreement with the majority which supports the government, it decided to abstain from voting on the pension reform bill, while *Alleanza Nazionale* and *Rifondazione Comunista* voted against it.

In September, however, *Forza Italia* returned to its strategy of pressuring the government with the aim of obtaining the much desired elections. Berlusconi stated explicitly:

> There was a promise, made by the President of the Republic in front of all Italians on December 31, that the March 27 vote would not be overturned. Thus, I do not see how parliamentary discussions can be held to attain a new majority which is different from the one chosen by the voters. I believe that after the *par condicio* the government has no alternative but to resign. Approval of the budget will be discussed, and I believe that it must be passed for the good of the country, but immediately afterwards we must go to the polls.[8]

He therefore announced that the party would carry out a rigorous opposition in Parliament, with a strict observance of rules capable of seriously limiting legislative activity. Just a few days later, Gianni Letta, Berlusconi's right-hand man,[9] inaugurated this umpteenth attempt at accelerating the elections by denouncing the agreement reached in July with the Center-Left coalition on the *par condicio* and RAI. The following day, however, he stated: "I hope that our work in Parliament will allow us to set out the text of the *par condicio* as soon as possible, amending the decree according to the agreements made, so that no-one may use this question as an excuse for not holding the elections, which should, at this point, be held by March 1996."[10] Of the same tenor are the statements of another moderate member of *Forza Italia*, Giuliano Urbani (political scientist, instigator of Berlusconi's entry into politics and ex-Minister of Public Administration) who, after having accusing Scalfaro and Dini are fooling the public, threatened the abandonment of Parliament by *Forza Italia*.

Again on November 27, in a letter to the *Corriere della Sera*, the leader of *Forza Italia* wrote: "We must establish when we are going to vote. Or better, we must place the Head of State in a position to fix the date of the next political elections immediately." He also proposed that the other parties to sign a document affirming

> the technical government has exhausted its functions, that there is no agreement on serious institutional reforms, that it is necessary to give Italy a stable and authoritative government which enjoys a real parliamentary majority [...] The main parliamentary forces feel the need to call new parliamentary elections immediately after the resignation of the Dini government.

No chance of equivocation or duplicity.[11] Parliament's consideration of the 1996 budget seemed to be the last chance in 1995 to bring down the government. *Forza Italia* and *Alleanza Nazionale* presented hundreds of amendments; the government was forced to a confidence vote in order to balance the budget in time. But on December 15 in the Chamber of Deputies, where on paper it had a majority, the *Polo* was beaten twice due to the absence of some of its deputies.

The defeat suffered on the occasion of the approval of the budget signalled the end of the year-long strategy which hinged on the request for elections "as soon as possible." Taking on the role of political "explorer," Berlusconi began a series of contacts with Prodi and D'Alema. On the eve of Dini's resignation, on December 28, the leader of *Forza Italia* phoned live to TG4 (a TV news program) and announced the new strategy: a new government of *larghe intese* (broad understandings) for institutional reform, primarily the form of government and the electoral laws. If such an agreement were reached, elections could be deferred for two years. A dialogue was begun with the PDS while disputes drastically worsened with AN, which remained isolated (together with *Rifondazione Comunista*) by its insistent requests for elections.

In exactly one year, *Forza Italia*'s strategy had run its course, and finished by reversing itself. The majority of party delegates declared themselves favorable to the change of course and were prepared to support an institutional government; however, they viewed the possibility of new elections less than two years from the previous ones, with a certain unease, given the necessity of a new electoral campaign and all that it would require in terms of commitment and expense. The opinion polls showed *Forza Italia* in decline and behind AN.

The Administrative Elections and Referenda

In the course of the year, *Forza Italia* had to confront two more very important challenges: the administrative elections of April 23 and the referendum of June 11. Both were demanding, though very different in nature. The outcome of the two challenges highlights perfectly, *Forza Italia's* strong points and endemic weaknesses. The administrative elections confirmed the difficulty which the party and its candidates had in gathering votes at a local level, especially in city elections; the referendum victory confirmed the outstanding ability of *Forza Italia's* leader and the efficacy of national campaigns with a strong symbolic content.

The three antiFininvest referendum questions were rejected by 57, 55.7, and 56.4 percent of the voters respectively. On other referendum questions, too, the vote was favorable to the positions supported by *Forza Italia* and the *Polo*. This referendum, which was preceded by an intense campaign by the three Fininvest networks, particularly on the subject of the regulation of commercial television, took on the appearance of a referendum for or against Berlusconi. The outcome demonstrated that in campaigns of this type, the appeal of *Forza Italia's* leader is very strong and that with the use of appropriate means and an efficient strategy of communication, he can do without the mediation of the party.

The case of the administrative elections, however, was very different and much more complicated. These involved the party in a much more direct manner and had important and immediate repercussions for it. On the whole, though not disastrous, the results of the administrative elections of spring were worse than expected and signalled a decline in popularity for the *Polo's* two main parties, *Forza Italia* and *Alleanza Nazionale*. In particular, with the PDS ahead by over two percentage points, *Forza Italia* was no longer the first party at the national level, and this fact was immediately interpreted as a clear rejection of Berlusconi's pretension of being the only politician legitimized by a popular mandate. The immediate political effect of the elections was *Forza Italia's* withdrawal of its request for elections in June, which had been sought to coincide with the referendum in order to exploit a presumed coat tail effect.

Forza Italia had been confirmed as a great national party, capable of gathering consensus throughout the country in a fairly homogeneous manner; its strongholds appeared once again to be the northern regions of the country, while in the south, the competition with *Alleanza Nazionale* was quite acute. Nevertheless, the results of the regional elections were less than outstanding, especially considering the fact that *Forza Italia* had presented itself together with the new *Polo popolare* led by Rocco Buttiglione, from whom a more consistent slice of votes was expected. The results of the elections for provincial councils were also negative. On a national level, *Forza Italia* on its own obtained 6.3 percent of the valid votes; together with the *Polo popolare* it obtained another 9.8 percent. The results of the administrative elections at the local level were even worse, in particular for cities with fewer than 15,000 inhabitants where *Forza Italia* as a distinct and autonomous party disappeared altogether.

The administrative elections highlighted a fundamental problem for *Forza Italia*, which still remains unresolved today: the weakness of its territorial presence. The problem was endemic and had already made itself evident during the two partial administrative rounds in 1994 (June and especially November), when *Forza Italia* was outclassed not only by the PDS, but also the *Partito Popolare* (then still united) and by *Alleanza Nazionale*. Its main difficulty was that of finding enough candidates of the quality necessary to compete in local elections. This inevitably forced *Forza Italia* to lean on older parties in order to nominate people with experience, contacts and presence at a local level. In reality, in contrast to the parliamentary elections, for the administrative vote all the parties relied on expert personnel. In fact, many of those elected in the regional councils, particularly those in the ranks of the major parties (DC, PSI, PDS and MSI), had many years in local administrations behind them. This was thus almost a necessary path for a young party which found itself facing accelerated electoral deadlines and a hard campaign. *Forza Italia* was forced to make the best of a bad situation and accept the candidacy of many people with previous political experience, above all, from the DC. This, in turn, necessitated the alliance with the *Partito Popolare* (in March, this was still its name) of Buttiglione, with whom it held laborious and complicated meetings on the subject of the candidacies. This alliance, however, provoked resentment, delusion and frictions within a party which found it hard to accept the presence of "recycled" politicians, to use a pejorative term. As one *Forza Italia* politician put it: "For me, we blew it the day the agreement with Buttiglione was signed." A party functionary expressed a similar sentiment: "Often, unfortunately, that's the way it went. We put in the money and the structures and they, with the yesterday's ability and the clientele, grabbed the votes."[12]

TABLE 5.1 Council Members Belonging to *Forza Italia* in the Six Ordinary-Statute Regions Where the Center-Right Coalition Was Victorious

Region	Winning coalition	President and vice-president	Forza Italia assessors out of total
Piedmont	Center-Right	P	5/11
Lombardy	Center-Right	VP	5/13
Veneto	Center-Right	P	5/11
Campania	Center-Right	VP	3/11
Puglia[a]	Center-Right	-	4/11
Calabria	Center-Right	P	2/9

[a] The President of the council, Salvatore Distaso, is officially described as "independent."

Source: Our own elaboration of information taken from *I governi locali*, October-December, 1995. Information updated on October 31.

As may be seen from Table 5.1, in the regional councils formed after the elections, *Forza Italia* obtained three presidencies, including those of Piemonte and Veneto, and two vice-presidencies. Without a doubt, this was a good result for the party, even if in its stronghold of Lombardia the President of the regional council was Roberto Formigoni, star member of the *Polo popolare* of Buttiglione. The number of assessors, however, notably lessens *Forza Italia*'s weight within the regional executives.

The ranks of *Forza Italia*'s local administrators became drastically thinner at the provincial level and the level of the larger city councils.[13] In all, by October 31, *Forza Italia* could count only eight provincial presidents out of a total of 103, none of whom were from the three great regions of the Center-North. Five were elected in the spring (L'Aquila, Latina, Benevento, Brindisi and Taranto) and three had been elected previously, in the June 1994 election (Reggio Calabria, Palermo and Caltanissetta). A total of nine mayors of provincial capitals were from *Forza Italia*, with only one elected on April 23 (Frosinone), a second elected on the occasion of the partial round of November, 1994 (Pescara) and the others in June 1994 in coincidence with the European elections (Como, Savona, Verona, Gorizia, Rieti, Enna and Cagliari). Among the mayors of provincial capitals, only four were not in the southern regions. They were elected at the time of *Forza Italia*'s maximum electoral appeal and represented, above all, a drop in approval for the *Lega* in northern regions.

Besides assigning candidates to the government of local bodies, the administrative elections have important internal implications for the parties. The offices up for grabs provide both important incentives for their participation and, if won, important organizational resources for the party. Those elected constitute, in fact, an excellent reserve of functionaries without any expense for the party, as well as a greenhouse for future professional politicians. Again, this is particularly true for a young party such as *Forza Italia*, which is large in terms of votes, but small in organizational structures. The spring elections also appeared unsatisfactory from this point of view.

The Party

Forza Italia was founded at the end of 1993 on the initiative of Silvio Berlusconi. The newborn party assumed the form of a personal-patrimonial staff directly dependent on its founder and leader.[14] Alongside the personal staff, but quite distinct from it, the "clubs" were formed. In the original model of 1993-94, the clubs were arranged as local electoral micro-committees, relatively uncoordinated among themselves, with only limited horizontal or vertical links. Strong tensions immediately arose between the two elements, as the clubs demanded autonomy, participation in decisionmaking and a role with regard to the selection of candidates.

Forza Italia showed itself to be a political organization capable of successfully managing a national political campaign, even a peculiar one such as that of March, 1994. But it also demonstrated some very clear limitations in competition at a local level; its capacity for mobilization and the stabilization of electoral approval in the medium to long term also appeared doubtful. The unsatisfactory results obtained in the administrative elections and the continual postponement of new parliamentary elections forced the party leaders to rethink the organization of the party and its functions. In addition, the growth of potential votes for AN had to be addressed.

All these factors militated in favor of a more stable, grassroots organization. And in fact, just at the beginning of 1995 a significant redefinition of the entire party and its internal workings took place, with concrete measures being taken between the summer and the autumn. Essentially these included the start of a process of organizational centralization and homogenization, which marked a clean break with the model of the first phase. *Forza Italia*'s second political phase coincided with a new, and still open, stage in its organizational history. Let us look at the salient features, starting with the central structure.

On paper, the organizational restructuring was extensive and changed the previous arrangement in some important respects by giving a systematic structure to the whole party and adapting it to the new characteristics of political competition.[15] The organizational structure was to be articulated on four fundamental levels: national, regional, provincial and constituency. The latter was to be the constitutional unit of the party base, in which would be situated the management nucleus responsible for local action. In each of the 475 constituencies electing deputies in the first-past-the-post system, there would be a "constituency delegate" who would serve as the real political and organizational lynch-pin at local level.[16] The constituency delegate would be assisted by four vice-delegates, divided according to function, and by a constituency executive. A constituency assembly was also planned. Thus, the structure was similar to that at the provincial and regional levels, each with a coordinator, vicecoordinators, an executive, and an assembly. This added up to a staff of several thousand people, including 2,300 just for the constituencies, counting the delegates and their assistants. This organization is far from being stable and complete. In the constituencies where there is a *Forza Italia* deputy (or Euro deputy from *Forza Italia*), that person is normally assigned the function of delegate; however, this covers little more than a third of the available posts. Other constituency delegates are recruited from the ranks of those elected to the regional and local administrations.

At present, the regional structure is the most consolidated part of *Forza Italia*'s apparatus.[17] At the end of 1995 there were active coordinators in all regions except for the Valle d'Aosta; in total, there are twenty-two regional coordinators, with three in Piemonte and two in Calabria. Among these there are two senators, twelve deputies and two Euro deputies; twelve of the twenty-two regional coordinators have been in office since last fall.[18] At a regional level the organization is filled out by an assistant coordinator and four vicecoordinators; among these there are many regional advisors. In all, therefore, a regional staff includes over one hundred functionaries. This is the backbone of *Forza Italia*'s structure and was the result of a year of laborious construction of the organization.

Another very important innovation in 1995 was the introduction of the figure of the party militant, officially called the "*Forza Italia* promoter." Most of these militants are drawn from the "electoral area managers," to whom are entrusted both the process of proselytising among the voters of the section and the representation of the list on election days. The area manager directs an electoral section manager and should be assisted by at least one other person.

The goal is to have at least two party activists for each of the 90,000 electoral sections (about 200 per constituency) into which the country is divided. According to sector manager Giovanni Dell'Elce, this grass-roots network was developed after a careful study of the structure of the PDS, which is at the forefront in this area.[19] Even in a minimal hypothesis of one promoter per section, this would mean having 100,000 militants available, a very considerable figure in a period of falling activism. Even though, despite optimistic pronouncements by the party faithful, the goal of having a grassroots network of territorial activists is still far from being realized, recruitment and preparatory work were effectively started by turning, first of all, to those enrolled in the clubs.[20]

An important aspect of this organizational structure is that *all* the office-holders in the party—from the section manager to the regional coordinators—are nominated by the next rung of the hierarchy. Thus, a rule of generalized cooptation exists; elective posts are not provided for. In this way, the constituency bodies are also deprived of the possibility of any real participation in political choices, either because they are composed of members already selected for a previous position or because they are denied the possibility of electing party heads.

At the top of the organizational pyramid is the party's national executive, comprising the president and president's committee. But effective power is, nevertheless, in the hands of a smaller body, the coordinating committee. While this body is without any official status and varies in composition, in reality, it is the directing nucleus of *Forza Italia*, the "president's team." This, in fact, is as it always has been.[21] In 1995 it was made up of substantially the same group of people as the year before: Senator Previti, ex-Minister of Defense, national coordinator of *Forza Italia*; the Hon. Mario Valducci, national vice-coordinator for organization and local bodies; the Hon. Domenico Lo Jucco, ex-Under Secretary of the Interior, treasurer; Giovanni Dell'Elce, director of promoters; the Euro deputy Alessio Gorla, director of communication and external relations; Guido Possa, director of the clubs; Dario Rivolta, ex-candidate for the European elections, director of candidate selection; Paolo Del Debbio, director of research.[22] What is important is that in every case these people are company men from within the Fininvest group, who are tied to Berlusconi by previous collaborative experiences and a strict bond of trust.[23] No form of election and/or control of these bodies is provided for on the part of the lower levels. In other words, the leadership of *Forza Italia* is, in the most literal sense of the word, autocephalous: it draws its origin from itself.

According to the plan announced in September, from the 1st to the 22nd October, the first constituent assemblies were to have been held. On the agendas of each of these assemblies was the nomination of three delegates to the first national assembly. These assemblies, however, never took place. Similarly, *Forza Italia*'s first national assembly was supposed to have taken place in Rome on November 25-26, but it too was post-poned for the umpteenth time until the Spring of 1996. In two years, although repeatedly scheduled, no assembly of *Forza Italia* was ever held. Even today, no nomination has been legitimized from the bottom up via any form of internal democratic procedure. Moreover, the assembly agenda only provided for: " 1) confidence motions in the president and his team (the president's committee); 2) approval of the completed or-ganizational structure; 3) delegation to the president's committee of the task of making the statutory modifications necessary to adapt the statute to the new organizational model; 4) approval of the final financial report and estimated budget." As noted before, the assembly merely ratifyies previously-taken decisions and is, therefore, completely deprived of power.

A brief description of *Forza Italia* as a "parliamentary party" is in order. Given the external origin of the party, it is not surprising that this is a weak link. *Forza Italia*'s members of Parliament owe their election, with very few exceptions, to Berlusconi's success. In as much as they are new politicians, they are almost totally without personal political resources and thus even more dependent on the party and its leader. This has contributed to the creation of two rather disciplined parlia-mentary groups. But signs of impatience and tension have arisen re-garding the party managers. At the beginning of August, this dissatis-faction was made public by the Hon. Podestà, ex University Minister who Left Parliament with a sharp polemic:

> In the bosom of *Forza Italia*'s parliamentary group, few meetings and (almost) no debate has ever taken place. Rather,[there have been] many boring monologues by the chief with his manifestation of a persecution complex, his reassurances of his good intentions, his firm will not to change, his admonitions to the undecided and his threats to the rebels (Della Valle) [ex-group leader]. To sum up the situation in *Forza Italia*'s parliamentary group in the Chamber of Deputies: lots of people tired of being used, lots of people deluded and lost.[24]

During 1995 the political factions with *Forza Italia*'s parliamentary group were consolidated into a Center and Right and liberal-radical wings. The moderates of the Center, led by Vittorio Dotti, group leader in the Chamber of Deputies, were the majority. But the other two com-ponents had influence within Berlusconi's tight circle of collaborators. This became clear in the frequent mediation between the groups. On the whole, the parliamentary group exerted a moderating effect on the party. The members of Parliament had to contend with a particularly heavy legislative agenda (including *par condicio*, regional electoral law, antitrust, pension reform, immigration, financial measures and the reorganization of the broadcasting system), which put the political staff, which was markedly inexpert and restricted by the electoral strategy of the party, to a severe test.

The Clubs:
Autonomous Associations or Local Branches?

In *Forza Italia*'s first phase, which roughly corresponds to the year 1994, the clubs cannot be in any way considered as *Forza Italia*'s territorial structures. They were in all respects external, or collateral, to the party; their tasks were clearly limited and did not in any way provide for a role in the definition of the political programs and strategies of *Forza Italia* nor, even, for any form of participation in its internal life such as the selection of directing bodies or of candidates. The point of contact between the clubs and the party consisted exclusively of the National Association of *Forza Italia* clubs (ANFI), which offered nothing more than membership, if desired by the local group, and a loose coordination of the activities of the clubs, which, however, remained autonomous.

In 1995, the clubs underwent a decisive transformation. For the first time, standardized procedures for the constitution of the clubs and their relations with *Forza Italia* were established. The *Forza Italia* club remained a "free, nonprofit association which seeks to develop, at a local level, cultural, social and political initiatives furthering liberal-democratic ideals in a spirit of openness and at the service of the citizens." The structure and the working methods of the clubs were formally fully democratic. The typical by-laws of a *Forza Italia* club, in fact, provided for bodies such as an assembly of members, a president, a steering committee and a college of adjudicators. In particular,

> the assembly of members is the sovereign organ of the Association. [It] defines the programmatic guidelines for all club activities and deliberates on any subject regarding associative life; it elects the club president and the other members of the steering committee; it elects the adjudicators; it deliberates on financial accounts and estimated budgets; it deliberates on proposals for a modification of the by-laws.

The club president and the members of the steering committee (from a minimum of 3 to a maximum of 15) are directly elected by the assembly, stay in office for two years and may only be elected three times consecutively.

A very important innovation in 1995, however, was the inclusion as members of the party of the presidents and members of the steering committees of the clubs. In this capacity they have a right to participate in local assemblies (constituency assemblies) in a measure proportional to the number of club members, up to a maximum of 15 people. Thus, the previously nonexistent figure of the individual *socio* or member of *Forza Italia*, similar to that of the traditional party member, was created. It should be underlined, though, that the clubs are a sort of "second tier" association, which is very selective both in terms of numbers and quality (presidents and members of the steering committees). Only a small portion of club members, and not all of those enrolled, may aspire to become party members as such and therefore to participate in its internal workings.

The other important new aspect of the clubs' relationship to the party is the so-called "affiliation relationship."[25] In fact, once constituted, in order to become a full-fledged *Forza Italia* club, the association *must* affiliate itself with the political movement. In this way, the clubs become stably inserted within the political movement and placed under the control of the central structure, preventing them from constituting themselves as independent electoral committees or personal electoral machines. Thus, the clubs were definitively deprived of power. Through affiliation, the clubs became the "recognized associations" of the political movement *Forza Italia*. The clubs' affiliation means "the acceptance of the political line deliberated by the organs of the Political Movement *Forza Italia*. In particular, the clubs may not support candidates, lists or political proposals of other parties or movements or lines which in any way in opposed to the Political Movement *Forza Italia*." The club presidents and members of the steering committees became subject to the by-laws of the party. In exchange, as we have seen, they obtained the right to participate in the assemblies at constituency level.

This redefinition of the relationship between the clubs and the political movement also coincided with the transformation of ANFI into the National Club Center. It would no longer be a second tier association made up of the clubs, but an internal part of the movement.[26] On the whole, this organizational structure was clearly different from the original and transformed the clubs into something very similar to the peripheral structures of a party. This process, however, has encountered resistance, and even now its outcome cannot be taken for granted.

What Identity?

The year's balance-sheet is contradictory. A year in opposition was in itself a serious problem for a party such as *Forza Italia*, which was absolutely unprepared for being out of government (as opposed, for example, to AN), and it certainly put the party, as well as its members and structures to the test. The strategic goal of holding elections as soon as possible was not reached. To this, it is necessary to add that the passage of a year has also allowed other parties to organize, or reorganize, themselves. Moreover, the neocentrist design followed by some parties and by Dini and President Scalfaro has also taken shape. In 1995, *Forza Italia* lost, perhaps once and for all, its initial momentum and with it, its declared ambition of radically transforming the Italian political system. The strategic turning point at the end of the year also signalled *Forza Italia's* political normalization, the accentuation of its centrist character and the dilution of its previous antiestablishment force. This is not to say that this change is a good thing for the Italian political system, in particular for the supporters of twoparty majority democracy.

The party is still seeking a political and organizational identity. Its political culture is still evanescent;[27] proposals on the main subjects of political and social life are almost nonexistent. On an organizational level, *Forza Italia* has begun a deep reordering of its structure, without having, however, resolved some basic problems. The original idea of the clubs was innovative with respect to the traditional methods of organization of the parties in Italy and is experiencing a growing, if yet uncertain, success (think of Romano Prodi's "committees for the Italy we want"). But this arrangement now seems to have been abandoned and, above all, the role of the grassroots associations in the internal affairs of the party has not been clarified. At the same time, the "party of the elect" has not come together either, because the elect are not yet autonomous enough. What is, instead, clear is *Forza Italia's* enduring character as the personal electoral machine of its founder.

Berlusconi continues to be the party's principal strong point, but also its main weakness. His outstanding ability in electoral terms, while falling, is still very high. Nevertheless, the intense identification between the party and its leader constitutes a debilitating factor for *Forza Italia*. In contrast to AN, which can count on coherent, tried and tested managing groups, at both the national and local levels, at Berlusconi's side, or behind him, there is still no such sufficiently autonomous and authoritative group. In other words, the personal staff is still the dominating element within the party. Although the time which has passed since the creation of *Forza Italia*, just two years, is still short; significant steps in the direction of an autonomous institutionalization of the party have not been taken. Despite everything, *Forza Italia* is still not capable of surviving the loss of its founding father.

Translated by Timothy Cooper and Susan Kertzer

Notes

1. See the poll conducted by the 'Istituto per gli studi sulla pubblica opinione di Milano', published in the *Corriere della Sera*, January 16, 1995.

2. *Il Sole 24 Ore*, January 25, 1995.

3. Statement by Silvio Berlusconi, published in *Il Sole 24 Ore*, February 18, 1995.

4. *Il Sole 24 Ore*, March 3, 1995.

5. *La Stampa*, March 4, 1995.

6. But not by the *Popolari* led by Buttiglione, who is concerned with the division in his party.

7. See *Il Sole 24 Ore*, July 22, 1995.

8. See *Il Sole 24 Ore*, September 19, 1995.

9. Gianni Letta was vice-President of Fininvest and Under-secretary to the Prime Minister during the Berlusconi government.

10. *Il Sole 24 Ore*, September 23, 1995.

11. *Alleanza Nazionale* immediately supported this decisive stand. In an interview, Fini stated: "We must vote by February [..] I am sure that Berlusconi wants to vote very soon." *Corriere della Sera*, November 30, 1995.

12. The information and quotes are taken from an investigation by Sari Gilbert of those elected to the regional councils of Lombardia, Veneto, Umbria, Molise and Calabria, published in four episodes in *Il Sole 24 Ore*, July 5-8, 1995.

13. This information is taken from *I governi locali*, vol. 8, n.27, October-December, 1995.

14. For a brief re-construction of the genesis and configuration of this personal apparatus, see my "Forza Italia", in G. Pasquino, ed., *La politica italiana*, (Roma-Bari: Laterza, 1995). See also P. McCarthy, "Forza Italia: nascita e sviluppo di un partito virtuale", in P. Ignazi and R. Katz, eds., *Politica in Italia*, edizione 95, (Bologna: Il Mulino, 1995).

15. See the document *Linee guida della struttura organizzativa del movimento Forza Italia a livello locale e regionale*, Roma, July 21-22, 1995.

16. In non-metropolitan constituencies with more than one local council, the post of council delegate is also provided for. In cities with more than one constituency, there is also the post of city coordinator.

17. The first regional coordinators had been nominated in October, 1994.

18. Note that two coordinators (Piemonte and Veneto) had to be replaced when they were elected presidents of their respective regional councils.

19. See *Corriere della Sera*, November 27, 1995. See also the investigation in *Il Sole 24 Ore*, October 31, 1995.

20. At the national headquarters in Rome, there is an active working group coordinated by Giovanni Dell'Elce. Between January and February of 1996, training meetings with promotion managers in the different constituencies are planned.

21. This is also the reason why only unofficial information on the composition of the group is available. See, among others, the stories published in the *Corriere della Sera*, "Supplemento Economia", March 27, 1995, and September 25, 1995.

22. Also part of this group, in various roles, are Gianni Pilo, Niccolò Querci (personal assistant to Berlusconi), Fabio Minoli and Gianni Letta.

23. To this, we may add that the coordinators in Lombardia, Lazio, Campania, Sicilia, Toscana and Trentino Alto Adige come from companies of the Fininvest group; the coordinator for Lazio is Berlusconi's ex-spokesman.

24. Letter published in *Il Messaggero*, August 3, 1995.

25. See the document *Regole del rapporto di affiliazione fra club Forza Italia e movimento politico Forza Italia*, Roma, 1995.

26. This transformation coincided with the replacement in the movement's executive of Angelo Codignoni, President of ANFI since November, 1993, by Fabio Minoli, director of the Centro nazionale club since January '95, and newly-elected member of the regional council of Lombardia.

27. On this rightly emphasized aspect see A. Panebianco, see "Tre mosse necessarie per un vero partito", in *Liberal*, n.4, July, 1995.

6

The Government of Lamberto Dini

Gianfranco Pasquino

On December 22, 1994, Prime Minister Silvio Berlusconi went to the Quirinale (the Presidential Palace) to hand in his resignation. His government, installed in May amidst great fanfare but only just scraping past a confidence vote in the Senate, had lasted just 225 days. While not one of the shortest-lived governments of the Republic it had certainly lasted less than the average government of the so-called First Republic, a figure which stands at around three hundred and fifteen days. The Berlusconi government's tormented, conflict-riven and largely unproductive term in office ended with the imperious request of the outgoing Prime Minister for immediate elections.[1] Wounded by the decision of "Judas" Umberto Bossi to sign a motion of no confidence against him, Berlusconi had from the very beginning of the crisis warned against any attempt at a *ribaltone*—a political turn-about which would have seen the parties that had been defeated at the ballot box on March 27, 1994 forming a government, thanks to the support of the *Lega*, which had betrayed the Freedom Alliance coalition. When (almost immediately) it became apparent that the President of the Republic, Oscar Luigi Scalfaro, was not eager to dissolve Parliament without having first exhausted attempts to create a new majority, Berlusconi announced his theory of the mandate.

According to this theory, the voters had conferred a mandate not only on the two-headed coalition Berlusconi had created with the names of *Polo delle Libertà* in the North (*Forza Italia* plus *Lega*) and *Polo del Buon Governo* (*Forza Italia* plus *Alleanza Nazionale*) in the Center and the South (though in truth, this latter coalition had presented itself somewhat unevenly in many of the single-member constituencies in the Center and the South), but had also conferred a *personal* mandate on him, Silvio Berlusconi, for the office of Prime Minister. If therefore it was impossible to go back to the polls immediately, Berlusconi claimed he had the right to be re-appointed—something the President of the Republic ruled out right after the first round of consultations—or, failing that, to remain in office to lead the country to new and early elections.

The pseudo-theory of the mandate has no basis in the electoral mechanisms and institutional procedures of parliamentary government and the Italian political system, where the only mandate (incidentally explicitly denied by the Constitution[2]) Berlusconi could possibly have claimed was from voters in his Rome 1 constituency. Though very shaky, the popular mandate theory seemed to find some support among public opinion, which for some time had been duped into thinking it could elect the Prime Minister directly. Not even the suggestion that, with the new first-past-the post electoral system, Italians had directly elected a coalition government and that, once overturned, a return to the ballot box was almost automatically required, can survive a multitude of political and constitutional objections.

In Italy, governments are formed on the basis of an agreement between the respective parliamentary parties, with the Prime Minister being appointed by the President of the Republic and his full powers taking effect only after he has obtained a vote of confidence in both Houses.[3] If a government no longer enjoys the confidence of even one of the two Houses, it must resign and may be replaced, as in all parliamentary democracies, by another government which does obtain the confidence of the majority in Parliament. As simple as that: no more, no less. Nevertheless, with a sense of constitutional and political responsibility, the President of the Republic did not try in any way to facilitate the formation of a *ribaltone* government that united the *Progressisti* and *Popolari*, who had lost the elections, with the *Lega*.

It is easy to imagine that when, during consultations, the leader of *Rifondazione Comunista*, Fausto Bertinotti, rejected the name of Romano Prodi (who, without the votes of *Rifondazione* would not have been able to win a vote of confidence), the President of the Republic breathed a sigh of relief. At which point, he found himself in the enviable position of asking Berlusconi which representative of the Center-Right was not totally disagreeable to him. Later, Scalfaro would underline how, in the course of the crisis, he had had to conduct himself in a way that took account of both the Constitution and the vote of March 27, 1994—i.e. the need to stick by and apply constitutional procedures and the imperative of not cancelling out the preferences voters had expressed less than a year before; not to have done so would have jeopardised the lot of any eventual Prime Minister. Furthermore, had he acted any differently, Scalfaro would have risked his own popularity and the prestige stemming from his impartiality which had already come under heavy and repeated attack from the "colonels" of *Alleanza Nazionale* and the many editorial writers favorable to *Forza Italia*.

The upshot of this complicated process and Scalfaro's skilful navigation between the Scylla of the Constitution and the Charybdis of the March vote was the appointment as Prime Minister on January 13, 1995 of Lamberto Dini, former Treasury Minister in the Berlusconi government. The crisis had lasted 22 days, about the average for the First Republic.

After the selection of twenty ministers, with the Treasury remaining in the hands of the Prime Minister, the Dini government was sworn in on January 17. It won votes of confidence in the Chamber of Deputies and then the Senate, on January 25 and February 1, respectively. In the Lower House the result of the vote was as follows: 302 votes for (*Progressisti, Popolari, Lega*), 39 against (almost all deputies from *Rifondazione Comunista*) and 270 abstentions (deputies from the *Polo del Buon Governo* including members of the *Lega* who had left Bossi). In the Senate 191 senators voted for the government (*Progressisti, Popolari, Lega* of Bossi), with 17 from *Rifondazione Comunista* against and one *Lega* dissident and one *Alleanza Nazionale* senator abstaining. The senators from the *Polo del Buon Governo* did not take part in the vote as a sign of protest.

Another "Technocratic" Government

The sixty-four year old Lamberto Dini is a technocrat who commands considerable respect. Having acquired wide international experience as Executive Director of the International Monetary Fund for many years up until 1979, he was then nominated Director general of the *Banca d'Italia*, an office which he held until 1994 when he accepted the job of Treasury Minister offered him by Berlusconi. Perhaps caught by surprise, though certainly forewarned of Scalfaro's intention of nominating Dini, Berlusconi failed to put a brave face on it all. On the contrary, he continued with his demand for immediate elections and his accusations of a *ribaltone* which had not in point of fact taken place. Precisely with a view to heading off accusations of a *ribaltone*, the government of Lamberto Dini went out of its way to highlight its "technical" credentials (i.e. a government made up of technocrats). Merciless, but probably accurate, the *International Herald Tribune* translated *tecnici* as "low-profile professionals" and, in effect, there were few technocrats of indisputable national standing in the Dini government. For a series of reasons, comparison with the government of Carlo Azeglio Ciampi immediately comes to mind.

A half-political government and therefore not one made up exclusively of professors but also of authoritative politicians with previous ministerial experience, the Ciampi administration was also a half technocrat government where the so-called "technicians" were essentially all famous professors—including some politicians—such as the Foreign Affairs Minister Beniamino Andreatta, professor of Economics.[4] The Dini government, on the other hand, included only a few ministers who were university professors, e.g. Tiziano Treu, Employment Minister, Elio Guzzanti, Health Minister and Giorgio Salvini, Minister for Universities; other professors took posts as undersecretaries, e.g. Piero Giarda in Finance and Carlo Maria Santoro at Defence. The prevailing tone was undoubtedly technical bureaucratic: a general at the Defence Ministry, Domenico Corcione, a prefect at the Ministry of Interior, Giovanni Rinaldo Coronas, subsequently replaced by another prefect, Antonio Brancaccio, a magistrate at the Justice Ministry, Filippo Mancuso, a tax expert at Finance, Augusto Fantozzi, director of a bank (the *Istituto Mobiliare Italiano*) at the Budget, Rainer Masera, a state advisor at the Public Agencies, Franco Frattini, and the Minister for Industry in the Ciampi government, Paolo Baratta, at Public Works and the Environment. Far from leaning to the Left, the Dini government seemed, on the contrary, to have an Andreotti-like cast, drawing on many of his followers from the bureaucratic and administrative corps in Rome.

The government of Carlo Azeglio Ciampi, formed immediately after the electoral referenda of April, 1993, focused its agenda on overseeing reform of electoral law, drawing up the single-member constituencies and proportional districts and preparing and passing a budget for bringing public finances under control.[5] It was therefore a government with a limited lifespan and a mandate which would expire not so much after a set period of time as when it had carried through a certain number of reforms. It complied with its mandate by resigning immediately after approval of the budget and the redrawing of electoral constituencies.

The duration of the Dini government also seemed to be limited from the start by a four-point agenda: 1) a budget to meet the shortfall resulting from the Berlusconi government's budget (for which Dini himself, as Treasury Minister, had to share some responsibility); 2) a decree on the so-called *par condicio*, giving all parties equal rights of TV access for electoral propaganda; 3) pension reform which, drawn up by Berlusconi and Dini himself, had met with fierce resistance from the unions and Italians to the point of becoming the main trigger of the previous government's crisis (and the Treasury minister could not completely deny his responsibility in this too); 4) the economic financial legislation plan to be presented before June, 1995.

The government promised, ahead of time, to hand in its resignation to the President of the Republic once its program had been completed. In the words of the Prime Minister: "To dispel any doubts or misunderstandings, I confirm that the government will consider its mandate at an end as soon as the four main points comprising its program have been achieved."[6] Dini received "long and ringing applause" from the *Polo del Buon Governo* when he added that "should it become clear that the above points are impossible to carry through because of objectively insuperable obstacles, the government would have to view this too as reason for handing in its resignation."[7] The hearty applause augured strong opposition on the part of the *Polo del Buon Governo* and its parliamentary deputies, especially in the Chamber of Deputies where the numbers did not appear to bode well for the technocrat government on particularly controversial issues.

Nevertheless, as the Prime Minister had cleverly divined, his government had also been called upon to play a therapeutic role: "to guarantee stability for the institutions and the markets" and "help calm febrile and emotional states detrimental to the stage of political civility our country, after so many trials and tribulations, has reached."[8] Such goals were to some extent shared by all the parties and members of Parliament, albeit to different degrees and with a different sense of urgency. Within the centerleft alliance, only the majority of *Rifondazione Comunista* deputies wanted early elections before June in the hope of capitalizing on the discontent of workers over the proposed pension reform. Neither the small groups of the Center-Left—the socalled *cespugli* ("shrubs") in the shade of the PDS oak-tree—nor, in particular, the *Lega*, fully aware of the risk of losing the vast majority of its single-member seats, were prepared to accept early elections. What is more, not even the smaller groupings within the *Polo delle Libertà* and *Polo del Buon Governo*, such as the Christiandemocrats and the *Unione Liberale di Centro*, seemed particularly keen on the idea of fighting a fierce political and parliamentary battle to impose early elections.

Finally, the President of the Republic himself had more than once declared he was against early elections—it would have been the second time he had dissolved Parliament in just two years—in the absence of firm rules on TV broadcasting and electoral propaganda, and in the knowledge that new elections would have done nothing to break the political logjam. Early elections without the proper rules threatened to reproduce the same balance between Center-Right and Center-Left parties that existed in the present Parliament. Naturally, speculation on the date of elections, fuelled by editors and commentators of the largecirculation newspapers, was fanned by the prevailing scepticism of politicians who, at least on this subject, always know more than journalists and have a greater influence on the outcome.

The Productivity of the Dini Government

Probably because of its technocratic nature, which was often, sometimes excessively, trotted out and flaunted, and most certainly because
of its actual timing, coming in the midst of a delicate political transition,
the Dini government was able to exploit some favorable conditions that
certainly helped it in its work. The supplementary budget of March
1995, which was not too painful but incisive enough, was approved
without any particular problems.

Greater difficulties emerged, because of the effect on the political
fortunes of the different alliances and the economic fortunes of the
Fininvest group, when the Dini government tried, unsuccessfully, to
regulate party political broadcasts on television for electoral campaigns,
a crucial part of the socalled *par condicio*.

The issue took on extraordinary importance in campaigning for the
regional elections, the results of which (besides leading to the formation
of new regional governments) could have been interpreted, if favorable
to the *Polo*, as an indication by the electorate that early general elections
should be called. In the absence of a parliamentary agreement between
the parties, the Minister of Post & Telecommunications, Agostino
Gambino, went ahead with a much criticized and strongly contested
decree severely limiting access to the television networks for electoral
campaigning purposes.[9] Shortly thereafter, a controversial sentence from
the Constitutional Court declared the decree to be inapplicable to the
referenda - much to the joy of the Fininvest networks that were busy
trying to defend themselves from the threats contained in the referendum questions: a limit on the number of advertising breaks during
television programs, limitation of the advertising market share and reduction in the number of television networks a single person could
own.

By the end of March, 1995, the Dini government had also managed
to preside over the passing of the new, almost indispensable regional
electoral law.[10] While this law can hardly be called a resounding success
either from a technical point of view—with all its drawbacks for forming governing majorities—or a political one—based as it is on the re-
introduction of a liberal dose of proportional representation and hence
hardly a step forward in the direction of authoritative regionalfederal
government—the Dini government had nevertheless, in just two full
working months, already achieved three of the four objectives it had set
itself. But it was now the turn of one of the thorniest problems in social
policy and one which affects not a few western democracies: the belated
reform of the pension system.

A detailed analysis of the pension reform and an assessment of its chances of curbing public spending in the longterm are beyond the scope of this chapter (but see the chapter by Onorato Castellino in this volume). What is important to emphasize is that by taking advantage of the parliamentary majority of the centerleft, which incidentally did not have the support of *Rifondazione Comunista*, Dini was able to conclude the whole laborious process of reform at the beginning of August. It is also interesting to note how the unions conceded much more to Dini's technocratic government than they would ever have conceded to a political one, even a sympathetic one (which perhaps, as such, would never have dared to ask for so much). At this point, the demands of those who were pressing for early elections might have seemed newly justified even, if for technical reasons, they could not have been held before the end of November, 1995.

In the meantime, however, not only was the law on the *par condicio* languishing, on account of fierce opposition from the *Polo*, but other important issues had come up that needed serious consideration. For example, the Senate had approved legislation on conflict of interests which was seen as anathema by Berlusconi and his supporters but which was probably an indispensable part of a working first-past-the-post democracy. The Chamber of Deputies was busy examining proposals to reform the procedures for appointing the Board of directors of the RAI. Moreover, aware of the need to change quite a few of the rules and provide each other with reciprocal political, as well as institutional, guarantees, the *Polo* and *Ulivo* had reached a series of informal agreements designed to stop the next majority from overwhelming the next minority both inside and outside Parliament. As a result, a none too sparkling or original debate on institutional reform took place in the Chamber of Deputies before the summer break in the course of which Berlusconi re-launched his proposals for *presidenzialismo* (presidential-style government), accompanying them with renewed demands for immediate elections.

Technocratic, Not Unpolitical

The popularity Dini acquired with his success in areas like pension reform—thorny issues for traditional "politicians"—turned him into a potential candidate for both alliances, looking as they were for a leader who was less of an embarrassment than Berlusconi and more tested than Prodi. Some sections of the Left, in particular the PDS, probably feared making the same mistake they had made with Carlo Azeglio Ciampi whom they had supported in Parliament and then abandoned when, in February-March, 1994, they had to choose the Progressive

Alliance's candidate for the office of Prime Minister (which was in fact not done ahead of time with fatal political and electoral consequences). There was however a fundamental difference between Dini and Ciampi. The former was a moderate, both culturally and politically close to the *Polo*. Ciampi was undoubtedly a progressive, as was the Center-Left government he led with the support of the PDS. However, the official leader of the *Ulivo*, Romano Prodi, rightly felt himself threatened by the musical chairs being played by some of his supporters, especially the editor of *L'Unità*, his number two man, Walter Veltroni, who was in favor of giving Dini a highprofile position in the Center-Left coalition. It is interesting to note that in response to Prodi's comment that Dini was just a technocrat and that early elections were necessary to elect a legislative government, Dini replied that Prodi too was a technocrat, while arguing that he had at least obtained the confidence of Parliament, hinting at his willingness to continue in government and not close the door on further political experience.[11]

The short but intense attempt at an "acquisitions campaign" in August, conducted while the Prime Minister was otherwise maintaining an Anglo-Saxon silence, did not of course lead to anything concrete. It did, however, strengthen Dini's position. In fact, at the beginning of autumn, it became clear that the government had almost automatically been given the task of pushing through the budget for 1996. Its work, in other words, could not be interrupted. Various voices, interested in the government's survival (and hence also Parliament's) called for guarantees that the government—headed by an authoritative, skilled and internationally acclaimed technocrat—should be allowed to continue, providing continuity during the Italian semester of presidency of the European Union (January-June, 1996). Buoyed by his popularity and the solidity of the parliamentary majority supporting him, and aware that parts of that majority were reform-minded, Dini went as far as to indicate certain measures that might be taken to reform Italy's parliamentary style of government.

His proposal, put forward in a speech given in October in Washington, consisted of seven fairly substantial changes: 1) to strengthen the role of the majority system in the electoral law with a view to reducing fragmentation; 2) to differentiate the functions of the two Houses; 3) to introduce the "constructive noconfidence vote" (as in the German model) to deter repeated governmental crises; 4) to strengthen the constitutional role of the premier in government with a view to ensuring unity of action; 5) to strengthen budget procedures via stricter constitutional rules; 6) to enlarge the responsibility of Parliament for general legislation, at the same time extending the government's powers in matters such as the reform of the public administration and implementation of

EU directives; 7) to significantly increase the regions' autonomy with greater federalism as regards taxation: more issues to be dealt with by regional legislation and fewer restrictions on the regions' power to determine their own institutional programs.[12]

Too caught up in internal wrangling and anyway deeply divided on the form and substance of the problems and their solutions, the various parts of the two *Poli* made short shrift of Dini's proposals which were not even given support by the Minister for Institutional Reform, Giovanni Motzo.

In the meantime, the first serious crisis affecting government and the relations between government and the parliamentary majority of the Center-Left was brewing: the case of Justice Minister, Filippo Mancuso. Repeatedly criticized, especially by the *Progressisti*, for the insistent and inconclusive inspections he had ordered of the *Procura di Milano* and for other remarks and measures he had made and taken against the magistrates most involved in the *Mani pulite* operation and the fight against the Mafia, Minister Mancuso finally became, perhaps belatedly, the target of a noconfidence motion presented in the Senate on October 4, a motion finally approved on October 17 with 173 votes in favor (*Progressisti, Popolari, Lega,* and *Rifondazione Comunista*).

During the debate, the minister fiercely attacked not only the Prime Minister, but also the President of the Republic. More than the criticisms levelled at Mancuso by the Center-Left alliance, what needs to be explained are Dini's appointment of Mancuso, the latter's stubborn resistance (over many months) to leave office, and the impassioned defense of the Minister by the Center-Right *Polo*, prepared to bring down the whole government just to save the Minister Mancuso. In the wake of the vote against Mancuso (the legitimacy of which was immediately contested by the Minister in the Constitutional Court), the Center-Right alliance decided to present a no-confidence motion in the whole government in the Chamber of Deputies, counting on the rifts that had developed within the Center-Left. At the beginning of December, the Constitutional Court came out against Mancuso, judging the individual motion of no confidence in a single minister to be constitutionally acceptable. The contradictions within the Center-Left grouping showed up immediately when the party executive of *Rifondazione Comunista* decided to vote in favor of the no-confidence motion of the *Polo* so as to be able to call immediate elections.

Replying to the Chamber, Dini sought to head off the no-confidence vote by promising what he had already pledged on several occasions: resignation of the government immediately after the budget and at the latest by December 31, 1995. The pledge to resign was accompanied by a call for Parliament to quickly approve the bill on the *par condicio*. The

Prime Minister significantly added that a "common willingness to press ahead with the necessary institutional reforms" could likewise emerge. If this had been the case, a *governo di larga intesa* (broad-based coalition), *di garanzia*, could have been put together with the appropriate reshuffling so as to "enhance its representativeness during the semester of Italian presidency of the European Union." Pressured by his members, who were overwhelmingly against *Rifondazione* votes going to support a motion by the *Polo*, the leader of *Rifondazione*, Fausto Bertinotti, struck while the iron was hot and announced his deputies' abstention from the vote, declaring himself satisfied with the "victory" that had been won with the government's formal undertaking to resign by the end of the year. It should be noted, however, that such an undertaking had always been on the government's agenda. What is more, it had been tempered by Dini's remarks reported above. The result of the vote, as can be seen in Table 6.1, revealed both the precariousness of the political balance in the Lower House and the extraordinary and unfortunate fragmentation of the parliamentary groups.

Naturally, the defeat of the no-confidence vote, so cleverly fended off, reassured the government. The budget was passed by the Senate—albeit

TABLE 6.1   Party Breakdown of Votes on the Motion of No-Confidence in the Government Presented by the *Polo* to the Lower House (October, 1995)

"No" to the no-confidence vote		"Yes" to the no-confidence vote	
Progressives	162	Forza Italia	110
Northern League	76	National Alliance	107
Popular Party	27	CCD and CDU	34
Democrats	19	FLD	25
Unitary Communists	14	LIF	11
SVP	3	Mixed	4
Mixed			8
Total	310	Total	291
Not voting	24	*Abstentions*	1
Communist Refoundation			

Key: CCD= Centro Cristiano Democratico; CDU= Cristiano Democratici Uniti; FLD=Fronte Liberal-Democratico; LIF=Lega Indipendentisti Federalisti.

Note: The Speaker, Irene Pivetti, does not vote; three other deputies did not vote: one constituency is unoccupied.

Source: Adapted from *L'Unità*, October 27, 1995, p. 3.

with some delay and after a walkout on November 17 of League senators, who demanded a tough decree against non-EU immigrants. The League obtained its decree, if not exactly as tough as its supporters would have liked, and, at the same, concessions were also made by senators from the *Polo*, who abandoned their obstructionism of the budget.

The Record

By the end of 1995, the Dini government had already improved on the average lifespan of Italian post-war governments which, as we have already seen, stands at about ten and a half months.[13] As all scholars of contemporary Italian politics well know, a government's longevity rarely goes hand in hand with its productivity. On the contrary, the governments which lasted longest have often been among the least productive. As elsewhere, so in Italy too, the power of government weighs most on those who actually exert it. With this said, the Dini government's record has been characterized by three elements: the personality of the leader, institutional dynamics and political consequences.

The Prime Minister's personal record was undoubtedly positive. His popularity grew both at home and abroad—so much so that the extra votes he would net for the alliance presenting his (re)candidacy for *palazzo Chigi* was estimated at around 4-5 percent, even if such calculations should be viewed with caution. The legislative record of Dini's government was just as impressive, especially if seen against the agenda it had set itself. If one excludes the extremely complicated issue of fair and equal access to television for all parties, the Dini government achieved all the goals it had set itself in the time it said it would. It should not, however, be forgotten that the real impact of the pension reform remains controversial and that the budget for 1996 has been criticised by many commentators for its lack of weight, making a supplementary budget indispensable for the end of the year.

More complicated, or rather mixed, is the political and institutional record of the Dini government. Is the relative cooling of the political tension between the two poles a permanent or just temporary improvement on the road to political transition? Did the Dini government succeed in its design to encourage a new consensus and balance between the political players, to create better and longerlasting conditions for the proper functioning, reform and reorganization of the Italian political system and to prepare the ground for a decent Republic? An affirmative answer to these questions can only be given if and when the socalled broad-based coalition becomes a reality. As regards the actual way of

TABLE 6.2   Number of Emergency Decrees per Government

Decrees	Governments		
	Ciampi	Berlusconi	Dini
Presented	98	193	223
Approved	5	54	38
With modifications	—	(42)	(27)
Without modifications	—	(12)	(11)
Expired	92	133	135
Rejected	1	5	3
Sent back to the government	11	24	8
Pending	—	—	47

Source: Elaboration of data from the *Ufficio informazioni parlamentari e Archivio legislativo del Senato*, November, 1995, pp. 8-10.

governing, the Dini government made excessive use—at times with the wilful acquiescence of Parliament, especially the Center-Left majority—of the oftcriticized *decretazione d'urgenza* (emergency decree). Table 6.2 shows data comparing the last three Italian governments (it was decided to limit data collection to the beginning of November, 1995 to have roughly similar time spans for the three different governments).

As is known, the emergency decree has customarily been used by Italian governments, on the one hand, to maintain unity even when the majorities backing them are divided on the remedies to problems and on the other, more frequently, to solidify the support from the selfsame parliamentary majority. Moreover, as Table 6.2 graphically illustrates, the exponential growth of the emergency decree, which so clearly characterized the working of the Dini government, ended up having a negative impact on the socalled presumed "centrality of Parliament." The technocratic government hardly empowered Parliament. In fact, it attempted to curtail its controls and escape its monitoring. Despite this, however, and especially because of the multitude of decrees and the inexperience and incapacity of the technocratic ministers and undersecretaries, the success rate of the Dini decrees, 16 percent, was markedly inferior to, for example, that of the Berlusconi government: 27 percent.[14]

It would be correct to deduce from all this that the technocratic government often showed indifference and, at times, disinterest in convincing Parliament of the urgency and quality of its legislation or indeed the need for it. It should be borne in mind that in order to resolve certain intricate issues, expedite the process of parliamentary approval,

TABLE 6.3   Confidence Votes on the Government's Amendments to the Budget (December 15, 1995)

	First vote	*Second vote*
Absent	28	19
Present	599	608
Total voting	598	607
In favor	306	310
Against	292	297
Abstentions	1	1

Source: adapted from *La Repubblica*, December 16, 1995, p. 3.

Notes: traditionally, the Speaker of the House does not express his/her vote.

In the first round, 20 deputies from the *Polo* were absent: 6 from *Alleanza Nazionale*, 5 from *Forza Italia*, 8 from the *Fronte Liberal-Democratico* and 1 of the *Cristiani Democratici Uniti*. The six absent deputies from the Center-Left were: 4 *Progressisti*, 1 *Popolare*, 1 *Leghista*, and 2 members from the *Gruppo misto*.

In the second round 15 members from the *Polo* were absent: 5 from *Forza Italia*, 5 from the *Fronte Liberal-Democratico*, 3 from *Alleanza Nazionale*, 1 of the *Cristiani Democratici Uniti* and 1 from the *Centro Cristiano Democratico*. Absent also were 2 members from the Center-Left: 1 of the *Progressisti* and 1 member of the *Lega*, plus the same 2 members from the *Gruppo misto*.

Three deputies are not included in the calculations: one deceased and not yet replaced and two who had resigned because elected to incompatible offices.

and call the bluff of the opposition, it had to resort rather frequently to the vote of confidence. The Dini government used a confidence motion no less than seven times: five in the Chamber of Deputies and two in the Senate. In the Chamber the no-confidence vote was requested on March 15 on the problem of employment and depressed areas and on the same subject in the Senate on March 21; in the Chamber on July 12-13 on pension reform; in the Senate on the October 4 on privatization; and in the Chamber on December 14-15 on the budget.

This last double vote merits particular attention because it represents the final desperate attempt by the *Polo*, led by Berlusconi, to precipitate a government crisis and achieve its objective of early elections. Instead, as is shown in Table 6.3, defections in the ranks of the *Polo* strengthened the government's hand and actually raised the possibility that the Dini government, or at least its Prime Minister, might enjoy an extension in term of office or begin a new one. In the traditional pre-Christmas press conference, Dini declared that he was not plotting or making plans and that he was answerable to the forces in Parliament. He also, however, outlined two possible scenarios for 1996: "Either we arrive at a broad coalition government where political parties of the Center-Right and the Center-Left can take part, or it will be difficult to change the type of government: in this case there would be a short-lived government which would lead to elections in a relatively short period of time."[15]

Dini's wholly technocratic government took advantage of the weakness both of the Berlusconi opposition, lacking the votes and unity to win a confidence motion, and the Center-Left (especially the representatives of the *Lega* and the *Popolari*) concerned about a quick return to the ballot box. But the Dini government neither knew how to improve, nor indeed wanted to improve, in any significant way on relations between the executive and Parliament. On the contrary, it went about its business exploiting the contradictions in the system without introducing any reform.

On a more purely political level, there is another reason why the overall evaluation of the Dini government is far from satisfactory. After the Ciampi government, which also won considerable praise—especially of its technical and professorial components (beginning with the role played by the Prime Minister himself)—the Dini government seemed, by virtue of its much vaunted technical nature, the behavior of some of its ministers and under-secretaries, and its reception in the public's eye, to support a feeling that was already rather widespread among the Italian electorate. Completely technocratic governments, i.e. governments made up exclusively of nonparliamentarians (including the head of government himself), which have never existed in any parliamentary democracy since the Second World War, imply, by their very nature, a suspension of politics. Paradoxically, if this suspension of politics is accompanied by efficient government, the message that comes through to the public is that it is preferable to keep politics and politicians away from the government of the country. It is this that generates that classic attitude of the majority of Italians: *qualunquismo* (populism of the average man), or rather antipolitics in its Mediterranean form. Naturally, the socalled suspension of politics cannot and should not be blamed on the Dini government and its president, but on the inability and weakness of the two opposing alliances and their leaders.

Nevertheless, at the same time as an "exciting" debate was going on about the direct election of the President of the Republic, or of the Prime Minister, or of the Prime Minister together with his majority, and about the need for a parliamentary political government, the government of Prime Minister Dini was busy flaunting its unifying capacity not as a simple matter of fact but as a prized trophy: none of its members, beginning with the Prime Minister himself, had been elected to Parliament, none of them had had to face the bruising electoral test. In Berlusconi's words, none of Italy's governing elite had in the course of 1995 received an electoral, popular, or political mandate of any description. There are certainly doubts about just how much and to what extent the Italian electorate is politicized, if by politicization we mean political interest and understanding and not just the strength of feeling of belonging to a party or a particular ideology or indeed hostility to an opposing one. There is however no doubt that "de-politicization," understood as the conviction that un-elected technocrats are better than elected politicians, does not encourage reform of the political system, improvement of Italian democracy and the completion of the transition.

Conclusion: Dini after Dini?

Technocratic governments may bring temporary solutions to situations of institutional ill health and real political crisis. Their reproduction, itself an indicator of crisis, ends up not resolving but simply aggravating the crisis. There is no reason to believe that, after the Dini government of 1995, the Italian political system will be in any better shape to tackle the urgent structural reforms it needs. On the contrary, there are very good reasons for believing that the Dini government, made up on the whole of low profile professionals, will end up being remembered as a government of transition in the transition.

In the future, the Dini government period may end up being seen as a transient experience between one government, that of Silvio Berlusconi with its aggressive champions of the business world, presumptuous neophytes in the world of politics, and a government of the same kind, perhaps even more rancorous and vindictive, or else a government composed of an inconclusive and argumentative Center-Léft grouping. While leaving both possibilities open, Dini's resignation, handed in as promised by the Prime Minister on December 30, does not exclude the eventuality of Dini temporarily succeeding himself. But if, in just a few months time, the Italian political system finds itself in the middle of fiercely contested new elections which are unlikely to resolve the transition, then the only real merit of the first Dini government will have been to keep the lid on political conflict for a year or thereabouts. If, however, the political temperature starts to rise once more, that merit will be seen as merely ephemeral and, with Italy's tumultuous and bizarre transition going on, the political record of Dini's technocratic government may actually be judged as having been counterproductive.

Translated by Timothy Cooper and Stephen Jewks

Notes

1. For more detailed information, see the introduction by P. Ignazi and R.S. Katz, "Ascesa e caduta del governo Berlusconi", in the volume edited by them *Politica in Italia. Edizione 95*, (Bologna: Il Mulino, 1995), pp. 27-48. For the problems linked to its formation, cf. S. Ceccanti and S. Fabbrini, "Transizione verso Westminster? Ambiguità e discontinuità nella formazione del Governo Berlusconi", in G. Pasquino, ed., *L'alternanza inattesa. Le elezioni del 27 marzo 1994 e le loro conseguenze*, (Soveria Mannelli: Rubbettino, 1995), pp. 257-284.

2. The reference is to article 67 of the Constitution: "Every member of Parliament represents the Nation and carries out his functions without constraint of mandate." In fact, by proudly rejecting party ties, Giulio Tremonti, elected as a deputy for the *Patto Segni*, had become the Minister of Finance in the Berlusconi government and Giuseppe Grillo, elected with the *Popolari*, became the under-secretary to the *Bilancio*. These are not the only examples of "rogues," but the most important and visible.

3. For the best treatment, see the chapter by S. Merlini, "Il governo", in G. Amato e A. Barbera, eds., *Manuale di diritto pubblico*, (Bologna: Il Mulino, 1994), pp. 419-461.

4. On this point, see C. Chimenti, *Il Governo dei professori. Cronaca di una transizione*, (Firenze: Passigli Editori, 1994).

5. Analyses and evaluations may be found in G. Pasquino and S. Vassallo, "Il governo di Carlo Azeglio Ciampi", in C. Mershon and G. Pasquino, eds., *Politica in Italia. Edizione 94*, (Bologna: Il Mulino, 1994), pp. 69-89.

6. From the stenographic record of the declarations regarding his program made by Dini to the Chamber of Deputies, January 23, 1995, p. 7516.

7. Ibidem.

8. Ibidem, p. 7507.

9. A well-documented, sober, and impartial account of the whole subject is given by E. Bettinelli, *Par condicio*, (Torino: Einaudi, 1995).

10. On this point, see the analysis by R. D'Alimonte, "La transizione italiana: il voto regionale del 23 aprile", in *Rivista Italiana di Scienza Politica*, n. 3, 1995, pp. 515-558.

11. Interview for *Panorama*, August 24, 1995.

12. The complete text may be found in *Milano Finanza*, October 11, 1995.

13. On this point, see my chapter I governi, in the volume I edited: *La politica italiana. Dizionario critico 1945-1995*, (Roma-Bari: Laterza, 1995), pp. 61-77.

14. For useful comparative data see V. Della Sala, "Governare per decreto. Il governo Craxi e l'uso dei decreti-legge", in P. Corbetta and R. Leonardi, eds., *Politica in Italia. Edizione 87*, (Bologna: Il Mulino, 1987), pp. 35-54.

15. Quote from the summary in *L'Unità*, December 24, 1995, p. 3.

7

Pension Reform: Perhaps Not the Last Round

Onorato Castellino

In the Fifties and Sixties, and throughout the following decade, Italian social welfare legislation proved to be both extravagant and shortsighted. The prerequisites for being awarded a pension and the size of the entitlement slowly widened to the point where Italian pensions became among the most generous in the world. No forecast, however, was made of the impact that such benefits would have on future generations and the problem was simply passed on to future governments making it increasingly harder for them to reform what public opinion saw as "acquired rights."

The first alarm bells started ringing back in the late Seventies after a series of private studies of the system by individual scholars. After a few years, the Commission for Public Expenditure added its voice to these warnings with a study predicting increasing difficulties for the system to pay its way. Finally, INPS and the Treasury ministry (General State Accounting Office) added the weight of their computerized data and projections to the forecasts on social welfare expenditure.[1] According to these projections, in the main pension regime (the *Fondo Pensioni Lavoratori Dipendenti* or FPLD—employees fund—which covers more than half of workers and pensioners), the actual rate of contribution necessary to cover pension outlay would have passed the 50 percent mark by 2010.

The system had also met with growing criticism for its redistributive aspects, over and above this general potential imbalance. In fact, the relationship between the pension received by a worker and the contributions previously paid in by him or her differed markedly from one regime to another and even between individual cases in the same regime—without such differences having anything to do with criteria of equity or standardization.

A great many reform programs were discussed by different governments in the Eighties, some of which even reached Parliament though none were approved. It was not until July, 1992, that the government of Giuliano Amato presented a proposal containing a series of measures on pension reform. The currency crisis of September induced the government to tighten its proposals and Parliament to approve them swiftly, leading to law no. 421, of October 23, 1992 and the subsequent decrees (in particular, no. 503 of December 30, 1992). The events of 1995 are substantially a continuation (but, as we shall see, not the definitive conclusion) of what had been begun in 1992 and it is thus from here that we must begin our investigation.

The Amato Reform and Unresolved Problems

There are basically two essential points that a law on pensions must cover (beyond, of course, those regarding its funding): the prerequisites for entitlement and the formulae for working it out. Tables 7.1 and 7.2 summarize the situation before the Amato reform, the innovations introduced by the latter and (anticipating, for the sake of comparison, what will be said later) the further changes introduced by the legislation of 1995.

The *pensione di anzianità* is a typical construct of the Italian pensions system which has very few equivalents in other countries. It is a pension which accrues after the accumulation of a certain number of working years, independently of actual biological age. The benefit has its origin in the public sector where it was introduced (in 1956, with further extensions made in 1973) on the basis of a very wide interpretation of regulations in which there is no real provision for such generosity (cf. Table 7.1). In the private sphere, the law is less generous than in the public sector but continues to appear profligate when compared to international norms; it came into being through direct legislation between 1965 and 1969.

The 1992 reform represents a decisive step towards reforming the system's financial imbalances and redistributive anomalies. Elevation of the age limit for the FPLD and of the length of service for public servants, the lower average value of pensions and the abolition of indexlinking of pensions to real salaries all contributed to the first objective. Making age limits the same for public and private employees and eliminating the differential advantages to favor "dynamic" careers (by calculating pensions as an average of salaries received over the employee's entire working life and not just during the final period) helped achieve the latter objective.

TABLE 7.1 Years Necessary for Pension Entitlement

	FPLD		*State*		*Self-employed*	
	Males	*Females*	*Males*	*Females*	*Males*	*Females*
	Before the Amato reform					
Old-age	60	55	65	65	65	60
Seniority	35	35	20	15	35	35
	Amato reform (regime)					
Old-age	65	60	65	65	65	60
Seniority	35	35	35	35	35	35
	Dini reform (regime)					
Old-age	57	57	57	57	57	57

TABLE 7.2 Pension Calculation

Before the Amato reform
a) for each year of service:
2% of the final pay-packet
N.B.: literally the last for the State;
average of the last 5 years for the FPLD;
average of the last 10 years for self-employed workers
b) index-linking of pensions:
to minimum contractual wage

Amato reform
a) for each year of service:
2% of the average wage (revalued on the basis of prices and a further 1% a year) over entire working life
b) index-linking of pensions:
to prices alone, were no special provision is made in the budget

Dini reform
a) conversion into pension income, according to life-expectancy criteria (thus taking account of retirement age) of the total amount of contributions paid, capitalized at the GDP growth rate
b) index-linking of pensions:
to prices alone, at least until 2009

It must be pointed out, however, that all the above measures were to be put info effect after a long and gradual transitional phase designed to cushion the blow for Italians and their generously understood "acquired rights." Furthermore, the legislature of 1992 had not had the courage to reform several anomalies present in the system, and especially:

- maintaining the age limit for women five years below that of men. This, alongside of women's greater longevity, limited the savings that could have been made;

- confirming the requirement in the FPLD regime of 35 years of service for a seniority pension. This, in many cases, made the increase in pensionable age irrelevant or at least less incisive and maintained distortions in pension yields favoring retirement at an early age.[2] Since a seniority pension was also foreseen for the categories of agricultural producers, artisans and tradesmen—instituted respectively in 1957, 1959 and 1966—entitlement to the same sort of treatment (35 years after the establishment of the respective categories) had just begun for the first category, and was about to start for the other two;

- the selfemployed, though entitled to pension payments equivalent to only roughly half of those paid by the FPLD, continued to enjoy the same criteria for working out pension rights;

- thanks to a provision (art. 1 of the legislative decree 373/1993) issued at a later date but still part of the law of 1992, salaries lower than 80 percent of the average were excluded when calculating the pensionable base. In this way, a distortion in favor of more dynamic and well-paid careers was—perhaps inadvertently—reintroduced.[3]

From the Berlusconi Government
to the Dini Government

In the course of 1994, new projections for the social welfare and pensions system became available, based on more uptodate information regarding macroeconomic variables and stretching to the year 2030 rather than 2010. The spectre of a contributive rate of around 50 percent, which the Amato reform seemed to have pushed back to 2010, was suddenly nearer at hand.

Quotas of these dimensions seemed too high to be borne by those of working age. The generosity of the system, even after the checks of the Amato reform, was in fact still excessive, mainly because of two factors (cf. Tables 7.1 and 7.2): the high rate at which pension provisions accrue (*coefficiente di rendimento* - 2 percent of the pensionable base for every year of service) and the low average retirement age (due to the 35 year limit for a seniority/service pension in the private sector and to the even more permissive transitional norms operating in the public sector).

The average age of retirement was approximately 59 years for men and 57 for women. If only service pensions are considered, the average drops to 54 years for men and 51.5 for women (the data refer to the *Fondo*

Pensioni Lavoratori Dipendenti). In some cases, this phenomenon was due to "early retirements," promoted as a means for dealing with crisis situations where workers were being laid off; in many others, it was simply a question of workers freely deciding to work in some other form or live off income generated in the family.

In the summer of 1994, the government set up a study Commission "for the prospective investigation of ideas to reform the social welfare and pensions system." University professors, public functionaries and experts appointed by trade union organizations representing employees and selfemployed workers and by the *Confindustria* were called in as members.

The Commission soon turned into a sounding board for discussion of issues that excited public opinion and which the press wrote daily about. Three issues deserve special mention.

In the first place, a whole range of different pension regimes continued to exist. If in one regime, the number of pensioners was low compared to active workers, better provisions could be offered for the same amount of contributions or lower contributions for the same amount of provisions. Craftsmen, shopkeepers and the selfemployed found themselves in this situation and paid in their contributions at rates markedly lower than those for employees, even though they enjoyed benefits determined by the same rules. In contrast, the regime of agricultural producers, with many pensioners and few active workers, drew heavily on state support.

The distinction between pension regimes, however, are not inevitable facts but rather simply historical accidents. If, instead of many regimes there were only one, there would be an automatic compensation of the different relations between pensioners and active workers, reducing both the possibility of more favorable contributionbenefit combinations and recourse to state subsidies. However, the mere mention of such an idea unleashed intense reactions from the professional categories which enjoyed a lower-than-average ratio.

A second problem hinged on the difference between *previdenza* (welfare/pensions) and *assistenza* (social security assistance). *Previdenza* usually refers to the series of benefits provided during or after a working life while *assistenza* refers to all the measures aimed at supporting those in situations of need. It is usually maintained that the costs of *previdenza* must be borne by the revenue generated from contributions, those of *assistenza* by taxes.

Consequences of great importance arise from this distinction as regards the actual burden citizens must shoulder. But where should we draw the line? Is guaranteeing a minimum pension to a worker (or to a worker's family) who has not paid in sufficient contributions *previdenza* or *assistenza*? Is intervening (as we have just mentioned) in favor of regimes suffering from a high pensioner-active worker ratio *previdenza* or *assistenza*? These are just two examples: there are many more borderline cases, all of them raising endless debate.

Another area of conflict regarded expectations which any reform must safeguard as "acquired rights." These, in order of decreasing immediacy, go from those who already have a pension book in their pockets to those who are about to leave work, from those who are halfway there to those who have just begun work. All of the above, if they are rational and farsighted, will have made choices and formulated plans on the basis of pension expectations. If past legislatures have been too magnanimous in making promises which seem to us today unbalanced, to what point should they be considered untouchable?

The greater the expectations of pensioners and those about to retire, the greater the burden on new contributors and those who will follow them in the future. The safeguarding of the elderly's expectations must, therefore, be limited by the just as important safeguarding of younger and unborn generations. Balancing these different interests can also be the subject of interminable debate.

Because of its heterogeneous make-up and the reluctance of those representing social interests to accept a solution which could have later undermined their negotiating power, the government Commission concluded its work at the end of September, 1994 without having succeeded in settling any of the open questions on its agenda.

In November, 1994, however, the government finally reached a decision and laid before Parliament not only a bill (with delegative powers) to generally restructure and harmonize the pensions system, but another to introduce, among other things, a penalty on the size of retirement/service pensions set at a rate of 3 percent for each year anticipated vis à vis the age for oldage pension.

Opposition to the bill from trade unions was strong; the parliamentary majority was accused (in a distortion of every official declaration or text presented to Parliament) of wanting to intervene not only on the criteria for settling future pensions, but also on the living standards of those already in retirement. After a period of attrition between government and unions, and the extraordinary success of the general strike called by the latter, an accord was reached on December 1, 1994 in which both parties accepted austerity measures, though the agreement was written in a language which was susceptible to differing interpretations. The following objectives were outlined in the text:

- to make the contributions paid by the individual more closely correlated to the benefits received;
- to relate pension levels to life expectancy at the date of retirement;

- to move towards equal treatment for the different categories of pensioners with sustainable contribution quotas.

Shortly after (December 16, 1994), the *Gruppo progressisti federativo* presented a bill to reform the pension system in the Chamber of Deputies which adhered to "the logic of a closer relationship between contributions and benefits" by moving "from a retributive pay-as-you-go system to a system based on actual contributions, calculated on a simulated capitalization-style basis."

In the meantime, however, the *Lega*'s withdrawal of support for Berlusconi and the worsening of relations between the government and trade unions quickly led to the executive's resignation.

During the first months of 1995, the unions held long and complex talks with the new government headed by Lamberto Dini in the course of which both the unresolved issues left over from the Amato reform and the above-mentioned causes of discontent again came to the surface. The meetings closed on May 8 with a new agreement that was much better articulated than the accord of December, 1994. This was promptly translated into a bill of law approved by the cabinet on the May 12 and later placed before Parliament.

Parliamentary discussion of the bill was long and arduous: the Right showed little interest in supporting the government, while the Left was torn between its recognition of the need for reform and the embarrassment of making itself responsible for a new *reformatio in peius* less than three years after the previous one. Law no. 335 of the August 8, 1995 was eventually passed without substantial changes to the original text, despite a series of noconfidence motions which, more than once, had forced the government to embody a whole series of different norms in a single (and thus rather botched) article.

The Dini Reform

The law laid down a new method for calculating pensions based on the sum of the contributions paid (from whence the name *sistema contributivo*) and its translation into pension yield.[4]

The *total amount* is obtained (cf. Table 7.2) by capitalizing pension contributions at the nominal rate of variation of gross domestic product (GDP): this means taking account both of increases due to inflation and real increases. It should be noted, however, that it is not contributions effectively paid which are capitalized but notional contributions obtained by applying a 33 percent quota to salaries for the FPLD and public servants and a 20 percent quota for self-employed workers. The currently applied quota is 32 percent in the first two cases[5] and 15-16 percent in the third.

A pension may be requested at *any age between 57 and 65 years*. The total amount is converted into income via coefficients which vary with age; these coefficients roughly correspond to life expectancy for a male pension, 60 percent payable in favor of the surviving spouse and calculated at an annual accrual rate of 1.50 percent.

Any evaluation of the reform from the point of view of *equity and incentives* must proceed from the understanding that the Amato reform, even at the end of the transitional phase, would have allowed the four systematic distortions mentioned in the first paragraph to remain.

The Dini reform brought an end to these distortions with the introduction of a contributive method applied differently for employees and the selfemployed and with conversion rates (of the total amount of income) differentiated by age but equal for men and women. In particular, the *pensione di anzianità* and its abnormal consequences as regards equity and incentives (through the payment of a sum related to an individual's contributions only and not to his or her expected lifespan) were substantially eliminated.

It would not have been difficult to obtain similar results by making appropriate changes to the previous calculation method though in this case the reformers would have come up against the "magic 2 percent figure" used to work out the rate of accrual (cfr. Table 7.2). Rather than confronting this obstacle head on, it was decided it would be better to go around it by adopting, or rather, returning to the contributive method. It should also be noted that the scale for converting the total amount into pensionable income reproduces roughly the same penalty (3 percent for each year under the age of 65) which had raised so many protests when it was included in the previous government's bill.

On the issue of *financial equilibria*, by beginning with the FPLD and looking at the regime situation (when, that is, the new norms come into force), we can examine the extent of cover (or replacement ratio), i.e. the ratio between the initial amount of pension and the final pay. This ratio is shown in Table 7.3 which considers four significant combinations of age and length of service, where "W" and "G" indicate, respectively, the percentage variation of individual salary and GDP.[6]

With a hypothetical GDP growth rate of 1.5 percent, the reform leaves the degree of coverage (established by the Amato reform) unchanged for a pensioner of 62 years of age and with 37 years of service. Using this as a benchmark, we find that:

- the application of differentiated rates of accrual according to age means that (for a GDP growth rate equal to 1.5 percent) the Dini pensions are lower (higher) than the Amato pensions for ages below (above) 62 years;

- since in the Amato reform, the pensionable base is calculated by reevaluating real salary at the preset rate of 1 percent while in the Dini

TABLE 7.3 Comparison Between Amato and Dini Norms

Age	Seniority	W	G	Cover%	
				Amato	Dini
57	35	2	1,5	58,6	50,2
		3	2,5	54,4	50,2
		4	3,5	51,4	50,3
60	37	2	1,5	61,3	57,8
		3	2,5	57,0	57,8
		4	3,5	53,6	57,9
62	37	2	1,5	61,3	61,7
		3	2,5	57,0	61,8
		4	3,5	53,6	61,8
65	40	2	1,5	65,9	73,7
		3	2,5	61,0	73,8
		4	3,5	57,2	73,8

reform the amount is obtained by capitalizing contributions at the rate of GDP growth, a rise in this latter has more of an effect on Dini pensions than on those of Amato.

A preliminary evaluation of the effects of the Dini reform when fully operative may thus be summarized as follows:

a) all pensions (excluding, obviously, those for invalids and surviving spouses) for those under the age of 57 years will disappear. This measure is of no small account if we consider that, taking all the regimes together (FPLD, self-employed workers, and public servants), pensions awarded in 1991 on the basis of *anzianità* (seniority) were almost equal to the number of old-age pensions;

b) for retirements between 57 and 61 years of age, expenditure will drop if, after 1995, GDP does not increase by more than 1.5 percent; for retirements between 57 and 59 years, expenditure will drop for rates below 2.5 percent; expenditure will go up in any case (though more markedly in the case of high development rates) for retirement after 62 years of age;

c) the distribution of retirements by age will in turn be influenced by the reform, causing people—even over the age of 57—to stay longer at work (as a result of eliminating incentives to retire early); this will have uncertain effects on the size of the average pension but will certainly bring about a fall in the number of pensioners and probably also an increase in contribution levels. Though it is often argued that each retirement leaves a job vacant, we must remember that many of those retiring on the basis of length of service continue to do the same kind of job as before either for the same or other employers or for themselves, without, that is, helping turnover and often without providing further contributions;

d) costs will be sensibly reduced for the categories of the self-employed. While the rules for calculating their pensions were previously the same as those used for the FPLD, the new regulations apply a notional quota of 20 percent compared to the FPLD's 33 percent.

We have yet to say anything about the important *transitional norms*. These were the result of the strong opposition shown by the trade unions during negotiations with the government towards any measures that would tangibly affect their members in the middle age range.

Workers who on December 31, 1995 have paid at least 18 years contributions will be entitled to a pension according to the previous pay-as-you-go retributive method, i.e. according to the Amato reform plus, if applicable, the transitional norms.

The new norms (contributive system) will apply only to those workers with less than 18 years of service at the end of 1995 and then only *pro rata temporis*. A pension will thus be determined by two addenda: one calculated in relation to seniority up to 1995, as per the Amato norms, the other in relation to seniority after 1995 as per the norms established by the Dini government.

What is more, the *pensione di anzianità* is also to be abolished gradually: in the private sector, the current requirement (35 years of service independently of age) is to be progressively modified in the following sense:

- with the 35 year service requirement remaining in force, an age requirement rising from 52 in 1996 to 57 in 2006 will have to be simultaneously satisfied; or, alternatively:

- in the absence of the age requirement, length of service will have to increase gradually from 36 years in 1996 to 40 in 2008.

For self-employed workers, the progression is much more rapid: the new age limit of 57 years will come into effect after the twoyear period 199697 when an age of 56 will be sufficient.

In the public sector, where the transition to the Amato legislation is still in course, and where, therefore, it is possible to retire with less than 35 years of service, norms for the gradual abolition of this privilege are also foreseen.

It should be noted that, in all these cases (besides one exception in the public sector), seniority pensions are calculated as per the previous norms and therefore—where the right exists—do not vary on the basis of age.

The Complementary Pensions

The Amato reform, like the Dini reform after it, had not only the compulsory pension system as its object but also *previdenza complementare*—complementary/supplementary pensions. The connection is clear: on both occasions, the legislature believed that a reduction in pension promises would have been more acceptable if accompanied by the prospect of recourse to a whole series of supplementary packages of one's choice.

It was again the *legge-delega* of October, 1992 which first made mention of provisions of this nature and it was on the basis of this law that legislative decree no. 124 of April 21, 1993 was issued, dealing with the "Forms of complementary pensions," or rather, as explained in its first article, "forms of *previdenza* for the provision of pension benefits to complement the compulsory public system with a view to ensuring higher pension coverage." The decree was welcomed by many as the creation of Italian pension funds.

In truth, many pension funds already existed, though they were mainly concentrated in the banking and insurance sectors. These, however, were not of any appreciable size and did not, therefore, play any great role in the economic system as a whole, however generous individual policies might have been.

The decree of April, 21, 1993 was designed to open the door to a broader development of complementary pension schemes. Of the many provisions contained in the decree, the following deserve mention:

- a clear choice was made in favor of forms of pensions—called *a contribuzione definita* (defined contribution)—whose provisions refer exclusively to the total amount of contributions paid in. Schemes *a prestazione definit*a (defined benefit) based on other variables and, in particular, income earned in the final phase of one's working life, were not expressly prohibited but were subjected to limits and conditions making their use more difficult;

- the funds must operate in a regime of capitalization, i.e. setting aside the reserves necessary for meeting commitment costs;

- the funds are financed by contributions from workers, contributions made by employers and the utilization of funds accumulated for severance pay.

The tax regime laid down by the decree was rather complex, being differentiated (as regards initial phase, i.e. contribution) according to the source of finance, and (as regards final phase) according to whether benefits were paid in the form of a lump-sum or income; the second option is compulsory for at least half of the accumulated sum.

Without for the time being entering into details, we should point out that the preexisting tax concessions were more generous, exempting all contributions paid by the worker or employer from taxation while the decree of 1993 placed severe limits on what was tax-deductible. For all contributions paid into the pension funds, the decree also established a tax of 15 percent which was held as a credit to be paid back to the contributor when benefits were paid.

The mechanism basically obliged the investor to loan the State, at market interest rate, 15 percent of the contributions paid into the funds. However, the unfortunate choice of the word "tax" to designate it meant that the regulation was negatively received. For this psychological reason, together with the more substantial reasons mentioned above, the 1993 decree not only failed to stimulate the creation of new pension funds—as was somewhat unreasonably expected—but actually paralyzed expansion of those funds already in existence.

Aware of this counterproductive effect, the 1995 legislation attempted to make amends. With the Dini reform, the tax of 15 percent was abolished, and taxation of workers' and employers' contributions slightly modified for the better, whereas nothing of any substance was modified as regards funding deriving from TFR quotas.

What forecasts can we formulate today about the future of pension funds and in particular about the positive or negative effects which the new tax regime will have on them?

For each of the three possible forms of financing, a comparison can be made, net of taxes, between the results obtained (either as lumpsum or income) from savings invested in a pension fund and those deriving (the burden on the contributor being equal) from an alternative method of providing for oldage.

A study recently completed by the Department of Economic and Financial Sciences "G. Prato" of the University of Turin compared two instruments: investment of contributions in State bonds and taking out a collective insurance policy offering payments which are considerably lower than those usually offered in individual policies.

Investment in state bonds does not initially enjoy any tax benefit but the interest which accumulates discounts only the "flat" tax of 12.5 percent, the final amount being exempt from taxes. The collective policy initially enjoys a tax deduction equal to 22 percent of the contributions paid; the interest which accumulates is not exempt from taxes; the final amount, whether it be taken as a lumpsum or as income, is subject to lower taxation rates.

The study shows that the pension funds perform better than State bonds, but worse than insurance policies. As we have assumed equal burdens for worker and employer, the differences can only be laid at the door of the tax treatment they receive. In other words, public finance "gains" and those interested lose if they choose the pension fund rather than the collective policy. This conclusion contrasts with the optimistic light that complementary pensions are often seen in and a robust development is forecast for pension funds with positive effects for coverage of old age pensioners needs and expansion of financial markets.

A Definitive Reform?

Not long after the presentation in Parliament of the reform bill, the Governor of the *Banca d'Italia* expressed himself in unusually frank terms:

> ...The regime system will continue to move away from that of other developed countries; in particular, the possibility of obtaining a pension at an early age will remain; the ratio between pensions and salary assured by the new system will remain higher. Should economic growth rates remain similar to those that have historically been achieved, for employees this ratio would turn out to be higher than that which, in the regime system, would be assured by the current legislation...[7]

Similar critical observations have also been made on different occasions by representatives of the *Confindustria*.

These observations cannot be defined as totally incorrect; in particular, the correlation between the pension/salary ratio and GDP growth rates—confirmed by a study of the *Banca d'Italia* and subsequently published[8]—also emerges from what was said in section 3 and in particular from table 7.3.

In order to attenuate this pessimism and, above all, to correct the mistaken impression that a lower rate of development is desirable to balance pension accounts, it should be borne in mind that if GDP trends affect pension expenditure they also affect contribution payments. In other words, it is perfectly true that for higher growth rates, the "degree of coverage," or rather the ratio between the *first* pension payment and the *last* pay-packet, is higher under the Dini than Amato regime. It is just as true, however, that—when each regime is considered separately—a higher rate of development means a more rapid rise in salaries of active workers vis à vis the last payment of each group of pensioners, and hence a more rapid decrease in the ratio between the *average* pension and *average* salary. This ratio, as is well known, represents one of the two fundamental determinants of the contributive quota imposed on the income of each worker for the payment of pensions (the other being the ratio between number of pensioners and number of active workers).

It should also be pointed out that, under the Amato reform, the reduction in the average amount of pension with respect to the previous norm was obtained (cf. table 7.2) by a double *deindexation*: the pensionable base was no longer linked to the final level of pay and the pension was no longer index-linked (as is still the case in the Dini reform) to real salaries. In the presence of yearly GDP rises of 3-4 percent, it would have been difficult—for the ever wider gap this would have entailed between the wages of active workers and the income of pensioners—to conserve this double deindexation. Comparison with the Amato reform is thus undermined by its doubtful longevity (in the presence, we repeat, of a fastgrowing GDP).

This said, the fact remains that the reformed system can only be considered effective and consolidated if the contributions for financing it can be sustained by the working population. The early provisional estimates iindicate that, comparing the Dini regime with the Amato reform with respect to the FPLD and the year 2030, the quota remains more or less unchanged (around the 50 percent mark) if GDP grows by 1.5 percent per year and increases slightly (4550 percent) if GDP grows at 2.5 percent per year.[8] If instead we consider the categories of craftsmen and tradesmen, the quota decreases quite markedly (by about a quarter).

Even if the results of such long-term projections should be analyzed with care, one has the impression that the Dini reform has still not provided that decisive contribution to balance the system, and that in the coming years further measures will be called for.

As for complementary pensions, it is possible that collective bargaining might look on the development of pension funds with favor (especially for their possible broader positive effects on industrial relations) and lobby for their establishment and development even within a legislative framework which, as we have seen, offers no substantial incentives from a tax point of view. Some of the clauses inserted in recently renewed national employment contracts seem to point in this direction. It is nevertheless clear that some relaxation of tax regulations would represent a decisive contribution to moving pension funds on from their current standing as extras on the Italian financial stage to a position as protagonists.

Translated by Timothy Cooper and Stephen Jewks

Notes

1. See from the last *Istituto nazionale della previdenza sociale (INPS), Le pensioni domani,* (Bologna: Il Mulino, 1993), pp. 113-172, and Ministero del Tesoro - Ragioneria generale dello Stato, "Linee di tendenza della spesa pensionistica",

in *Conti pubblici e congiuntura economica*, n. 3, July, 1993.

2. It is clear that contribution history—and thus the size of the pension—being equal, a lower retirement age means a longer life-expectancy and thus a higher rate of yield on the contributions paid.

3. In fact, the higher the average rate of increase in salary (retribution) in the course of one's working life, the higher the number of years excluded, and thus the higher the ratio between the pensionable base (the average of residual retributions) and the general retributive average.

4. A calculation method based on the contibution history of the pensioner had been applied, for the FPLD, from the institution of the regime (1919) until 1968. The "new" method is therefore a return to the past, though with substantial modifications.

5. For the FPLD, the quota has risen from the previous 27 percent to 32 percent via the devolution of five percentage points which were originally destined for the management of temporary benefits (family relief, unemployment benefit etc.).

6. If we assume that the working population and the distribution of the PIL between income from work and other incomes remain constant, "G" is also the rate of variation of average salary and the difference between "W" and "G" is attributable to career progression in terms of seniority.

7. Banca d'Italia, *Relazione del Governatore sull'esercizio 1994 - Considerazioni finali*, Roma, May, 1995, p. 24 of the proofs.

8. See "La riforma del sistema pensionistico", in *Banca d'Italia*, n. 25, October, 1995, pp. 4*-19*.

9. As we have pointed out, higher development rates make the equilibrium quota decrease, but more markedly under the Amato regime than the Dini regime.

8

The Stone Guest: Italy on the Threshold of European Monetary Union

Pier Virgilio Dastoli

Storm clouds heading towards *Palazzo Chigi* (the premier's residence), Admiral Boom would have yelled at Lamberto Dini if our Prime Minister—on the eve of the Council of Ministers for Economy and Finance meeting on September 18, 1995—had ventured out onto the streets of London frequented by Mary Poppins.

Unfortunately for him, Lamberto Dini had instead passed the weekend of September 16-17 holed up in *Palazzo Chigi* putting the final touches to his government's budget and the Italian strategy aimed at winning the European Commission's favor for its attempts at reforming public finances.

The first warnings of the storm therefore arrived unexpected, though with good Teutonic timing, while the economic and finance ministers of the Fifteen were gathered in Brussels working on the final timetable and technical decisions for the third stage of economic and monetary union.

In a long interview on September 18 with *Handelsblatt*, German Finance Minister Waigel suggested drawing up a new treaty between the members for monetary union which—in line with the Schengen model—would ensure greater financial discipline and tighter control of member state budgets. The reference to Schengen was not accidental and Italians—excluded from the agreement on the free movement of people for lack of credibility[1]—should have immediately sensed the gathering storm.

Instead of answering German worries, the Italian authorities—in what was reported by the Italian press as hard news—put it abroad that the EU authorities considered Italy's finances to be in a state that left hope for the country's immediate participation in the third phase of economic and monetary union.[2]

The storm clouds hardly abated and indeed the wind from Frankfurt to Rome blew harder with the publication—in the *Frankfurter Allgemeine* on September 20, 1995—of a detailed and hard-hitting analysis of the systemic weakness of Italian public finances.

The storm finally broke out of Bonn on the same day, September 20, in the form of a press release from a functionary at the Bundestag. Theo Waigel was reported as saying to members of a parliamentary finance committee that the third phase of economic and monetary union would begin only for those countries that—as of 1997—met the convergence criteria set out in the protocols attached to the Maastricht Treaty (a simple restatement, to this point, of the Treaty itself),[3] adding that the state of public finances in certain countries (Italy, Belgium, Spain) would make it extremely difficult for them to join those that were ready to start on January 1, 1999.

Italy in the Second Division?

German Minister Waigel's words reverberated round the international markets, already shaken by speculation on the dollar that had seriously weakened the Italian lira. The Italian currency repeated the record lows of September, 1992 (when the lira and sterling left the European Exchange Rate Mechanism) and August, 1993 (when the exchange rate bands of the European Monetary System were widened from 2.25 percent to 15 percent with the lira's subsequent failure to rejoin the exchange rate agreement).

The storm triggered by Waigel's words pointed up a question the Italian authorities had, till then, tried to exorcise, trusting in the good will of the partners to interpret "politically" the criteria set down at Maastricht in December, 1991: the unpostponable and inevitable start of the third phase of economic and monetary union limited to those countries meeting such criteria and the feared relegation of Italy into *serie B* (the second division).

This then is how the financial consequences appeared of following the agreements underwritten by the Twelve four years previous and negotiated with the conscious and active participation of Italy's monetary authorities in the monetary Committee (Carlo Azeglio Ciampi) and of Italy's political authorities in the Council of Ministers of the economy and finance (Guido Carli).

Aware of the clear impossibility for Italy in the short/medium term to curb its public debt below the 60 percent limit, Guido Carli and Carlo

Azeglio Ciampi had however successfully requested that this criterion be examined in the light of the trend each country showed; they did, however, fully accept the rigid implications of all the other criteria proposed by the monetary Committee, especially the 3 percent limit on budget deficits.

Carefully assessing the implications of Italy's financial system joining economic and monetary union and well aware of the fact that Italy began with a budget deficit of 8.8 percent in 1991[4] the Amato government made a remarkable effort at reforming public finances by cutting the deficit by 1.9 percent of Gross Domestic Product (GDP), bringing it below the 7 percent mark (6.9 percent). The Ciampi government sought vainly to move in the same direction but was hindered by the onset of economic recession and the subsequent slow-down in GDP growth.

As often happens in Italy, the risk of seeing the country relegated to *serie B* and the prospect of being excluded from the negotiating table of economic and monetary union immediately sparked off angry and offended reactions from the press and politicians.[5]

This indeed was what happened when Chancellor Kohl's party, in August, 1994, put forward the idea of a core group of European countries, trimming down the list of seven countries (the six founders and Spain)—indicated a year earlier by the then Foreign Minister Beniamino Andreatta[6]—'choosing" only Germany, France and the Benelux countries and thus dealing a serious blow to the already damaged international credibility of the Berlusconi government.[7]

The "German Model"

In order to impose the German model—claimed Eugenio Scalfari (director of the influential daily newspaper, *La Repubblica*), casting himself as defender of wounded Italian pride[8]—the German political and financial classes "dictate the rules for everyone, make the choices, and set the agenda, creating a German model that looks less and less like Europe and more and more like a big deutsche mark area where the economy and above all the currency have supplanted politics."

Most of the comments in the press were, however, based on an erroneous assumption that the criteria for getting on board the train for a single currency—and hence the list of those who will be admitted—are a German whim and not the inevitable result of an international agreement (the Maastricht Treaty) signed by eleven heads of government and a head of State and ratified by nine national parliaments and three referenda.

Besides the heated comments in the press, many financial experts, a large part of the trade unions, and some politicians seized on the controversy raised by Waigel's words to attack the Maastricht Treaty and the criteria ("senseless," someone wrote) for achieving a single currency. Thus there were some who felt that the deflationary and social consequences of a tight spending policy and tax increases were more damaging than the benefits to be had from joining a stable European monetary area.

There were others who saw the criteria laid down in the Maastricht protocols as economically groundless and, finally, those who regarded the path chosen as being the least efficient way forward for achieving satisfactory short-term results in terms of economic reform.

Antonio Martino's *Big-bang* and Beniamino Andreatta's "Political Substance"

The main criticisms to the Maastricht Treaty came from Antonio Martino in line with the foreign and economic policies already in force when he was at the *Farnesina* (Foreign Office). According to Martino, the strategy pursued by the treaty of Maastricht has no chance of success and runs the risk of actually splitting Europe.

The ex-Foreign Minister of *Forza Italia* believes the convergence criteria are completely arbitrary and are neither a necessary nor sufficient condition for arriving at a single currency: convergence is not necessary if we consider that Luxembourg and Germany—the only two countries apparently able to meet all the Maastricht parameters—have different currencies, and it is not sufficient if we consider that the country with the highest debt-GDP ratio in Europe—Belgium—and the one with the lowest—Luxembourg—have had the same currency for years. In other words—Martino argues—convergence is possible without having the same currency and it is possible to have the same currency without having convergence.

If a single currency is to be achieved, then, the strategy for monetary union needs to be changed: the path Martino has singled out on more than one occasion is that of the so-called *big-bang*, i.e. the creation of a single currency at the beginning of the convergence process in manner similar to what happened in Germany at the beginning of the unification process between West and East.[9]

Antonio Martino's arguments are certainly not lacking in theoretical grounding or references to international reality; if monetary union were to be realized by choosing those countries of the world that meet the Maastricht criteria, only five would be ready for the single currency right away: Germany, Luxembourg, Taiwan, Argentina and Singapore.

The *big-bang* idea could then resurface if in 1998 it turns out that, not only Italy, but not even France meets the conditions set by Maastricht. In this case, the governments would be faced with three possibilities: postponing the start of the third phase of EMU (but this is not foreseen by the treaty), tempering the Maastricht criteria (but this would mean modifying the criteria, something Germany would certainly not agree to) or else setting fixed exchange rates between certain currencies (those of the deutsche mark area and the French franc), speeding up introduction of a single currency in order to fight international speculation on the money markets (the *big-bang*).

It seems however that what escapes Antonio Martino is the political substance of the problem: and that political substance—in the words of the PPI party leader in the Chamber of Deputies, Beniamino Andreatta[10]—"is the diffidence of German public opinion regarding replacement of the Bundesbank and *deutsche Mark* by Community institutions and a Community currency."

"Germany—Andreatta adds—has represented a monetary anchor for Europe, has provided the other countries with an anti-inflationary marker they have been able to tie their own policies to, has techniques for managing liquidity that are devised and in line with the behaviour of market operators—trade unions and enterprises—convinced of the credibility of the monetary authorities and hence quick to adapt to the behavioural changes of these authorities."[11]

Germany—warns Andreatta—"does not want the governors of the future European central bank to be tempted by lax monetary policies to help manage, in their own countries, public debt, by somehow using the weapon of inflation to reduce the actual weight of the public debt."[12]

"This is the trade-off that is happening in Europe—concludes Andreatta—and while running away from this might be all right for a few professors meeting on the other side of the Atlantic, it means turning your back on reality for a European politician."[13]

There is, moreover, something else fundamentally wrong with the critical reactions following Waigel's words in Italy: reforming public finances should be considered a goal for every country to pursue, independent of the realization of economic and monetary union. Since the recession that affected all the countries of Western Europe at the beginning of the 1970s, public debt has been rising progressively with the growth in budget deficits and many countries—starting with Italy—today spend three to five times more on interest payments than they do on public investments.

Cutting budget deficits—by means of curtailing expenditures and redistributing the tax burden—has direct implications for the reduction of public debt and the reduction of public debt means that resources—today used to cover interest payments—can be freed up in the medium term for productive investments.

Italy in *Serie B*

The presentation at the end of September, 1995 of the budget for 1996 and the forecasts for reductions in inflation and the budget deficit in 1997 confirmed the hypothesis put forward by Theo Waigel in his remarks of September 20, 1995—that Italy would not be able to respect the Maastricht criteria in 1997—and drew criticism of Dini's budget package from politicians like Romano Prodi, Mario Segni and Giorgio La Malfa, and from figures from the economic and financial communities like Antonio Fazio and Gianni Agnelli.

The Governor of the *Banca d'Italia*, Antonio Fazio, also triggered debate about the need for a supplementary budget some time before the end of 1995. Fazio's idea, shared by Roman Prodi, was initially rejected by Dini and refused by D'Alema, conditioned by the need to keep under control the many voices within the PDS protesting against an "excess" of financial rigor. In the debate taken up by the newspapers, D'Alema reached the point of putting down the idea of a supplementary budget to journalistic disinformation. Fazio, however, had stated categorically to the House that "after checking the results of the tax amnesty in December, 1995 a supplementary budget could well be called for. According to preliminary calculations—Fazio added—this could well turn out to be about half the amount of the budget passed at the beginning of 1995. Achievement of the goals set for the current year and for 1996 is indispensable for winning the confidence of the currency and financial markets, bringing down inflation and stabilizing the exchange rate."[14]

A supplementary budget was in fact introduced by the Dini government before the end of 1995, held up temporarily in the House by an amendment of *Forza Italia* and the Northern League, and eventually passed with public spending cuts and tax increases. Despite this supplementary budget, the forecasts of the Dini government for 1997 still point to a budget deficit of 4.4 percent (compared to the 3 percent required under the Maastricht criteria) and an inflation rate of 3.7 percent (compared to the 3.1 percent of the Maastricht criteria). This means that the measures to reduce the budget deficit—which will have to be introduced by the government in office in autumn, 1996—will have to reduce the deficit by 2.8 percentage points of GDP vis à vis 1996. This percentage could be raised or lowered depending on the state of revenues (more revenue = greater tax receipts = smaller reduction in expenditure) and the discount rate (one point off the discount rate=15,000 billion lire off the budget deficit).

Notwithstanding these uncertainties and even allowing for favorable economic circumstances, it is very unlikely Italy will be able to meet the budget deficit target of 3 percent of GDP in 1997. Such a target could be achieved in 1998 and the reduction could continue in subsequent years with direct effects on cutting public debt.

It is well known that the Council of Europe meeting in Madrid on December 15-16, 1995 accepted the suggestions put forward by the European Monetary Institute, the Commission, and the Council of Ministers for Economy and Finance to the effect that "the Council, meeting at the level of heads of state and government, will confirm as soon as possible in 1998 which member states satisfy the conditions laid down for adoption of the single currency."[15] According to the terms of reference set out by the Council, the Commission and the European Monetary Institute "the heads of state and government should decide on the participating member states on the basis of the most recent and reliable effective data for 1997."[16]

This means that, even in the unlikely event of the Council of Europe reaching a decision at the end of the first semester 1998,[17] it will be the actual 1997 results that will be taken into account and not the forecasts for 1998. Italy could, therefore, find itself provisionally in *serie B,* as happened in 1978 when the European Monetary System was launched and Premier Andreotti was forced to postpone Italy's joining it in the face of opposition from the PCI, PSI and the *Banca d'Italia.*

We said above that the budget deficit target of 3 percent of GDP could be achieved in 1998 and that would allow Italy to ask its partners to consider again whether it meets the convergence criteria and decide on its return to *serie A* (the First Division).

The third phase of economic and monetary union will begin on January 1, 1999 when the currency exchange rates of the participating countries are fixed irrevocably, one with the other and against the single currency, the Euro. As of that date, monetary and exchange rate policies will be carried out in Euros, use of the Euro will be promoted on the money markets, and the participating member states will issue new negotiable bonds in Euros. Euro banknotes and coins, however, will begin to circulate on January 1, 2002,[18] together with national banknotes and coins: six months after at the latest, national currencies will be completely replaced by the Euro in all participating member states and introduction of the new currency will be complete.

These deadlines show that Italy can get back into *serie A* before the single currency begins to circulate and that this would most likely happen some time before the end of the century, allowing the country to take part in working out all the fundamentals of monetary policy in view of the date of January 1, 2002.

"I'm coming too, ...wait for me"

Perfectly aware of this situation, Lamberto Dini sought to extract an undertaking from the partners, and especially France and Germany, that the date of commencement of the third phase be postponed if the original group of participating countries is too small, i.e. if Italy is not ready for January 1, 1999. The Prime Minister, trusting in German reticence, for four months embraced the idea of those who urged that "it is more important the criteria be respected than the timetable" and his "crusade" did indeed find some supporters here and there in France and Germany.

Thus it was that on September 22, 1995 Lamberto Dini dashed off to the informal summit of heads of state and government at Formentor, feeding journalists the unlikely story that the Council of Europe was sympathetic to Italian ideas; and a few days later he went to Valencia to wring a promise from the economy and finance ministers for deferment. In both cases Dini's ideas remained completely isolated and indeed both Chirac and Kohl repeatedly upheld—despite domestic difficulties (the public sector strikes in France and the nationalist swing by the SPD in Germany)—the scenario of January 1, 1999.

Isolated in Europe, Lamberto Dini then tried to get the support of the Chamber of Deputies, trusting in the critical position of many parts of the Right and in the reticence of part of the Left. "The Italian government," said Dini in his report to Parliament on December 5, 1995, "believes that the meeting of the Council of Europe, originally scheduled for Spring 1998, should not be anticipated so that the decision for admitting each member state to the final phase of economic and monetary union can take full account of the economic-financial results for 1997." "In any case," Dini subtly added, "we should try to avoid a situation where at the very time of decision the Council of Europe finds itself faced with a serious dilemma: on the one hand the need to respect the parameters set by the Maastricht Treaty to ensure that monetary union works properly and avoid the emergence of divergences and tensions that would undermine its very survival; on the other realization that, should the number of member states meeting the Maastricht criteria be too low—i.e. if monetary union involves only very few countries—the economic and political significance of the operation would be undermined." The Council of Europe—Dini concluded—needs to bear in mind that undue haste could aggravate the dilemma.[19]

And, recalling his personal view of the Formentor summit, the Prime Minister drew the House's attention to his worries over the economic stability of the Union in the case where "half the member states are included and half excluded from monetary union: when it comes time to decide it will be necessary to bear this risk in mind and realize that it will be less critical the more countries take part in the third phase."[20]

Confident in the traditional line of Italian diplomacy which at crucial moments in the process of European integration has sought to play off the Rome-London accord against the French-German axis, Lamberto Dini then flew to Florence to convince the already convinced Major about adopting a cautious position at Madrid on the timetable for economic and monetary union.

The vote in the Chamber of Deputies on December 7, 1995 pointed up some important differences between the views presented by the various political groups, and the resolution of the Center-Left (Andreatta and others) passed by a vote of 270 to 181. Besides an appreciation of the "strong European convictions" of the Italian government and formal approval of the prime minister's remarks, the original text of the Center-Left—drawn up in large part by PDS foreign affairs spokesman Piero Fassino, on the basis of frenetic consultations with *Palazzo Chigi* and the Farnesina—urged the Italian presidency to work for "an economic and monetary union based on a common currency[21] in line with the convergence criteria laid down in the Maastricht treaty,"[22] i.e. with no reference to the timetable set out in the treaty.

Having exhausted the possibility of agreement with the Center-Right—initially sought by Fassino—and hence the possibility of a practically unanimous vote that would have strengthened the Dini government's hand, the text that was finally approved no longer expressed appreciation for the strong European conviction of the government and approval of its communiqués, but urged the government to work for "an economic and monetary union, according to the criteria and timetable set out in the Maastricht treaty, taking full account of the economic-financial results achieved in 1997 and making every effort to ensure that the passage to a single currency was not carried out by too small a number of countries, undermining its economic and political value."[23] With this in mind the Chamber of Deputies held that "policies aimed at reforming public finances are necessary to allow our country to take part in the third phase of economic and monetary union in 1999."[24]

The Indifference for Europe

The debate that took place in the House on December 5-7, 1995 on the government's statements regarding the Italian semester of the presidency of the European Union—ending with the passing of five resolutions (Pezzoni; Costa; D'Onofrio; Strik Lievers and Andreatta)—and the debate following on the remarks of Theo Waigel on September 20, 1995 are certainly not proof of a sudden Italian interest in European affairs.

The overwhelming majority of speeches in the House focused on the question of the imminent resignation of the Dini government; and the political parties' interest in the semester of Italy's presidency of the European Union appeared somewhat instrumental even on the part of many of those who asked for general elections to be postponed until the end of the semester.

The possible negative impact of a governmental crisis and an electoral campaign during the semester was in fact only understood belatedly by Italy's politicians after publication of a series of articles by EU commissioner Mario Monti in the *Corriere della Sera* (August-September, 1995). Those supporting the need for early elections wrongly cited the example of Germany and France, overlooking the fact that in both countries the dates of the federal (Germany) and presidential (France) elections could not be extended and that for almost two months EU activity had been virtually paralyzed first during the German semester (September-October, 1994) and then during the French semester (April-May, 1995). Those on the other hand advocating the need to delay early elections nevertheless accepted the possibility they could be set for May-June, 1995, overlooking the fact that the most important work in a semester is packed into the last two months culminating in the concluding meeting of the Council of Europe, while the actual launching of the Intergovernmental Conference at the end of March is only of cosmetic interest.

Aside from the argument between ex-foreign ministers Martino and Andreatta, the debate in the Chamber of Deputies focused on questions of domestic policy; by contrast, the significant decisions reached with the passage of at least two resolutions (Andreatta and Strik Lievers) aroused no interest among the political forces. A similar lack of interest was also shown by the Italian press which covered all the political maneuvering surrounding the Dini government in minute detail and failed to accurately inform their readers on the content of the mandate the House had given the government for the European semester.[25]

The Italian political system's lack of interest in Europe had already been graphically shown in the foreign policy programs of the parties for the general elections of March 27-28, 1994, when the whole issue of economic and monetary union had practically been ignored by *Forza Italia*, had rekindled the opposition of the then MSI to the Maastricht treaty,[26] and had been the subject of insignificant discussion by the Democratic Party of the Left.[27]

The Berlusconi government's European policy was influenced not only by the opinions of the foreign Minister, Antonio Martino, but also the approaches of the parties in the coalition government, especially *Forza*

Italia and *Alleanza Nazionale*. For *Forza Italia* "the end of bipolarism means the international scenario has much less of an effect on our foreign policy: from being a country belonging to one of two blocs, we are once more in a position to make our own foreign policy decisions."[28] In this spirit "it is a question of systematically identifying in the various areas the national interests that can be achieved by renewed diplomacy." For *Alleanza Nazionale*—who say "taly should be reunified just as Germany was, to achieve once more its own unity and hence national independence"[29]—European unity should be first and foremost political "by devising a Confederation of States, because never as today have the affairs of the continent been so influenced by a political strategy and the respect and glorification of history, traditions, nationality... It is in fact ridiculous to found Europe on the breaking up of nations and the decadence of States."[30]

Outside these statements "of principle" the Berlusconi government was unable to influence: the chronic lack of internal coordination of Community policies and the corresponding coordination of the Italian position vis à vis European institutions;[31] Italy's perennial difficulty in transforming EU directives into national law; the waste of community funds; and the bad habit of designating Italian members in the European Commission on the eve of the body's first meeting, thus leaving the others completely free to decide the "portfolios."

The end of Berlusconi's term in office and the advent of Lamberto Dini's "technical" government brought Italy back into line with the pro-European tradition of the First Republic, a position in fact confirmed by the new Foreign Minister, Susanna Agnelli, in her very first address to the Chamber of Deputies on February 23, 1995. On this occasion, Minister Agnelli said she was in favor of the Commission's presidency being strengthened and the number of commissioners reduced,[32] and came down against the practice of opting out and the permanent nature of exemptions.

Outside these statements, the proposals Minister Agnelli put forward on February 23, restated in a subsequent debate in the Chamber on May 23 and confirmed by Dini himself in the aforementioned debate on December 5, pointed up a very cautious approach at the institutional level, giving substantial support to the intergovernmental model in foreign policy and legal cooperation (the second and third pillars of the Maastricht treaty).

At the institutional level and in particular as regards the role of the European Commission, Lamberto Dini actually seemed to take a line closer to the traditional British position than to the supportive stance long shown by Italian governments towards the Brussels executive. After criticizing excessive community regulation, Lamberto Dini put forward an original version of his own of Italy's poor record in applying EU directives, claiming that "in some cases the measures needed to apply these laws seem to be excessively expensive. Since compliance with EU regulations has not been the same in all member states—claimed Dini—the impression is that distortions in competition, rather than dropping, have actually increased. In some cases the citizens themselves have reacted negatively to what they see as undue intrusion by the Brussels bureaucracy. The principle of subsidiarity and its proper application, therefore, are once again the order of the day."[33] The Italian government's position on this point would have been more credible if the government itself had in the meantime met its obligation of presenting the "community law" for 1995.

It is significant then that, having linked the strengthening of the Commission's presidency to the European Union's visibility abroad, Minister Agnelli wholly accepted the Gaullist idea of entrusting the intergovernmental secretary for foreign policy and common security with powers of analysis and forecasting and judged it "not indispensable to go beyond the intergovernmental level of foreign policy."

Contrary to the opinion expressed by Jacques Delors, the European Commission and the traditional pro-European allies of Italy, such as Belgium, the Netherlands and Luxembourg, the Dini government stuck to its approach in favor of the intergovernmental nature of foreign policy and the need to distinguish the role of representation, analysis and proposal from the "internal" powers of the European Commission. This approach was moreover facilitated by uncertainty among the political parties supporting the Dini government, if it is true—for example—that the PDS foreign affairs spokesman, Piero Fassino, became an uncritical spokesman for the Foreign Office's position, while Giorgio Napolitano regretfully observed that the text passed by the European Parliament on May 17, 1995[34] "made no mention of the passage appearing in the original text approved by the institutional affairs commission, proposing for consideration the creation of a position of commissioner in charge of foreign affairs and another in charge of common defense, who would also exercise authority as general secretary of the EUO and which would be appointed by the Council of Europe by the same procedure that applied to the President of the Commission."[35]

In the Andreatta resolution, passed by the Chamber of Deputies on December 7, 1995, the rigid intergovernmental position expressed on February 23 and May 23 by Minister Agnelli and confirmed by Dini on December 5 was however significantly changed since the House asked the government to work for "a foreign and common security policy (FCSP) which would enable the Union to speak with a single voice and respond to the new dangers threatening Europe's stability and security while, at the same time, allowing the European Union to talk and co-operate with the different actors on the international scene: it is essential—the resolution went on—that the intergovernmental conference takes decisions to encourage a greater EU role in Fcsp through the establishment of a highly qualified figure charged with singly represent-ing and carrying out foreign policy and all external relations of the European Union; a united Council-Commission entity for forecasting and planning able to analyse international dynamics and put forward the necessary European policies."[36]

What to Do about the Intergovernmental Conference

The caution of the Dini government changed to open hostility over the question of a two-speed Europe, raised with a hue and cry by the CDU/CSU parliamentary group in the document of autumn, 1994. Coming down firmly in favor of a "single institutional system," Minis-ter Agnelli rejected in February "every attempt to constitute directo-rates on the part of any country." The Italian "philosophy" of differen-tiated integration was more widely developed by Susanna Agnelli in her address to the Chamber on May 23, 1995: "especially within the perspective of enlargement—said the minister—it would seem difficult to avoid a degree of differentiated integration in the new policies (for-eign, security, justice and internal affairs), with different timetables and fixed courses. Here lies the key to solving the dilemma deepening-enlarging, unity and flexibility and preventing the formation of a weak Europe, limited to areas of free trade and made up of different sub-groups."[37] The premise for a differentiated integration—and this is the heart of the Italian philosophy

> remains the principle of institutional unity: same Council, same Parliament, same Court of Justice, enjoying the flexibility needed to run policies that not all the member states participate in... In a word, it is the whole Community *acquis* that needs to be saved in such a way that the logic of strong central cores (of the CDU/CSU, reporter's note), the strategy of separation, the distinction between Europe as space and Europe as power (the expression used by Valéry Giscard d'Estaing, reporter's note) does not also prejudice economic and financial cohesion, encouraging an Archipelago of Europe and losing the challenge of number and diversity.[38]

In Andreatta's resolution, the ritual remark on the "federal vocation" of the European Union was accompanied—in line with the philosophy of the Italian government—by reference to the criterion of "flexibility within unity, that enables each member state of the Union to take part in every phase of the integration process, while at the same time allowing those countries—who so wish—not to participate in particular aspects of the integration process without this standing in the way of the other member states pressing ahead with integration measures already decided on; to promote provisions and procedures that make different degrees and speeds of integration by single member states to integration policies compatible with a process of progressive harmonization and convergence within a single institutional framework."[39]

The position so clearly expressed by the British government on the rules for the functioning of the single institutional framework casts a great deal of doubt on the possibility of introducing in the treaty, by the unanimous vote of all member states, those changes that would concretize the federal vocation of the European Union. It was for this reason that Jacques Delors on several occasions drew the attention of governments and political parties to the wisdom of establishing, alongside the idea of differentiated integration within a single institutional framework, the idea of two Europes: the greater Europe and the Federation of nation-states. It was for this reason that the European Parliament—worried in case all the referenda (at least seven) called to ratify the results of the intergovernmental Conference might end in several "no"—put forward the idea of self-exclusion by one or more member states from the European Union.

The work of reflection carried out by the Westendorp group and presented to the European Council in Madrid confirmed the possibility of a crisis scenario during the intergovernmental Conference or at its conclusion. If significant changes do not take place in the attitude of certain governments—including the Italian government—the likelihood is that the intergovernmental Conference will end with an agreement on the lowest common denominator. This means that enlargement to the East will come about in the worst way possible and that the British view of a large free-trade area will inevitably prevail: weak institutions do in fact mean weak common policies and hence a step backwards for the idea of common European solidarity.

Is it possible to imagine an alternative to that of the European Union being diluted into an area of free trade? In order to do so, it would be necessary to run the risk of precipitating a crisis within the Union, by forcing the development of a stronger common position in a majority of governments. This is the approach indicated by Altiero Spinelli in the treaty project of February, 1984; and it is the idea that François Mitterand launched in May, 1984, aimed at realizing a Union "among those who actually want it."

Translated by Stephen Jewks

Notes

1. After ratifying the Schengen Agreement with considerable delay (September 30, 1993), Italy then had to tell its partners (statement of Interior Minister, Nicola Mancino, on November 29, 1993) it was not able to enforce the Agreement on 1 February 1994 because the funds for connecting its police files to the Schengen computerized system had not yet been approved. The same Mancini had unwisely announced that the "the appropriate transit corridors, at the airports of Milan and Rome, for passengers from countries which are part of the Agreement would be ready between 1994 and 1995." At the end of 1995 these corridors were still not ready.

2. This was what was reported, at the suggestion of Italy's permanent EU delegation, by most Italian correspondents in Brussels in the articles of September 19, 1995.

3. "The criteria," wrote Fabio Colasanti in *Il Mulino/Europa* 2/1995, "are the result of an economic logic shared by the overwhelming majority of economists," according to which "high budget deficits reduce the margins for maneuver in economic policy, undermine productive public expenditure because of the increasing effect of interest payments on public debt and do not help economic growth" while "high levels of public debt create risks of instability and expose public accounts to strong shocks when interest rates are varied."

4. Colasanti points out (*Il Mulino/Europa*, 2/1995) that "the Maastricht 3 percent in the 1960s would have seemed an irresponsible level: hardly any country exceeded it and those that did exceed it did so only slightly because of investment expenditure, given that all the countries had current accounts in the black." Colasanti further points out that "the six countries of central and east Europe (Czech Republic, Slovakia, Poland, Hungary, Bulgaria and Romania) have in 1995 an average deficit equal to about 3 percent of GDP and that the country with the most serious situation, Bulgaria, reached 7.2 percent (Italy: 7.4 percent)."

5. "The fascination with negotiation tables—wrote Barbara Spinelli in *Micro/Mega n. 4/1995*—is so indestructible and so much an end in itself for Italy's ruling classes that foreign policy becomes one of the many occasions for securing a place at the table."

6. First at the annual summer conference in Cernobbio (August, 1993) and then in *Il Mulino* (September, 1993).

7. For a description of the debate following the German document, see P.V. Dastoli in *Il Mulino/Europa*, n. 2/1994.

8. In *La Repubblica* of September 24, 1995.

9. The way forward indicated by Antonio Martino does not even seem to have won over supporters in the *Forza Italia* ranks if we are to believe the statement made on December 7, 1995 by the honorable Di Muccio on behalf of *Forza Italia* on the government's pronouncements. According to Di Muccio "the single currency should come about only through a natural evolution and with the full support of all the participating nations" (taken from "Stenographic report of the House of December 7, 1995").

10. Address on the "statements of the government regarding Italy's semester of presidency of the European Union," on December 5, 1995 in the Chamber of

Deputies. "Stenographic report of the House of December 5, 1995."

11. Ibidem.

12. Ibidem.

13. Ibidem.

14. *Il Sole 24 Ore*, October 15, 1995.

15. Conclusions of the Council of Europe of December 15-16, 1995 taken from *Agence Europe* of December 17, 1995.

16. Ibidem.

17. The presidency of the Council of Europe for the first semester of 1998 will be held by the United Kingdom and hence by the government that emerges from the general elections that will take place before April, 1997. What is more, general elections to re-elect the National Assembly in France will have to be held before May, 1998 and general elections to renew the Bundestag in October, 1998 (in an "electoral" year, also featuring general elections in Denmark, Sweden and the Netherlands); these two national deadlines would seem to indicate that it will be in the interests of Chirac and Kohl for the decision on the beginning of the third phase of economic and monetary union to be taken as early as possible at the start of 1998.

18. The Council of Europe in Madrid said "at the latest," but it seems extremely unlikely that—given the date of January 1, 2002—the financial markets and banks will be able to anticipate this deadline. The three-year interval between the beginning of the third phase of economic and monetary union and the circulation of the single currency, however, reflects political caution more than any technical-monetary motivation.

19. "Stenographic report of the Chamber of December 5, 1995."

20. Ibidem.

21. In EU terminology "common currency" means "parallel currency" and not "single currency."

22. The original text of the Center-Left has not been formally deposited and was circulated in the Chamber as a typescript, to be negotiated with the Center-Right coalition.

23. The final resolution of the Center-Left appears in the official records of the Chamber with the number Ris 6-00033.

24. Ibidem.

25. The disinterest of the Italian press for European affairs has in fact emerged for years in the studies carried out by international bodies. Recent research carried out by the European Press Association in the period October, 1994-March, 1995 analyzed 3,427 texts devoted to Europe by 24 European dailies (with a total circulation of 7.5 million copies per day). The average *European interest* is 4.17 percent with a high of 10.5 percent (360 pieces out of a total of 3,427) in the Danish daily *Dagens Nyheter*, followed by *Die Welt* (8.35 percent), *Frankfurter Allgemeine* (7.03 percent), *The Times* (6.97 percent) and *Figaro* (6.27 percent). The daily bottom of the list is the Portuguese *Diario de Noticias* (0.53 percent or 20 articles in 6 months) which beat by a few decimal points the record lows of *La Repubblica* (0.93 percent or 32 pieces) and the *Corriere della Sera* (0.96 percent or 33 pieces).

26. "We have rejected the attempts, graphically present, of one EU member state abusing others by means of financial speculation or partial political ac-

cords... Maastricht sought to premise the future of Europe on the predominance of large economic-financial groups which exacerbated divisions and led the single states to accept and underwrite the treaty from different positions. One need only think of the exemptions granted all the contracting parties except Italy," taken from *L'Italia nella politica internazionale: 1993/1994*, edited by Istituto Affari Internazionali.

27. "We believe what is called for is a courageous initiative to update and enrich the Maastricht treaty...in the financial field, supporting the launch of the European Central Bank and the creation of instruments for collectively governing exchange rates," taken from *L'Italia nella politica internazionale: 1993/1994*, cit.

28. The texts of the party programs have been published in *L'Italia nella politica internazionale: 1993/1994*, cit.

29. Ibidem.

30. Ibidem.

31. *Forza Italia* had proposed "proceeding with the creation of a Ministry having increasingly wider powers and competencies, the head of which should have the rank of vice-President of the Council and be authorized to define the Italian position for all the different sectors of activity" (taken from *L'Italia nella politica internazionale: 1993/1994*, cit.). The usual ministerial market preceding the formation of a government led, however, to confirmation of the inconsequential Ministry for the internal coordination of Community policy and appointment of the Northern League's Comino. It was in this way that victory once more went to the Farnesina which—since the very first appointment of Minister for European affairs (Vincenzo Scotti, spring 1980)—has always been opposed to creating a Ministry like those existing in the majority of EU countries.

32. "Stenographic report of the House of May 23, 1995."

33. "Stenographic report of the House of December 5, 1995."

34. The Martin/Bourlanges resolution on preparation of the Intergovernmental Conference published in the verbal proceedings of the European Parliament session of May 17, 1995.

35. "Stenographic report of the House of May 23, 1995."

36. Andreatta resolution Ris 6-00033 (cit.).

37. "Stenographic report of the House of May 23, 1995."

38. Ibidem.

39. Andreatta resolution Ris 6-00033 (cit.).

9

Stopping the Judges

David Nelken

Throughout 1995 the *Mani pulite* investigations into political corruption proceeded despite considerable setbacks, but there were increasing calls for what was described as either a legal or political "solution" to *Tangentopoli*. My main aim in this chapter will be to attempt to account for the narrow failure so far of the various efforts to stop the judges or to agree or to impose such a solution. But this enquiry will also throw into relief a number of interrelated features of Italian law, politics and culture whose significance transcends this specific episode in the history of the post-war relationship between judges and politicians.

Tangentopoli's Success as a Problem

The survival of the *Mani pulite* enquiries for yet another year was a highly contingent outcome of a series of events which might have spelled their conclusion. The most serious blow to the legitimacy of the investigations came as the year ended when the prosecutors at Brescia finally announced that they had decided to bring forward charges, including corruption, against Antonio Di Pietro—the symbol of anti corruption even though no longer a member of the judiciary. (They also recommended more minor charges against three of the existing members of the Milan pool.) But this was not the first blow that *Mani pulite* had suffered. If discussion of the end is itself part of the end then the signs that *Tangentopoli* was on the skids were there for all to see. Already, before resigning in December, 1994, Di Pietro had said that collaborators were no longer coming forward and that the investigations had little future. Throughout 1995 the *Mani pulite* judges were regularly put on the defensive, as much trying to safeguard their power to continue the investigations as with demonstrating evidence of political corruption.

The struggle over stopping the judges was inevitably also a competition over how to circumscribe the significance of *Tangentopoli* and who owned the right to do so. Even deciding when it had really begun depends on how the initiative is to be classified. Attempts to identify corrupt politicians had after all been going on in all the years since the Second World War, even if the 1990's had seen a sharp increase in the proportion of those requests to Parliament to proceed against deputies which referred to crimes involving administrative and financial irregularities rather than to other types of offences.[1] *Tangentopoli* could therefore be seen as just another instalment in a continuing power struggle between judges and politicians—the judges' response, for example, to Premier Craxi's successful use of a referendum in 1987 to oblige them to take responsibility for judicial errors, or to President Cossiga's efforts in the early 1990's to curb their powers of self-government.

On the other hand, for all its revolutionary effects on the political system *Tangentopoli* had required no more than the application of existing (under-enforced) criminal laws,[2] and so it was not as easy to call a halt as it is when genuine revolutions draw lines concerning the prosecution of acts carried out under a previous regime. In the same way the fact that it was not essentially an initiative piloted by or on behalf of one of the political parties—such as the PDS—meant that it could not end, as most anti-corruption campaigns do, with the take over or consolidation of power by the sponsoring party (and the much called for emergence of a new political class was not something that could happen overnight). If anything, it was the extension of attacks to the PDS which was more likely to add them to those who called for a return to "normality" where the judges' influence on politics was curbed.[3] Given the way the phenomenon of *Tangentopoli* had taken on a life of its own as a sort of "moral panic"—its future depended not only on what the judges did and the politicians said (or vice versa), but even more on whether media attention moved on, perhaps after a new general election or another major scandal, so that people no longer bothered even to discuss whether it had ended.

For some, the judges' intervention had fulfilled its function by unblocking the political system and getting rid of a political class who had outlived their usefulness (who it was they were no longer useful to was rarely spelled out, but included businessmen, who had grown impatient of the ever higher tribute in kickbacks they were forced to pay at a time of economic recession and increasing foreign competition, the Americans, who had lost interest in propping up the Christian Democrats after the fall of the Berlin wall had robbed Italy of its strategic significance, and even the Sicilian Mafia, who had lost confidence in the power of the Christian Democrats to "fix" trials in which their leaders risked ending up in prison). The investigations had had the useful effect of (temporarily) reducing the element of bribes which went to make up the overall costs of public works (the costs of building the Milan underground railway, for example, were said to have halved following *Tangentopoli*).[4] But now routinized corruption was returning, and the costs of those corrupt transactions which had continued to take place all along had no doubt gone up to compensate for the increased risks of judicial intervention.

For others, on the other hand, the evils against which the *Mani pulite* judges struggled had come to represent all that was wrong with the previous political system and democracy "Italian style"—ranging from the dominance of the political parties over civil society, the way they co-opted each other into spoils—sharing and so ran up the public debt, the enormous level of tax evasion and fiscal malpractices of the business world, the dubious methods used to select and control a desperately inefficient administration, the conflicting loyalties of a conspiratorial secret service, and even the overextended role of judiciary itself. Thus not everyone was in a hurry to find a solution. Apart from those parties, politicians and businessmen who considered the continuation of the investigations to be to their advantage (especially as far as they aggravated Silvio Berlusconi's judicial problems), there were some who regarded the *Mani pulite* judges as honorary members of what they called the "party of legality" engaged in the battle against the Faustian agreements which politicians on the other side had entered into with corrupt business, organised crime and deviant parts of the secret services. For them it would not be safe to talk about ending the investigations until the previous system had been thoroughly dismantled.

For most commentators, however, it was a only a question of when, not whether, *Tangentopoli* would end. Much of the talk about ending these investigations assumed that it was enough to show that they were now causing harm, irrespective of whether they had accomplished all that they could have been expected to. But there was a lack of any clear vision of what would come after. In general, many editorialists complained that periods of collective soul-searching had to have a limit and that living under emergency conditions was exhausting (even if this was not really so unusual in Italy where matters are typically described as critical without being serious). There was concern that parliamentary democracy had been replaced by "the rule by judges" in that what now counted in politics was the ebb and flow of criminal charges rather than the cut and thrust of political competition. It was also argued, with some reason, that prosecutors and judges were good at repressing misbehaviour but institutionally incapable of planning the future.

In concrete terms, *Mani pulite* was accused of having had a variety of counter-productive effects. Although the main targets chosen for investigation were politicians, or business-politicians such as Berlusconi, many large and small businessmen had also been caught up in the inquiries and yet others waited uneasily to see when a limit would be set to the chance that they could find themselves under investigation for illegal practices which had once been (and probably still were) widespread.[5] Likewise many administrators were cautious about taking on responsibilities in the granting of new public works contracts for fear of incurring what could turn out to be criminal proceedings for their decisions.[6] This raises the question of to whom these contracts were going. Some observers alleged that administrators may really have been waiting for a time when the taking of bribes or exchanging of favours would become less risky. Difficult as this is to prove, there was some evidence, in Emilia Romagna as elsewhere, that building contractors, fallen on hard times for lack of public works in this period, were at risk of being bought up by organised criminals who could thereby consolidate their hold on large parts of the building industry.

The sharpest criticisms, however, concerned the way the *Mani pulite* judges pursued their investigations[7] and what success had done to them. Particular judges were vilified in parts of the media for their alleged cruel treatment of suspects before and in prison, as well as for their failure to safeguard the secrecy of their investigations. Complaints were made that judges behaved like inquisitors, that they had grown too fond of the limelight[8] and had neglected the many everyday cases of judicial injustice. The familiar charge that the judges had become politicised (with a left-wing slant) seemed all too clearly demonstrated by the way they had taken on so much power. (In fact neither Borrelli nor Di Pietro of the Milan Pool could be described as left-wing sympathisers. Even opinion amongst the left-leaning judges of *Magistratura Democratica* had actually been tending for some time to define the judge's role less as the "scourge of the powerful" and much more as the protector of Italian institutions and above all of the independence of the judiciary[9]—though obviously, as in these investigations, these two goals could coincide). Reference was made to systems of checks and balances which limited the role of judges elsewhere as compared to the exceptional Italian situation.[10] On the other hand, it was difficult to deny that prosecuting judges had expanded their role precisely because of the irresponsibility of the politicians and the weakness of other institutional controls.[11] Many of those currently leading the attack on the judges plainly had a vested interest in seeing the investigations brought to a close. And many of the methods tried, from the defamatory to the ham-handed, tended to discredit those opposed to the judges even further.

Many judges, for their part, insisted that there was either nothing to be ended and/or no possibility of ending it. They stressed how much

Mani pulite was simply an aspect of the correctly functioning ordinary activities of the prosecutors and the courts—"stealing was stealing," even if carried out by highly-placed people, or for the sake of the Party.[12] In these terms it made no sense to talk of closing it down. The fact that corruption had been shown to be systematic (the "corruption of politics" rather than merely '"corruption in politics") did not make it any less true that each trial dealt with an individual or set of individuals who had broken specific criminal laws. This struggle, like that against organised crime, was one which would continue for the foreseeable and perhaps indefinite future and there was no lack of work still to be done. Apart from the way the Milan Pool steadily added to the charges being levelled against Berlusconi and his companies, and the tentative extension of *Tangentopoli* by other judges (such as Judge Nordio in Venice) to involve parts of the co-operative movement and the PDS leaders, many other examples of corruption going back to the First Republic continued to be discovered. Amongst many other cases were those involving the well-connected fraudsters of the *Cassa di Risparmio* of Florence; the business and organised crime ring at Bari, connected to Rino Formica, former Socialist Minister of Finance; the arrest of Cirino Pomicino, one of the most powerful of the leaders of the ex-DC, in October, 1995, at the time apparently collecting kickbacks which he needed to use to pay the plea bargain he was hoping to arrange for his past offences; and the charges brought in December against Riccardo Misasi, another ex-DC minister, accused of having been involved with high functionaries of the Ministry of Education in a trillion lire fraud which doubled the price of computers bought for use by the state schools in 1991. Throughout the year Bettino Craxi was still fighting a rearguard battle from Hammamet, Tunisia, helped, it seemed, by still loyal functionaries in Italy with access to reserved documents.

Understood as a war against corruption, *Tangentopoli* could neither be won[13] nor abandoned, especially if the definition of corruption was extended to include business[14] and administrative corruption at all levels. Francesco Saverio Borrelli, the head of the Milan pool of judges, in an interview with *La Repubblica* in December, 1995, rejected calls for the ending of *Tangentopoli* in the following terms:

> Nobody desires anything like throwing in the sponge except those who would reap direct benefit. Every day we see new discoveries of types of corruption. Here has taken root not only large-scale corruption but also smaller forms: tips, bribes, the exchange of favours. None of this is foreign to our customs. We must start by trying to put things right now, but the fruits will be seen perhaps by our children, if not by our grandchildren.

But even the clear evidence that corruption had far from disappeared would not have been enough in itself to guarantee the continuation of these investigations. On the one hand it showed the need for *Tangentopoli*, but, on the other, it also prepared the way back to a "normality" composed of the regular discovery of flagrant examples of corruption, each of which became in its turn no more than a short-lived scandal.[15] What mattered more was the political situation.

Competing Legitimacies

The most plausible explanation of the fact that the judges were able to keep going with their anti-corruption campaign is to attribute this to the weakness of the forces arrayed against them: the balance of power was still too uncertain to allow the political system to recover the effective control which had previously ensured its immunity despite the formal independence and powers of the judges. 1995 served as a year of pause and transition in which the political parties (and factions and alliances) fought a careful war of position in the shadow of Dini's government of technocrats. There was what we might call an (un)"elective affinity" between the technocrats and the judges involved in clearing up the financial and the legal mess left behind by the politicians of the First Republic. Those who approved the role of the technicians usually also supported the continued central role of the judges, and the opposite was true for those who saw the technicians as having outlived their usefulness. Dini was also strongly supported by President Scalfaro, who, it was said, had little enthusiasm about inaugurating a new Berlusconi administration, and may have been trying to freeze the political situation so as to allow the ex-Christian Democrats or others time to regroup and move Italian politics back to the Center.

For their own reasons the two rival coalitions (and the minor parties in their alliance) could not agree on the date for a general election, which each at different times feared to lose. Given the roughly similar strengths of the two sides, neither was certain it wanted to move towards a two party alternation, without adequate guarantees for the loser, rather than the less risky pattern of co-operation (and spoils sharing). Businessmen and others likewise waited to see who would emerge as the new political references and mediators to replace those "criminalised" by *Tangentopoli*. The struggle of the Milan judges to continue their investigations and the efforts of Berlusconi to defend his political credibility took place as long as this stalemate persisted. By the end of the year it had become clear that both sides had their own source of legitimacy (and support) and neither for the time being possessed the strength to deliver the knock-out blow. The judiciary, flushed by its early successes against the discredited politicians of the First Republic, and reinforced in prestige also as a result of the struggle against the Mafia,[16] represented "the Law." On the other side Berlusconi and other politicians could draw on the legitimacy of democratic consensus and the fact that everyone knew that sooner or later it would again be necessary to trust them rather than the judges to represent the popular will. Former Premier Berlusconi's political fortunes went up (as when winning the referendum on the media) or down (as in the regional elections), in ways that seemed only loosely connected to the stories carried by the media of his legal battles with the judges. The Milan pool tried to complete their unfinished business with Berlusconi and managers of his companies, alleging corruption of the Financial police to oblige them to overlook tax evasion and other fiscal crimes, the use of undeclared slush funds for corruption or for paying high transfer fees for football stars, the existence of large funds sent abroad including some which finished in Craxi's bank account, and so on. Berlusconi and others responded with countermoves aimed especially at the Milan pool and its former star Di Pietro.

Although there is substantial truth in this theory of "competing legitimacies"[17] it does not fully capture some of the complexities and paradoxes in the relationship between the judges and politics which developed in the wake of *Tangentopoli*. One complication is provided by the fact that for most of the year the politicians with the main interest in ending the investigations were not part of the government in power and lacked the legitimacy that comes from this. (The Ministers in Dini's administration, on the other hand, had all been appointed rather than elected and therefore could only appeal to yet a third form of legitimacy based on their professional competence). We also need to make distinctions amongst both politicians and the judiciary rather than assume them to be two united blocs. The PDS (like the National Alliance) had been relatively spared by these investigations. As the year advanced the PDS came more under investigation (mainly regarding allegations of financial crimes or collaboration with organised criminals made against the cooperative movement). There was even talk of a switch of policy so as to distance themselves from the judges, which was given some credibility by their supporting a new law curbing judicial powers of preventive detention.

For most of the year, however, politicians of the Center-Left (and probably also Dini and his technocratic government), could only gain from the continuation of the *Mani pulite* investigations at the expense of the leader of the rival coalition (to be exact it was in their interest that Berlusconi should be under investigation but remain a weakened leader rather than be driven from the leadership). At the same time there were also politicians from the other side, such as Mirko Tremaglia of the right-wing National Alliance (a personal friend of Di Pietro), who strongly supported the investigations continuing. In June the parties did manage to agree on a new law restricting the use of preventive detention (which was passed over the opposition of some judges though not their representative body).[18] But, at the same time, when the investigations of the judges of the Milan pool were actually obstructed by Filippo Mancuso, Dini's Minister of Justice, who persisted in a single-minded campaign of inspections against them, the PDS came swiftly to their defence (as did President Scalfaro). In May, Mancuso had asked the Supreme Council of Judges (known as the CSM) to bring disciplinary actions against the Milan pool for a variety of charges including oppressive tactics in gathering evidence, the failure to respect secrecy of investigations, intimidation of Ministerial inspectors, and other abuses of their official position, but the Court of Cassation and the CSM both found in favour of the judges.[19] Very soon the PDS was demanding as the price for its support that Dini get rid of his vexatious Minister and, finally, in October, a motion of no confidence in Mancuso in the Senate forced his dismissal.[20] On the other hand, just as many politicians supported the judges so there were some judges who chose or were manipulated into opposing or investigating their colleagues for complex reasons of duty, interest or rivalry. (Fabio Salamone, the Brescia prosecutor with the greatest media exposure, for example, had gained prestige fighting the Mafia in Sicily. But those who looked for hidden explanations underlined the fact that Di Pietro had been indirectly responsible for the corruption investigations which had created legal problems for Salamone's businessman brother in Sicily).

Fighting Law with Law

An important and paradoxical feature of the struggle over *Tangentopoli* was thus the way judges and politicians competed on the basis of each others' legitimacy. If the "party of the judges" included both representatives of politics and the judiciary, those most opposed to them tended to justify their stand by citing the need to do the utmost to protect the rights of those suspected of crime (so called *garantismo*), a principle held as sacred also by some on the political Left.

It is of course understandable that judges' representatives should take interest in proposed political solutions which affect their privileges, their powers of investigation or the outcome of particular classes of cases under investigation. (The judges on loan to the Minister of Justice also play the main part in drafting any laws which politicians might propose). But the political profile of the judges went well beyond this, continuing what had been one of the most remarkable features of *Tangentopoli* right from its outset—the way the judges and not the existing opposition parties had used the law to provide an effective political opposition. As time went on they increasingly sought to capitalise on their popular legitimacy (with deliberate appeals to the media or Parliament), and Di Pietro, although he had resigned as a judge, made political interventions which drew on the prestige he had gained whilst acting as a prosecutor. Their political opponents, by contrast, after the failure of the decrees intended to end *Tangentopoli*, made their crusade one fought in the name of all criminal suspects, and increasingly resorted to *ad hoc* proceduralistic tactics as part of a general effort to delegitimate and discredit the judges.

The methods used against the judges in the course of the year in fact covered a wide spectrum, from the violent (as in the foiled ambush to kill Gerardo D'Ambrosio of the Milan pool), the defamatory (as in daily television broadcasts), to attempts by other judges to show that their colleagues themselves were guilty of crimes, (as in charges eventually brought against Di Pietro). Those seen to be orchestrating attempts to delegitimate the *Mani pulite* judges through the slow leaking of "dossiers" of accusations, included Craxi himself, and Carlo Taormina, the defence lawyer in some of the most important corruption cases. Later Di Pietro's astonishing resignation was retrospectively explained as the result of a blackmail campaign allegedly organised amongst others by Previti, Berlusconi's Minister of Defence and lawyer to Fininvest, and Paolo Berlusconi. Throughout the year Vittorio Sgarbi and other media personalities, journalists and political allies offered vitriolic character assassinations of leading judges from the safety of Berlusconi's television channels. Other problems for the Milan judges came when the higher courts stopped giving them automatic cover, choosing for example to move crucial cases involving corruption charges against Berlusconi from the Milan court to Brescia. Likewise they were put on the defensive when Minister of Justice Mancuso sent in inspectors to reopen and question earlier investigations.[21]

A burning issue of media attention throughout the year was the question whether Di Pietro would use his immense popularity to enter politics. At first he used his new—found freedom to teach a law course at a private University and accepted numerous invitations to speak and write broadly on the theme of corruption and what could be done about it (including a much publicised program of reform laid out at a conference in Cernobbio in September). Whilst willing to take on various semi—official roles such as consultant to the Parliament's Committee on Terrorism (in some cases becoming involved in polemics), he steadfastly refused an open declaration of political alliance or willingness to stand for Parliament or serve as a Minister. Alongside this attention to his potential political impact, however, from April (the date of his formal departure from the Magistracy) onwards, there also began to circulate stories of investigations into his conduct being carried out by Judge Salamone of Brescia. At first these seemed only to concern improper methods he may have used during the *Mani pulite* investigations such as pressurising witnesses to inculpate Silvio Berlusconi.[22] By the end of the year, however, it became clear that Di Pietro himself was to be charged, on the basis of a dossier relying mainly on the depositions of Giancarlo Gorrini, a failed Milan businessman, for a series of allegedly corrupt acts or otherwise improper use of his influence. He was said to have taken advantage of ex-Minister Gaspari, to have favoured the use of a firm, with which he had strong connections, for the job of introducing information technology into the Milan prosecutors' office, to have taken loans without interest and a Mercedes from Gorrini, and to have helped a friend become head of the Milan Municipal police force. Whatever the eventual outcome,[23] the bringing of these charges was itself crucial in weakening Di Pietro's credibility as a political competitor above the standards of mere politicians, even if his popularity remained high. Given Di Pietro's strong political prospects but uncertain loyalties, Craxi was by no means the only politician or ex-politician pleased at these developments.

Corruption, Anti-Corruption
and Italian Legal Culture

A further problem with explaining the survival of *Mani pulite* only in terms of the stalled political situation is that this can easily become a tautology. If we argue that *Tangentopoli* was (just) able to continue because the politicians were too weak to stop it we cannot then use this fact as evidence of them being weak. What this explanation fails to account for is the power of the judges to act independently of other power holders. The continuation of *Tangentopoli* may have been made possible by its falling in the transition period between the two republics but it was also itself one of the factors which prolonged that period (and not only because it perhaps provided a useful distraction from more significant developments).

The successes of *Mani pulite* could certainly not have been achieved without the institutional protections enjoyed by judges and prosecutors in Italy. In common law systems political influence over the judiciary is exercised through recruitment and appointment. In Civil Law systems, given that recruitment by open competition after University makes this method impossible, it is achieved through internal bureaucratic controls. The steady dismantling of hierarchical controls in Italy since the Second World War has, however, made them formally much freer than in comparable Continental countries such as France.[24] In fact, both prosecutors and judges are guaranteed promotion in salary and formal status on the basis of seniority, regardless of the work they are doing, so as to remove the temptation to collude with political corruption. Self-government is organised through the CSM which allocates the senior appointments and carries out internal discipline. Its built- in majority of judicial representatives can normally be relied on to unite behind the corporate interests of judges, whatever the political or other differences which may otherwise divide them. Most important, prosecutors in Italy belong to the same profession as judges, with whom they regularly interchange roles. They have the same autonomy and are not responsible to any central authority or Ministry. Despite the introduction in 1989 of a new code of criminal procedure modelled along accusatorial principles, the prosecutors continue to think of their role as being like that of the judge, as concerned with "jurisdiction," the ideal of working to ensure respect for the law, rather than that of being functionaries whose task is to act simply as the official counterpart of the defence lawyer. (The importance of the prosecution stage in *Tangentopoli* can be appreciated if we remember that the major political damage was done well before any trials had been brought to a conclusion). In addition, a stringent rule of mandatory prosecution of all offences (supposedly) excludes the exercise of discretion for any reason. This meant that the Minister of Justice could not try to argue the case for "the public interest" in non-prosecution even where he himself came under investigation.

If these factors made it more difficult for politicians to block corruption investigations in Italy than it would have been elsewhere, they could also be turned to their advantage. The unpredictability and independence of prosecutors, and the obligatory rule of investigation of crimes, meant it was only a matter of time (and encouragement) before prosecutors began examining the work of their colleagues. The delays built into the system, the number of semi-autonomous and overlapping organs (or levels of hierarchy) responsible for handling particular controversies, the insistence on a sharp formal separation of powers between institutions (leaving their actual relationship to be worked out by negotiation or conflict) together with the media thirst for novelties, which once helped drag out the notoriety of accused politicians, now had the same effect on the investigations targeted on the judges themselves.

But in various ways the *Mani pulite* judges had also gone beyond their formal independence so as to exploit their margins for manoeuvre "in the shadow of the rules," as in their use of confessions and preventive custody and by making strategic use of opportunities to make public information about the bringing of charges. Here the politicians (and defence lawyers such as Taormina) showed themselves even more adept at inventing dirty tricks. They could not so easily, out of government, mobilise the unwritten system of threats, deterrents and diversions to "safe courts" which had been sufficient to discourage over-zealous judges in the period before *Tangentopoli*.[25] But they followed a similar strategy. In addition, the politicians had always benefited from the sheer length of time taken for a case to reach final sentence ("Political time" and "legal time" were made to coincide by the *Mani pulite* judges only through the use of the media). One of the disturbing facts of 1995, as compared to the early years of *Tangentopoli*, was thus the return to the previous practice of not necessarily resigning when accused—seen most clearly in the behaviour of Berlusconi but also given some support by the PDS.

Finding a Suitable Ending

By this stage, the question posed by *Tangentopoli* was no longer how best to deal with corruption, or even how to finish off the enquiries in progress, but rather where and how to draw a line between the past and the future, to find a way of starting anew with a fresh script. The incessant parade of accusation and counter-accusation was producing cynicism ("gossip has taken the place of moralization,") and even commentators on the Left were becoming increasingly impatient with the political importance which had been assumed by the judges.[26] If the roles of politician and judge had got confused, it was important that new lines be written that each could recite convincingly (at least at first). If *Tangentopoli* in its first years represented "good theatre"[27] (as always in the theatre, stage management was also essential, as shown by the Cusani trial), the story line was now becoming confused, and even in danger of being rewritten.[28] Instead of representing the moralizing "forces of light" against the political "forces of darkness," the differences in the Magistracy were now coming to light as judges turned on one other. Judge Salamone was bringing charges against Di Pietro, and eventually D'Ambrosio of the Agrigento Court in turn accused Salamone of having used his influence to help his brother, Judges Nordio and Ielo were making reciprocal accusations of political bias, and so on. After surviving a series of attacks, Di Pietro now risked being finally revealed as an idol with feet of clay. The media mixed up the roles of players and spectators as if in a play by Pirandello (but with less skill)—everyone was invited to offer a solution to *Tangentopoli*, politicians, whether in or out of prison, defence lawyers, even if they were building secret dossiers against the judges, or senior judges, including those who had let the problem of corruption get out of control in the first place.

The search for "solutions," as if *Tangentopoli* were a puzzle to be solved, rather than a matter of reconciling competing interests or changing entrenched (and often functional) behaviour patterns, faithfully reflects the Italian idealist and intellectualised way of dealing with what Anglo-American culture calls "social problems." But it does seem to be the case that one of the difficulties in closing down *Tangentopoli* was the need to find a solution which recognised the limits of what law could achieve when faced with widespread disobedience but did so without also openly acknowledge such limits (and thus selling out the anti-corruption ideal which had been fought for). What was required was an amnesty which wouldn't be seen to be one. At least in part then various possible pragmatic solutions and compromises were not taken up because "the Italian art of getting by" is never considered appropriate as a theoretical solution. The use of amnesties, and the "condoning" of crime in return for confession and repayment, is of course a well-established feature of the Italian legal system. But whilst this was routine for tax evasion or administrative irregularities, and could just about have been accepted for illegal financing of the political parties, it was harder to stomach when what was involved was massive embezzlement and the deliberate betrayal of political trust.

Amongst immediate solutions canvassed (but not taken further) were such ideas as organising a general confession, offering pardons in return for information about other cases of corruption, or introducing special procedures for speeding up cases rather than letting them take their course through the normal three court stages. But these suggestions all faced considerable technical problems. Would it be fair to treat future cases of those tried for political corruption in ways which were not extended to the first offenders sent for trial? How far could one group of offenders be treated more favourably than others (and what would be the consequences of offering the same terms to other types of criminals?) For the longer term Di Pietro proposed regular checks on the level of property and wealth of members of the public administration. Others argued for changing and possibly depenalising the rules about illegal political financing and other fiscal crimes. There was considerable debate over solving "the problem" of the judges' eruption into politics by separating the careers of prosecutor and judge or looking again at the rule of compulsory prosecution. But little or nothing was said about creating other agencies for the control of corruption or finding ways of making other types of administrative control more effective and incisive.

A common distinction made was that between "legal" and "political" solutions, but where the line was to be drawn between these was often left ambiguous. On one view what was being indicated were different types of solution: there were two alternatives for getting beyond *Tangentopoli*: either by legal decree or by political agreement. On another interpretation what was important was the division of roles: the judges had to be left to find a way of dealing with past cases of corruption whilst it was up to the politicians to find means to prevent repetition in the future[29] (though of course some relationship between the two solutions was inevitable). But it was exactly this separation of roles which the *Mani pulite* judges had helped to muddle. It was common to find judges—and ex-judges such as Di Pietro—proposing answers both to the past and to the future, just as it was more than likely that politicians (in or out of government) would be found bending their efforts so as to end the existing investigations rather than make plans for the future. Posing the alternatives as either a legal or political solution thus reproduced the basic problem; how far had the *Mani pulite* judges proved the value of maintaining the "political" and "legal" as counterbalancing forces? How far had they shown the need for new arrangements to stop either side invading the territory of the other? And, (most difficult of all) could there be any way of judges and politicians arriving at an honourable collaboration in the public interest?

Insofar as *Tangentopoli* was seen as essentially a problem of previous political irresponsibility then it was up to politicians to find the answer. But relying on a "political" solution itself seemed to imply political interference in what was the competence of the judges. For Berlusconi it also looked suspiciously like attempting to interfere in favour of his own interests or that of his brother or managers. Attempts which were made to end *Tangentopoli* by government decree met with strong public disapproval. On the other hand, Giovanni Flick, a leading defence lawyer—and friend of Borrelli of the Milan pool—was one of those who put forward a "legal solution" which he claimed was in the interests of the investigations themselves. His suggestion was for plea-bargained agreements to be based on disbarring offenders from future political office and requiring them to return their illicit gains in return for freedom from prosecution. (In fact the Milan judges had themselves put forward a stringent version of this solution early on in the enquiries. But by this point they were worried that talk of an amnesty would discourage politicians from voluntarily repatriating the funds which were supposed to provide the basis of a plea bargain). To those who complained that this was letting criminals off Flick claimed that there were already examples of "silent amnesty" at some lower and local levels; for example, deals based on plea bargains were already being worked out (under trade union pressure) so that tax officials involved in corruption could keep their jobs. He went on to warn that in the absence of a solution there was a very good chance that the judges would soon be unable to do anything about most of the crimes committed before 1990 since these would fall into prescription by 1997 at the end of their 7 year prescription period, well before they had reached the stage of final and definitive sentence.

If *Tangentopoli* is to be ended formally it will require some such solution, packaged in a way that satisfies certain narrative requirements which allow it to be "rhetorically managed." The climax may arrive if Berlusconi is convicted in a new show trial ("I fought the law and the law won.") Alternatively, the charges against Di Pietro may be used to show that no one, not even the most admired judge, has "Clean hands." Either result could make it easier to proceed to a formal conclusion. But we cannot take any clear-cut ending for granted, for how many other events and scandals are still awaiting satisfactory closure in the "Italy of mysteries?".

Notes

1. See F. Cazzola and M. Morisi, "Magistratura e classe politica. Due punti di osservazione specifici per una ricerca empirica", *Sociologia del Diritto* XXII, 1995, pp. 91-145.

2. See D. Nelken, (1996) "A Legal Revolution? The Judges and *Tangentopoli*", in S. Gundle and S. Parker, eds., *The New Italian Republic: from the Fall of the Berlin Wall to the Rise of Berlusconi*, London, Routledge, or D. Nelken, "Judges and Corruption in Italy", in M. Levi and D. Nelken, eds., *The Corruption of Politics and the Politics of Corruption*: special issue of the *Journal of Law and Society* 23, 1, 1996, pp. 95-112.

3. Already by the beginning of January Judge Carlo Nordio of Venice had sent notice of pending investigations to the National President of the League of Cooperatives as well as to the President of the Venetian Committee of the League. These and other inquiries, which rumbled on throughout the year, extended also to the present and former leaders of the PDS, and led to suggestions, on the one hand, that there might be proceedings brought against the Milan pool for their failure to prosecute the PDS and, on the other, to claims that Nordio was acting in concert with Craxi in his fight back against *Mani pulite*.

4. According to *Il Resto di Carlino* (10/2/94), even in areas where public works were largely in the hands of communist co-operative construction companies costs went down in the period June-September, 1993 by 20 percent in Bologna, 30 percent in Ferrara and 20 percent in Ravenna.

5. On the other hand, some businessmen regarded the investigations simply as a threat to be contained. Giovanni Agnelli, leader of industrial capital as head of FIAT (as well as owner of two of the major daily newspapers), announced in

December, 1995 that he was retiring and handing over control to Cesare Romiti, the manager credited with successfully steering the car company through the difficult early 1990's. He brushed away as unworthy of reply a question from an incautious journalist who asked him whether he was disturbed by the fact that Romiti had just been informed that he was under investigation by Judge Maddalena from Turin concerning the alleged existence of a 30 billion lire slush fund for purposes of bribery.

6. The blockage of public works was felt mainly in the South, which fell even more dangerously adrift as the economy in North and Central Italy revived strongly on the back of an exports boom made possible by the devaluation of the lire.

7. G.M. Flick, *Lettera a un procuratore della Repubblica*, (Milano: Il Sole 24 Ore, 1993).

8. The Milan pool made regular recourse to the media in their battle against Berlusconi or unwelcome government measures which they saw as threating their powers of investigation. But there were also ill-advised attempts by some judges to prosecute those who attacked them in the media, as in the charges brought by Calabria judges against parliamentarians Sgarbi and Tiziana Maiolo for allegedly objectively helping the Mafia.

9. See e.g. E. Fassone, "Essere a sinistra oggi nella giurisdizione", *Questione Giustizia* 4: 1987, pp. 835-847; L. Grassi, "Magistratura progressista negli anni '90", *Questione Giustizia*, 4: 1991, pp. 951-959; G. Scarpari, "Crisi della Sinistra e prospettive della giurisdizione", *Questione Giustizia*, 1, 1992, p.177.

10. See G. Di Federico, (1991) "Obbligatorietà dell'azione penale, coordinamento delle attività del pubblico ministero e loro rispondenza alle aspettative della comunità", *La Giustizia Penale* XCVI: 147- 171; and C. Guarnieri, (1993) *Magistratura e Politica: pesi senza contrappesi*, (Bologna: Il Mulino).

11. S. Senese, "Sovranità popolare e potere giudiziario", in G. Azzariti et al. *Il Potere dei Giudici*, (Rome: Il Manifesto, 1994), p. 71.

12. G. Colombo, P. Davigo and A. Di Pietro, "Noi obbediamo alla legge non alla piazza", *Micromega* 5/1993, p. 7.

13. In *Il Corriere della Sera* (17/10/ 92) it was estimated that 100,000 people lived directly or indirectly off political corruption. This was about one tenth of those employed by the submerged illegal economy as a whole. See generally F. Cazzola, *Della corruzione*, (Bologna: Il Mulino, 1988); D. Della Porta, *Lo Scambio Occulto: Casi di Corruzione Politica in Italia*, (Il Mulino, 1992); D. Della Porta and A. Vannucci, *Corruzione Politica e Amministrazione Pubblica*, (Bologna: Il Mulino, 1994).

14. In his lectures and journalistic writings Di Pietro laid particular emphasis on what he called the hypocrisy of a business world which made regular resort to secret slush funds, false balances, fictitious consultants and inflated invoices. Here "the real problem is to convince the business world that they have above all a social function in a real liberal democracy. They must not think only of trying to achieve maximum profit passing like a bulldozer over the collectivity", A. Di Pietro, "Corruzione e ipocrisia", *Micromega*, 3/1995, p. 239 at p. 244.

15. J. Chubb and M. Vannichelli "Italy: A web of scandals in a flawed democracy", in A.S. Markovits and M. Silverstein, eds., *The Politics of Scandal: Power and Process in Liberal Democracies*, 1988

16. Whatever the actual overlap with the fight against the Mafia, judges did not hesitate to rhetorically link the two. The appeal to Parliament by 200 prosecutors at the time of the draft law setting limits to their powers of preventive detention began as follows: "the undersigned magistrates, daily involved in the difficult task of searching and checking for the truth in a country infested with the ever spreading phenomenon of organised crime as well all sorts of political administrative, economic and financial illegalities, feel it their duty to represent all of their unease and concerns respecting the draft law on preventive custody under examination by the Senate" ("Appello dei 200 p.m."), *Questione Giustizia* 2, 1995, p.421.

17. See F. Cazzola and M. Morisi, see note 2.

18. The law's terms—for example that there had to be proper recording of interrogation, and that the investigating judge had limited access to the suspect in prison, that suspects could only be kept in prison for 30-90 days awaiting confirmation charges, and that the courts had "only" 9 years (and not 20 as before) to reach final sentence—did not appear too harsh on the judges. In practice given the way the system operated they could create real formal and substantive obstacles for prosecutors, but, when D'Ambrosio of the Milan pool said that *Mani pulite* would not have been possible with such a law, he only confirmed suspicion that *Tangentopoli* had relied too much on oppressively induced confessions .

19. Though Judge Fabio De Pasquale of Milan was subjected to further investigations over the suicide in prison of Gabriele Cagliari.

20. Mancuso failed in his legal appeal, which argued that a no-confidence vote cannot be limited to only one minister but must bring down the whole government. Nor was he any more successful in his attempts to embarrass the government by claiming that his inspections had been secretly approved or that Dini had prevented him from proceeding against the Northern Leagues for treason. For the April, 1996 general election he was put forward as a candidate for Berlusconi's *Forza Italia* in Catania.

21. Obviously politicians and others also exploited to the full all the many possible legal methods for delay and obstruction, especially regarding getting information from foreign bank accounts or overseas business branches. Compliance with such rogatory requests to foreign governments was becoming increasingly problematic throughout the year; Mauro Vaudano, the judge in the Ministry of Justice who dealt with these requests, had been deprived of his post there by Alfredo Biondi (Berlusconi's Minister of Justice) for reasons which the CSM found totally spurious.

22. Strangely, Berlusconi himself claimed that Di Pietro had privately confided to him his disagreement with the appropriateness and timing of the charges which he had been served with whilst presiding at an international conference on criminality. Di Pietro's initial failure to deny this led to a rebuke from his former colleagues of the Milan pool.

23. On February 22, 1996 it was decided that there was insufficient evidence for Di Pietro to be sent to trial on the first two of these charges, the most serious ones. Judge Salamone has announced that he will appeal. On March 6 the same decision not to proceed was made concerning another two of the counts against him.

24. See Guarnieri in note 9.

25. See e.g. M.A. Calabrò, "Il porto delle nebbie", *Micro Mega* 5/1993: 89.

26. See e.g. Napoleone Colajanni, *Mani pulite: Giustizia e Politica in Italia,* Mondadori, 1996, and Pietro Folena, *Il Tempo della Giustizia,* Riuniti, 1996.

27. See the brilliant study by Robin Wagner-Pacifici (*The Moro Morality Play: Terrorism as Social Drama,* Chicago, University of Chicago Press 1986) in which the Moro affair is analysed as an example of "bad theatre".

28. Giuliano Ferrara (a former minister in Berlusconi's government) began arguing in his specious way that *Tangentopoli* had been launched by Achille Occhetto against Craxi's Socialist party as the only way of saving the PCI from losing out to its rival on the Left after the collapse of the Berlin wall had sent world communism into crisis.

29. Onida, V. "Mani pulite anno 3", *Politica in Italia 1995,* p.175.

10

The Confederated Trade Unions and the Dini Government: "The Grand Return to Neo-corporatism?"

Michael Braun

In the last fifteen years, talking about the Italian trade unions has meant talking about the crisis in their ranks. Since the beginning of the 1980s, confederated trade unionism has undergone a crisis in strategy and representation, with rifts developing in the relations between the three confederations: CGIL, CISL and UIL.[1] Unlike trade unions in other countries, the Italian unions, while not having had to face a sharp drop in their organizational force, have certainly been faced with a long, slow decline. And if it is true that the confederations have been able—though at times with great difficulty—to hold their own with businessmen and defend their positions in collective bargaining, it is also true their political clout has been seriously undermined. The confederations, which in the 1970s had acquired a power of veto over government economic and social policy, were no longer able in the 1980s to exercise such an influence.[2] Torn by internal division on questions of union strategy, split along party political lines, incapable of restoring ties with the union grassroots organization (for years new elections had not been held for the factory committees), and buffeted by competition from autonomous trade unions and COBAS, the confederated trade unions seemed to have boxed themselves into a crisis there was no way out of.

It is therefore all the more surprising that the three confederations managed to bounce back in 1995 to play a central role on the political scene and that, as one observer has commented, Italy has seen "the grand return of neocorporatism."[3] CGIL, CISL and UIL in fact played a crucial role in the survival of the Dini government in the following ways:

- They made a decisive contribution to the defeat of the Berlusconi government. The very successful general strike of October, 14, 1994 and the massive protests culminating in the huge demonstration of the November, 12 of that year in Rome forced Berlusconi into a humiliating retreat over pension reform.

- During the government crisis, CGIL, CISL and UIL made a clear stand in favor of a *governo di tregua* (a "truce" government) and welcomed the appointment of Lamberto Dini as premier.

- The Dini government accepted the confederated trade unions as primary interlocutors in the negotiations on pension reform and recognized that it would have been impossible to press ahead with reform without union consent. It was on this basis that the government and trade unions on May, 1, 1995, after twenty years of trying in vain, reached agreement on a complete overhaul of the pension system.

- Finally, as the budget was being prepared the confederated trade unions had their role as privileged interlocutors with the government confirmed. They returned this recognition on the part of the government by adopting an attitude never before seen: openly welcoming the government's proposals and foregoing those symbolic protest actions that had become part of Italy's industrial landscape.

In this way, following the brief interlude of the Berlusconi government, there was a rekindling of the government-trade union rapport that had begun under the Amato and Ciampi governments and that had two distinguishing features: on the one hand, affirmation by the trade unions of a new strategy of *concertazione* (cooperation between political and labor organizations); on the other, the establishment of close ties between government and trade unions, helped by the "technical" governments' need to secure union support and hence legitimation from social groups.

The "rise and fall of the unions"[4] thus seems to have ended in a somewhat unexpected way. The trade unions seem to have finished the trek they set out on fifteen years before: they have redefined their strategy in terms of *concertazione*, rediscovered strategic unity and reforged—through the massive protests against Berlusconi—a strong link with the grassroots, reemerging as front-line actors on the political stage.

If one looks at the history of Italian trade unionism this result cannot help but seem paradoxical. Precisely at a time when the First Republic has reached a crisis point, when many of the traditional parties are disbanding, when new political forces are coming to the fore and the whole political climate has become more heated, the situation as regards the trade unions is exactly the opposite. The traditional leaders have not been replaced—indeed they have strengthened their positions—and relations between trade unions, government, and business have reached a level of stability never before seen.

Even though CGIL, CISL, and UIL were closely tied to the political parties of the First Republic, they have not been contaminated by the crisis that has engulfed these parties. "The last sanctuary of the First Republic"[5] has not been dragged into the crisis of legitimacy; on the contrary, confederated trade unionism seems to be more alive than ever following the collapse of the party political referents of the CISL, the UIL, and the socialist part of the CGIL.

At the same time as the political system, upheld by the parties, has been running into trouble, the system of industrial and government-labor relations has, after years of vainly trying, entered a phase of con-solidation; as the temperature of political debate rises with a lamentable lack of rules to cushion and govern the clash between Right and Left, industrial unrest has reached its lowest level since the Second World War, a result made possible by the common acceptance of rules govern-ing the relations between labor and business.

But precisely because of the fluidity of the political situation it would be premature to talk about the creation of a new framework of tripartite relations; in the course of 1995, there was no shortage of signs indicating just how fragile the unions' newly-acquired position in the political arena is and to what extent trade union unity is still threatened by repercus-sions that political developments have on the confederations. The four referenda of June, 1995 on trade union rights (three regarding company representation and one the automatic deduction of union fees from pay-checks) caused new rifts between CGIL, CISL and UIL. Moreover, the problem of relations with political parties (existing or in the process of being formed) acted as a brake on attempts to overcome trade union divisiveness.

From Conflictual to Participatory Trade Unionism: The Long Crisis of the Eighties

The beginning of the long crisis for the confederated trade unions is marked by a symbolic date: the defeat of the unions in the strike at the FIAT works in 1980. The famous "35 days," which ended with the equally famous "march of the forty thousand" against the trade unions, brought a traumatic end to the era of conflictual trade unionism.

In the 1970s, CGIL, CISL and UIL had placed all their hopes on their ability to mobilize workers and affirm their demands through conflict. The trade unions' strong point in the Seventies was the solid base they enjoyed in the big factories—their being *sindacato dei consigli,* that is, unions composed of many factory councils. At that time, even the trade unions' relationship with government was marked by a "disputational" approach: the trade unions entered into negotiations with government armed with a raft of demands regarding economic and social policy and resorted to political strikes whenever the government opposed the unions' position. Any move towards introducing models of more formalized participation of workers at the company level or promoting cooperative relations between enterprise, trade unions and governments was at odds with this type of conflictual trade unionism. Indeed, such models were criticized as being harmful to "union autonomy."[6]

By following this line, the confederated trade unions had managed to achieve the great conquests of the 1970s, but the conflictual framework in which they worked proved inadequate for managing the crisis, dealing with job cuts, and fighting inflation; it was even less well adapted to providing a model for a future where the big factory was no longer so important and where new professional figures were emerging who did not coincide with the archetypal union member (male, worker, heavy industry employee).

A re-definition of trade union strategy was in itself a difficult undertaking because it affected the interests, convictions, and ideological taboos of the hard core—i.e. of the "worker masses"—around which the confederations had built their strength in the Seventies. "Hands off the *scala mobile*" (linking automatic wage increases to an inflation index) was the slogan then in vogue, though other rights were also not to be touched: the inviolability of jobs in heavy industry and the "rigid" structure of salaries and working hours.

But there was a second factor which made any attempt at changing the union line even more difficult: the political heterogeneity of the trade union movement. The three confederations had managed to patch together a fragile unity under the roof of the "CGIL-CISL-UIL Unitary Federation," founded in 1972, but only by coming up with a formula that stated the unions' basic party political neutrality. According to this formula, the unions followed their own political agenda without bowing to anyone and without taking heed of the interests of the government or the opposition. Such a formula could only seem credible as long as the confederations claimed complete freedom of movement in the political field, as long as they adopted a "disputational" framework in their relations with government, as long as, in a word, the unions demanded government policies without promising something in return or proposing direct trade union participation in forms of tripartite government of economic policy.[7]

When, however, in 1980, CISL—in the wake of the defeat at FIAT—took a definite moderate turn and began to talk of an anti-inflation pact with the government and business, a "political exchange" of wage containment for economic policy concessions, the strategic unity of the three confederations fell apart.[8] CGIL, in fact, came out against any neocorporatist shift for a series of union and political reasons: CGIL represented the majority of workers in industry who were loathe to sacrifice past conquests, beginning with the *scala mobile*, but the CGIL was at the same time the union closest to the PCI (Italian Communist Party), a PCI that had only just emerged from its experience of "national solidarity." The PCI could hardly welcome the development of close trade uniongovernment collaboration, just as the CGIL had no reason to see a credible counterpart for a *concertazione* strategy in the fiveparty governments of the day.[9]

Given that CISL proved inflexible on the need for a strategic change and that the communist majority in the CGIL proved just as inflexible on the need to prevent it, the first half of the 1980s saw the spread of antagonism between the two great confederations.

Even if many observers hailed the grand accord of January 22, 1983 between trade unions, businessmen and government as the beginning of *concertazione* in Italy, the opposite was true. The agreement was not based on any new strategic consensus within the unitary Federation and did not mark the start of a new era of industrial relations in Italy, but was only a step in the long-running CISL-CGIL conflict: CGIL had signed not because it agreed with CISL's strategic design on political dialogue but only because in 1983 the leaders of the confederation thought the eventual breakup of the Unitary federation would be more damaging than the accord itself.[10] In fact, in the following year confederation unity fell apart when CISL and UIL signed the Saint Valentine's day agreement with the Craxi government. CGIL opposed the operation, not so much because it cut three points off the *scala mobile*, but, as a matter of principle, out of its oppposition to the strategy of *concertazione*.[11]

Both sides turned out to be losers in the dispute: the neocorporatist agenda of CISL was unachievable as too was the CGIL's idea of making the union movement a bulwark for protecting the gains made by workers and a social opposition to complement the political opposition of the PCI. If the unions suffered a serious loss of political power the confederations also remained on the defensive vis à vis business: for years they struggled to negotiate collective contracts both at a company and sectorial level.[12]

The Italian Road to *Concertazione*

There were two factors which, despite the tribulations of the 80s, encouraged the new climate of cooperation between government and trade unions. The first was that the CGIL, under the leadership of Bruno Trentin, undertook radical revision of its strategy—completed with the congress of 1991—and declared its willingness to rethink its relations with business and government. "Codetermination" became the new buzzword for this the largest confederation; only the internal minority of the *Essere sindacato* (Being a Union) faction continued to defend the idea of the union as antagonist of enterprise and governments.[13]

But the trade union impasse had been caused by a series of reasons both internal (the question of whether to maintain the conflictual line of the Seventies or go down the road of cooperation) and political (the question of whether to accept the five-party coalition governments of the '80s as credible interlocutors of the unions). Overcoming the strategic block, therefore, also required a change on the political scene.

In the debate on the reasons for the failure of the attempts at political dialogue undertaken in the mid-1980s, many observers dwelt on the question of whether the existence of a "pro-labor" government was a prerequisite for such political exchange. On the one hand, it was asserted that dialogue could only work if the party most representative of the workers, i.e. the PCI, was part of the government coalition; on the other, it was argued that a government of parties that were not "antilabor" was enough for dialogue to take place.[14]

The events of 1995, like those of 1992-1993, suggest a third answer: the Italian trade unions are unable to push ahead with policies of cooperation with party political governments precisely because they are closely tied to the parties. Only when Italy had two executives removed from the political party sphere, first with Giuliano Amato and then with Carlo Azeglio Ciampi, were the trade unions able to enter into a policy of *concertazione*. This is what occurred with Lamberto Dini.

In July, 1992, CGIL, CISL and UIL agreed with the Amato government that the *scala mobile* be suspended and talks started on the final abolition of this contractual institution.[15] One year later, the "Ciampi protocol" of July 3, 1993 came along which not only finally dismantled the *scala mobile* mechanism, but represented an ambitious attempt to completely overhaul industrial relations and the relationships of labor organizations with government within the context of *concertazione*.[16] The "Ciampi protocol" did in fact re-define negotiation levels and the issues to be discussed at each level; it set in place triangular procedures to fight inflation via an "incomes policy;" and it re-ordered the representation of workers at a company level by introducing the *Rappresentanze sindacali unitarie* (RSU) in place of the factory committees.[17] At the very time *Tangentopoli* was putting the traditional ruling parties out of the game, the trade unions were recapturing clout on the political scene.

In the Italian case, it took "technical" governments to bring about *concertazione* and this for two reasons:

Firstly, technical governments showed themselves to be technically more prepared and professional; the Amato and Ciampi governments—in marked contrast to the patronage practices of the *pentapartito* (five-party) coalition governments—launched a policy for the reform of public finances which affected dependent workers but did not spare the self-employed either, as these were hit, for example, by the introduction of the minimum tax (even if this latter was later to be abolished). Political measures such as the introduction of the minimum tax were essential for the trade unions—at a time when government concessions could not involve lavishing material benefits but rather seeing to it that the burden of any recovery policy was more fairly spread—if they were to demonstrate to their members that they were not pursuing a policy of unilateral surrender but rather one of political exchange.

Furthermore, the main obstacle to attempts by the unions to develop policies of *concertazione* was removed: the everpresent question of whether an agreement with the government represented an advantage for this or that party. In fact, the DC and the PSI were no longer parties of government, while the PDS no longer acted as an opposition party; thus for the first time in fifteen years, union leaders were freed from the problem of whether their signature on an agreement was an advantage for a government party or if their nonsignature was a service rendered the opposition.

The Confederated Trade Unions and the Berlusconi Government

If the old party-political divisions of confederated trade unionism had temporarily lost all relevance and if, for a large part of the union factions, their party political reference points had disappeared, this did not lead to political unification of the main trade unions. The candidacies of union leaders in the electoral campaign of 1994 testified to the fact that political pluralism within the confederations was destined to last: the candidates from the CGIL entered the contest in the lists of the PDS, CISL activists presented candidates with the *Partito Popolare,* and the UIL gave strong support (without much success) to the lists of *Alleanza Democratica.*[18]

None of the three confederations, however, supported the Center-Right forces who turned out to be the victors of the elections. While with the Amato and Ciampi governments none of the confederations—for the first time in the history of the Republic—had had ties with an opposition party, this time no trade union was allied with any of the parties in government.

The damage that political change caused newly-found trade union unity was bound therefore to be limited. And yet the prospects for the strategic design of *concertazione* were rather gloomy, even if the new Prime Minister, Silvio Berlusconi, had initially declared he wanted to continue the dialogue with the trade unions in the wake of the "Ciampi protocol." In fact, the Berlusconi administration continued its predecessors' practice of consulting the confederated trade unions on social and economic policy, though the dialogue broke down quickly after the government launched its reform of the pension system.

The trade unions vetoed the government's demand that the reform be coupled with the passing of the 1995 budget—calling for a complete reform kept distinct from short-term budget considerations; and since the government sought to demonstrate it was able to push through reform even without the consent of the unions, a head-on confrontation was inevitable. The trade unions organized a wave of protests, strikes and demonstrations that unexpectedly showed their ability to mobilize support. The call for a general strike on October 14, 1994 was heeded by numbers that had not been seen since the heady days of the "hot autumn" of 1969, and more than three million people took part in the union rallies. The demonstration of November 12, 1994 passed into legend as the largest ever in the history of the Republic.[19]

While the pictures of crowded piazzas might lead one to think that the Italian trade unions had returned to a strategy of conflict and mass mobilization, the opposite was in fact true. In the same months that the confederations prepared themselves for the clash with the government, they also provided proof of their desire not to abandon the path undertaken with the "Ciampi protocol." In the negotiating of contracts they remained faithful to the principle of dialogue: the negotiations for the new national contract for metalworkers was concluded in July, 1994 without even a single hour's strike, a unique event in the history of the postwar years.[20]

As regards relations with the government, CGIL, CISL and UIL did not opt for a merely oppositional strategy or simply refuse to participate in talks on designing pension reform, but rather used the conflict in the name of *concertazione*: they acted in defense of their right to co-decide reform.[21] The plan worked perfectly: the Berlusconi government was forced to sign an agreement, which was immediately labelled the "Surrender protocol,"[22] and to withdraw its reform project; government and trade unions agreed to tackle reform by the first quarter of 1995.[23]

In this way, the trade unions not only contributed to the defeat of the Berlusconi government but came out of the whole period with a very positive balance-sheet. If the previous phase had served to lay the foundations for the strategy of *concertazione* and recreate effective unity among the confederations on the political scene, the experience of the Berlusconi government allowed the trade unions to reforge ties with their grass-roots, reaffirm their authority as representatives of dependent workers, and demonstrate to their government counterparts that attempts to do without union consensus could turn out to be very expensive.

The Trade Unions and the Dini Government: Final Acceptance of *Concertazione*?

After the trade unions' experience first with the technical govern-ments and then with Berlusconi's administration, the strong support given by the confederations to the formation of a new Dini government was not at all surprising. Like the forces of the Center and Left, the trade unions feared immediate elections. A Berlusconi government re-legiti-mized by the ballot box and no longer dependent on the support of the Northern League would certainly have had much greater freedom of movement, especially as regards the trade unions. The CGIL, CISL and UIL, therefore, came out immediately in favor of Lamberto Dini, first with a letter to the parliamentary groups asking for the "formation of a government capable of managing—for the period necessary—pressing economic and social issues and urgent reforms,"[24] and later with the position struck by the CISL secretary general, Sergio D'Antoni, who hailed Dini as a "technocrat of great competence."[25] Finally, the trade unions asked, with anti-Berlusconian irony, that Dini "be allowed to get on with the job."[26]

As Michele Salvati pointed out, the Dini government shared two peculiarities with the Amato and Ciampi governments that made a good rapport with the trade unions possible. On the one hand, the government was little conditioned by the parties that supported it, either because they were in the process of dissolution (like the parties of the *pentapartito* of 1992-94) or because the majority was politically heterogeneous (as was the case with the alliance of the *ribaltone* between Northern League and the Center-Left), and therefore capable of pursuing a coherent policy of stabilization. On the other hand, the government, not being able to count on party political channels, needed the labor organizations to guarantee it the consensus necessary to press ahead with its austerity reforms.[27]

In fact, Dini paved the way for agreement on pension reform in long negotiations with the trade unions before turning to Parliament in May, 1995. In this way, despite the lack of a solid and homogeneous parlia-mentary majority, he succeeded in an undertaking that the governments of the last twenty years had all failed in, i.e. a complete overhaul of the pension system.

The fundamental change was altering the way pensions were calculated from a "retributive" system to a "contributive" one: pensions will no longer be calculated on the basis of wages earned in the final working years, but on the basis of the contributions paid throughout a worker's working life.

Agreement was also reached on the gradual abolition of the so-called *pensioni di anzianità*, the possibility of leaving work after 35 years of activity but before reaching retirement age. Instead a flexible retirement age, starting at 57, will be introduced.[28]

Both of these measures mean sacrifices, some heavy, for many workers; nonetheless, the unions have not refused their support. In fact, they have done more: the three confederations organized a referendum on the reform. From May 29 to June 1, 1995 all workers and pensioners—not just those registered with the confederations—were called to express their opinion on the draft reform agreed by government and trade unions. The main aim of the referendum was to organize grassroot support from members for the union leadership, but it is obvious that the Dini government also benefitted. For weeks, the trade unions organized assemblies and gave out leaflets informing millions of people of the inevitability of the cuts, the unsustainability of the old system and the reasonableness of the proposed reform.[29] The vote of four million people—65 percent of whom approved the reform (even though the "yes" vote among active workers dropped to 60 percent)—could also be considered a vote of support for Dini, just as the high level of "no" votes among active workers (40 percent overall, with peaks of 50 percent in some regions of the North and certain categories such as the metalworkers) was proof of the fact that the trade unions had stuck to their line of support for the government even at the cost of creating strong internal dissatisfaction.[30]

A posteriori, the confederations demonstrated once again that their opposition to Berlusconi had not been, as was often suspected, a "rearguard action"[31] aimed at defending systems which were by now indefensible, but was rather a battle fought to affirm union rights in helping decide incomes policies. In fact, the size of the savings achieved through the Dini reform was only slightly less than what would have been achieved with the reform proposed by Berlusconi.

Dini took the same tack with his budget: before taking his proposals to Parliament he made sure he had the support of the CGIL, CISL and UIL for his budgetary savings measures. This time Dini met the trade unions halfway, not only by recognizing them as primary interlocutors in the drawing up of the government's policy, but by approving many of the confederations' demands. The budget aimed to save approximately 30,000 billion lire, i.e. a relatively low figure but, above all, Dini renounced any attempt at making these savings exclusively via cuts (which would have affected social security levels). Instead—and this was a point very dear to the trade unions—he strengthened the fight against tax evasion.

The trade unions returned the government's solicitude with full support for the budget. With the Ciampi and Amato governments, with whom they had always enjoyed close dialogue leading to the start of *concertazione*, the trade unions had regularly organized protests, called for changes, and expressed their dissent on budgets. With the Dini executive, even such symbolic protests disappeared. Raffaele Morese, assistant secretary general of the CISL, stated that the government had "all the cards for passing a budget with our support:" "This budget is based on a logic of incomes policy, with special protection for the lowest income groups."[32] Natale Forlani welcomed "a budget which is finally fair" and commented: "What a singular fate for the budget of '96: supported by the trade unions and criticized by the parties."[33] Sergio D'Antoni, secretary general of the CISL, took his cue from the budget bill to draw a more general picture of the relationship between government and trade unions: "With Dini we have a relationship that has led to a budget which is fairer than past ones. But there is no special treatment on our part: rather, it is this government which has shown us more attention than those which preceded it."[34]

The dialogue between the Dini government and the unions was therefore much more than a simple repetition of the experiences with Amato and Ciampi. While these latter had begun the process of *concertazione* (Amato) and defined its formal framework (Ciampi), the Dini government actually carried it through. Both the issues dealt with and the consensus reached between the parties seem to point to a consolidation of cooperative practice. Furthermore, a factor which had made early steps towards an incomes policy problematic was now lacking: the violent disagreement over the results achieved from within the union structure and activist base. In 1992 the then secretary general of the CGIL, Bruno Trentin, in order to overcome internal resistance to abolition of the *scala mobile*, had had to resort to the threat of resignation; and the union demonstrations of 1992-93 had been marked by violent attacks by groups of demonstrators against the union leadership.[35] In 1995 the confederations presented a much more united front. The dissent expressed by a group of CGIL leaders against the agreement on pensions remained just an isolated episode,[36] while grassroot discontent was felt only through the channels set up by the union executive, that is, in the union referendum on pensions.

Union leaders, however, not only maintained their cooperative course of *concertazione* with the government, they also respected income policy guidelines in their dealings with employers. If, in fact, the agreements on pensions and budgetary policy made it possible to press ahead with the reform of public finances, the containment of wages by the unions meant that the repercussions of the devaluation of the lira on inflation remained limited. In fact, according to ISTAT, gross salaries rose by just 3.9 percent from November, 1994 to November of 1995 compared to an increase in the cost of living of 6 percent.[37]

In this way, the confederated trade unions have shown that they have concluded the long process of revising the conflictual framework that dominated the Seventies. They have rediscovered their strategic unity—this time on the basis of *concertazione* and incomes policy—and they have succeeded in reaffirming themselves as political players.

It is therefore not surprising, in this light, that discussions regarding trade union unity and the unification of CGIL, CISL and UIL in a new *Confederazione* have returned to the fore in 1995. Just as in the first half of the Seventies "organic" unity (never achieved) was supposed to have sanctioned acceptance of the model of the "union of committees," that is of the union movement reborn in the struggles of the hot autumn of 1969, so unification of the confederated unions was today supposed to mean acceptance of the new model of participation, *concertazione* and incomes policy.

There are still two factors that exist which have stood in the way of unification and which could therefore hinder future development of the policy of *concertazione*. Firstly, there are still differences on the approach to union action, especially on how to understand the relationship between the union organization and its members, whether registered or not. Secondly, the political pluralism still present in the union movement could return to divide the different factions on the very question of the unions' political action.

The potential for conflict over the first problem was revealed when CGIL, CISL, and UIL had to formulate a common position on the four referenda regarding the unions which were part of the referendum package of June, 1995. One question—on the abolition of the article in the Worker's Statute providing for the automatic deduction of union fees at source—had been promoted by the political forces of the Center-Right. The other three questions regarding the privileged positions of the confederated unions in representing workers in companies—privileged positions reserved for the most representative trade unions at a national level or those who at least were signatories of national or provincial collective contracts applied at a company level—had been championed by left-wing forces opposed to confederated unionism. Two of the these referenda garnered support not only from *Rifondazione Comunista*, but also from large parts of the PDS. Thus the CGIL, to avert internal strife, declared itself neutral, recommending a "no" only on the other two questions, while CISL and UIL called for a "no" vote on all four referenda regarding the unions.[38]

But beyond the question of the referenda, the differences that reemerged between the confederations have brought to light the problem of what trade union democracy should consist of in a future united confederation. CISL and UIL favor the model of the *sindacati degli iscritti* (the members' trade union) where the union leaders have a mandate from, and are responsible to, members of the union only and are free to negotiate contracts and agreements both with business and government, authorized as they are by the members and elected by the union congress. Thus CISL proclaimed that "...the power of decision must remain entirely in the hands of the union."[39] The CGIL model, on the other hand, is that of the *sindacato di classe* (class trade union), i.e. a union which also acts on behalf of non-members, and which is not authorized to conclude agreements without securing from time to time the consensus of all workers—even those outside the unions—via popular referenda on specific platforms and agreements.[40]

The significance of these differences for the future of *concertazione* is obvious: CISL and UIL claim complete freedom of action for union leaders to sign agreements with business representatives and politicians, while the CGIL model would make it possible for the base, perhaps even a base outside the union, to repudiate any agreement made by their leaders: this would make *concertazione* a much more uncertain process. And this was the criticism the CISL leveled at the CGIL: of seeking to keep the door open so as to be able to "play a part in both drawing up agreements and in opposing them," and of being incapable "of assuming the responsibility which behooves great union organizations"[41] because still subject to "a certain nostalgia for conflictuality."[42]

The second factor mentioned above may also continue to be an obstacle both to the unification of the three confederations and to their adopting a common policy on the political front: the party political pluralism within the trade union movement. It is no fluke, it is said, that the presence of a technical government provided the ideal conditions for the development of *concer-tazione*. CGIL, CISL and UIL have not had to worry about their actions handing an advantage to this or that party associated with one of the factions within the union. But this felicitous state of affairs of having a government-trade union rapport that is not mediated by the political parties is not destined to last. The substantive unity, therefore, of the trade unions in the political arena, an essential condition for pressing on with *concertazione*, can only be maintained if the three confederations manage to reach agreement on the nature of their future relationship with the party political universe. In 1995, despite their general support for the Center-Left parties, the unions were divided on certain issues.

The CGIL (which felt the lack of a political counterpart least) urged the unions, in tones which recalled the CISL of the Seventies, to adopt a rigorous position of neutrality towards the parties, a "radical autonomy that (has) no specific connection to the political system,"[43] and declared itself contrary to any union attempt to remodel the party political scene. Should union neutrality be compromised, said secretary general Sergio Cofferati, then the prospects for unity would come under threat.[44]

The CISL, on the other hand, set itself "the problem... of how to take part in politics, in the construction of alliances,"[45] and committed itself, under the leadership of Sergio D'Antoni, to support the *Ulivo* coalition of Center-Left parties. With a resolution of its General Council on June 127-28, 1995, CISL threw its support behind the construction of a new "Center which seeks well-balanced alliances with the Left," a moderate force which can act as a counterweight to the PDS in a Center-Left coalition.[46]

Pietro Larizza, secretary general of UIL, went even further out on a limb by announcing in December, 1995 the formation of a *Lavoro Società* movement, the direct expression of UIL in the political arena.[47]

Just how two contrasting ideas such as the attempt to create a unified trade union and the move to commit the union to a specific niche in party politics unrepresentative of a large part of union membership would actually be able to coexist is a dilemma neither CISL nor UIL has to date been able to find an answer to. Only when CGIL, CISL, and UIL have succeeded in reaching agreement on internal rules for decision-making, in resolving the conflict between unions composed of members and those representing a whole class, and in determining the nature of their relationship with the party political system, will the confederations have built a united front on the basis of the strategy of *concertazione*. Only then will they be able to enter into a dialogue with a political government in the same way they did with the technocratic government of Dini. And only then will the "grand return of neocorporatism" be something more than just a brief hiatus brought about by the anomolous situation created by the Dini government.

Translated by Timothy Cooper

Notes

1. See for example, A. Accornero, *La parabola del sindacato,* (Bologna: Il Mulino, 1992); C. Mershon, "La crisi della CGIL il XII congresso nazionale", in

S. Hellman and G. Pasquino, eds., *Politica in Italia. Edizione 92*, (Bologna: Il Mulino, 1992), pp. 137-166.

2. See G. Baglioni, "Il sistema delle relazioni industriali in Italia. Caratteri ed evoluzione storica", in G.P. Cella and T. Treu, eds., *Relazioni industriali*, (Bologna: Il Mulino, 1989), pp. 17-45.

3. M. Salvati, *Crisi politica, risanamento finanziario e ruolo della concertazione, Il Mulino*, XLIV, n. 359, May-June, 1995, pp. 431-436, here p. 433.

4. The title of the work by Aris Accornero, see.

5. G. Cazzola, *I piccoli Frankenstein del sindacalismo nostrano, Il Mulino*, XLIV, n. 360, July-September, 1995, pp. 643-650, here p. 644.

6. For an overview of the confederated unions in the Seventies, see G. Bianchi, *Storia dei sindacati in Italia*, (Roma: Editori Riuniti, 1984); M. Regini, *I dilemmi del sindacato*, (Bologna: Il Mulino, 1981); S. Turone, *Storia del sindacato in Italia. Dal 1943 al crollo del comunismo*, (Roma-Bari: Laterza, 1992).

7. On this trend which at most led to models of "conflictual participation," See A. Cantaro and M. Carrieri, "Sindacato, accumulazione, democrazia industriale", *Democrazia e diritto*, year XX, September-October, 1980, pp. 591-632; L. Mariucci, "I rapporti tra sindacato e Stato", in G. Ferrante, ed., *Il futuro del sindacato*, (Roma: Ediesse, 1986), pp. 19-40.

8. The growing strategic divergence between the two largest confederations is documented in the three volumes by M. Mascini and M. Ricci, *La via del consenso, Lo scambio alla prova, La grande sfida*, (Roma: CEDIS editrice, 1984-1985). See also M. Dal Co, "Crisi dell'unità sindacale e prospettive delle relazioni industriali", in M. Carrieri and P. Perulli, eds., *Il teorema sindacale*, (Bologna: Il Mulino, 1985), pp. 43-54.

9. For the position of the PCI in this phase cf. G. Chiaromonte, *Quattro anni difficili. Il PCI e i sindacati 1979-1983*, (Roma: Editori Riuniti, 1984).

10. See M. Cicala et al., *Il grande accordo*, Dossier Adn Kronos, year II, n.5, May, 1983;

11. See T. Treu, ed., *Il patto contro l'inflazione*, (Roma: Edizioni lavoro, 1984); E. Santi, "Dal decreto al referendum l'ipoteca del primato della politica sull'evoluzione delle relazioni sindacali", in CESO, *Le Relazioni sindacali in Italia, Rapporto 1984/85*, (Roma: Edizioni lavoro, 1986), pp. XVII-XXXII; M. Carrieri, "Accordi non conclusi, accordi non efficaci, accordi non voluti. La logica negoziale dei governi nelle relazioni industriali", in M. Carrieri and P. Perulli, eds., *Il teorema sindacale*, (Bologna: Il Mulino, 1985), pp. 129-163.

12. See P. Lange, "La fine di un'era: il referendum sulla scala mobile", in P. Corbetta and R. Leonardi, eds., *Politica in Italia. Edizione 86*, (Bologna: Il Mulino, 1987), pp. 127-150.

13. For the CGIL 1991 congress see the two issues of *Nuova rassegna sindacale*, n. 38/39 of 28-10-1991 and n. 40 of 11-11-1991 and also C. Mershon, "La crisi della CGIL il XII congresso nazionale", see.

14. Among the many works on the subject, see M. Regini, "Le condizioni dello scambio politico. Nascita e declino della concertazione in Italia e Gran Bretagna", in *Stato e mercato*, n. 9, December, 1983, pp. 353-384; M. Regini, "Sindacati e governi in Italia che cosa cambia negli anni ottanta?", in M. Telò, ed., *Sindacato, politica e corporativismo in Europa 1970-1980*, (Milano: F. Angeli,

1983), pp. 263-279; M. Carrieri, *L'azione politica del sindacato fra vecchie immagini e nuove incertezze*, ibid., pp. 281-298; T. Treu, *Valore e limiti della politicizzazione del sindacato negli anni settanta*, ibid., pp. 245-261; E. Benenati and C. Sabattini, *Sindacato e potere contrattuale*, (Roma: Ediesse, 1986); G. Giugni, "Concertazione sociale e sistema politico in Italia", in G. Ferrante, ed., *Il futuro del sindacato*, (Roma: Ediesse, 1986), pp. 271-283.

15. See R.M. Locke, "L'abolizione della scala mobile", in C. Mershon and G. Pasquino, eds., *Politica in Italia. Edizione 94*, (Bologna: Il Mulino, 1995), pp. 233-245, here pp. 239ss.

16. See R.M. Locke, see, pp. 241ss.

17. For the text of the agreement see "Il protocollo punto per punto. L'intesa e il commento", *Nuova rassegna sindacale*, n. 27, 19-7-1993, pp. 8-21.

18. See "Tutti gli uomini del sindacato", *Nuova rassegna sindacale*, n. 10, 21-3-1994, p. 9.

19. See S. Zero, "Lo sciopero generale del 14 ottobre. La marcia dei tre milioni", *Nuova rassegna sindacale*, n. 38, 31-10-1994, pp. 12-14; B. Ugolini, *1.500.000 nella storia*, *L'Unità*, 13.11.1994; A. Orioli, *Più di un milione a Roma contro la legge finanziaria*, *Il Sole 24 Ore*, 13.11.1994; G. Musmarra, "Lavorate, non scioperate", *La Voce*, 13.11.1994.

20. See F. Liuzzi, "Un contratto senza scioperi", *Nuova rassegna sindacale*, n. 27, 18-7-1994, p. 5.

21. See e.g. R. D'Agostini, "Stop al governo. Intervista a Sergio Cofferati", *Nuova rassegna sindacale*, n. 36, 17-10-1994, pp. 5-7.

22. Giuliano Cazzola, *Il ruolo politico del sindacato*, Il Mulino, anno XLIV, n. 357, January-February, 1995, pp. 47-52; here p.49.

23. See "Il testo dell'accordo", *Nuova rassegna sindacale*, n. 44, 12-12-1994, pp. 7-10.

24. See Francesco Gagliardi, "Il verdetto di Scalfaro", *Conquiste del lavoro*, 10-1-1995.

25. See Marco Reggio, "E ora le riforme", *Conquiste del lavoro*, 15-1-1995.

26. This is the title of the article by Marco Reggio, *Conquiste del lavoro*, 26-1-1995.

27. See Michele Salvati, see, p. 433s.

28. For a detailed analysis of the reform see E. Ga., "Arriva la pensione flessibile", *Nuova rassegna sindacale*, n.19, 22-5-1995, pp. 8-10.

29. For a good overview of the campaign, see *Nuova rassegna sindacale*, n. 19, 20, 21, respectively of 22-5, of 29-5 and 5-6-1995.

30. For a detailed summary see *Nuova rassegna sindacale*, n. 23, 19-6-1995.

31. See G. Cazzola, *Il ruolo politico del movimento sindacale*, see, p. 52.

32. See Giampiero Guadagni, "La parola alle Camere", *Conquiste del lavoro*, 27-9-1995.

33. N. Forlani, "Una Finanziaria finalmente equa", *Conquiste del lavoro*, 4-10-1995.

34. See Giampiero Guadagni, "Una manovra che sceglie il lavoro", *Conquiste del lavoro*, 28-9-1995. Sergio Cofferati, general secretary of the CGIL, expressed an equally positive judgement speaking of a "Budget which for the first time in years has respected working incomes," quoted from Federico Rampini, "Bene così, avete salvato i redditi dei lavoratori", *La Repubblica*, 30-12-1995.

35. See F. Matteini, "Grandine di bulloni e uova su Trentin", *La Stampa*, 23-9-1992; L. Lonardi, "La rabbia della piazza colpisce anche D'Antoni", *La Repubblica*, 14-10-1992.

36. See M. Tulli, "CGIL, separati in casa", *Conquiste del lavoro*, 18-6-1995; M. Tulli, "Progetti di unità sindacale. Ecco il momento delle verifiche", *Conquiste del lavoro*, 19-6-1995.

37. See "Occupati in calo, salari sotto i prezzi", *La Repubblica*, 29-12-1995.

38. On the four referenda and the position of the CGIL see G. Rispoli, "Due no dalla CGIL", *Nuova rassegna sindacale*, n. 22, 12-6-1995, pp. 4-5; on the position of the CISL and UIL cf. F. Guz., "Ma PDS e CGIL con chi stanno?", *Conquiste del lavoro*, 25-5-1995, M. Tulli, "No, Si Boh. Il voto della CGIL", *Conquiste del lavoro*, 26-5-1995.

39.CISL, "Consiglio generale del 27/28-6-1995, Documento finale", *Conquiste del lavoro*, 9-7-1995; cf. also N. Forlani, "Unità sindacale. Cosa sta accadendo?", *Conquiste del lavoro*, 20-10-1995. For the position of the UIL cf. the speech by the secreatry general of UIL, Pietro Larizza, to the "Assemblea dei quadri e dei delegati della CGIL" (Roma, 16/18-10-1995), Supplemento a *Nuova rassegna sindacale*, n. 41, 20-11-1995, p. 15.

40.See the interview with the secretary general of CGIL metalworkers, Claudio Sabattini, "Una nuova confederalità", *Nuova rassegna sindacale*, n. 36, 16-10-1995, pp. 9-12; G. Rispoli, "Divisi sulla legge", *Nuova rassegna sindacale*, n. 24, 26-6-1995, p. 8.

41. N. Forlani, "Unità sindacale. Cosa sta accadendo?", *Conquiste del lavoro*, 20-10-1995.

42. R. Morese, "E ora discutiamo sui confini tra legge e contratto", *Il Progetto*, anno I nuova serie, n.2-3, pp. 1-3, here p. 2.

43. Claudio Sabattini, "Una nuova confederalità", *Nuova rassegna sindacale*, n. 36, 16-10-1995, pp. 9-12, here p. 9.

44. See Daniela De Sanctis, "Cambiare si può insieme al sindacato", *Conquiste del lavoro*, 4-3-1995.

45. Sergio D'Antoni, secretary general of the CISL, "Discorso all'Assemblea dei quadri e dei delegati della CGIL" (Roma, 16/18-10-1995), *Supplemento a Nuova rassegna sindacale*, n. 41, 20-11-1995, pp. 36s.

46. CISL, "Consiglio generale del 27/28-6-1995, Documento finale", *Conquiste del lavoro*, 9-7-1995.

47. See Enrico Marro, "Larizza presenterò il mio 'Lavoro Società'", *Corriere della Sera*, 8-12-1995.

11

The Church and the End
of the Catholic Party

Sandro Magister

In Italy, 1995 marked the end of the Catholic Party. *Democrazia Cristiana* (the Christian Democratic Party) had already perished in 1994, and by March, 1995 the *Partito Popolare* (the Popular Party), its struggling offspring, had shattered as well. For the Church, which had invested enormous pastoral and political energy to maintain a unitary Catholic Party during the years after the war, it was the end of an epoch. Having lost its greatest, decades-old political arm, the Italian Church suddenly found itself having to totally redesign its public role. For this purpose, at the end of November it called a week-long meeting in Palermo of bishops, clergy, and laypersons, the *stati generali*.

Instead of speaking of this issue in terms of the Church and *stati generali*, however, it is more accurate to discuss the ecclesiastical hierarchy and the Catholic world, or indeed, the ecclesiastical hierarchy alone, which in turn can be reduced to its highest officers: the Bishop of Rome and Primate of Italy, Pope John Paul II, and his Cardinal Vicariate and President of the Italian Episcopal Conference (CEI), Camillo Ruini. In 1995, in fact, the Italian Catholic world had arrived at the end of a more than century-long journey, or at least at the end of its ideal as taking a unitary political form. This outcome, which was summed up by the dissolution of the Catholic Party, has produced the paradox of an ecclesiastical hierarchy which had become more politically active than ever in the midst of an Italy which had never been more secularized.

It Started Like This...

In Italy, the Catholic world is, in the strict sense, that set of associated entities which, from the beginning of the last century, developed around the Catholic hierarchy and the papacy to serve as their protection and militant reserve in the face of a common enemy. This enemy originally consisted of forces of the *Risorgimento*, who, against the backdrop of the demon of liberalism and the dreaded new order introduced by the industrial revolution, had dethroned the pope and laicized the new unitary state.

What distinguished this organized Catholic world from the much larger and varied population of the faithful were its proclaimed confessional involvement in politics and the hierarchical mandate which connected it to the bishops and the Holy See. This mandate was so binding that, when the hierarchy put an end to its conflict with the state with the Concordat of 1929, it did not hesitate to sacrifice, as a *sine qua non* of the reconciliation, the most original and laical expression of this same Catholic world, the *Partito Popolare*, forcing its founder, don Luigi Sturzo, into exile.

After the Second World War, the hierarchical tie worked in the opposite direction, not by liquidating but by marrying a party: offering the DC of Alcide De Gasperi the exclusive right to serve as the unitary political representation of Italian Catholics, this time against the new enemy ommunism. In the postwar period, the substitute Secretary of state for the Vatican, Giovanni Battista Montini, forced the initially reluctant hand of Pope Pius XII in this direction. Elected as pope himself in 1963, with the name of Paul VI, Montini turned out to be "not only a fully Italian but, in a certain sense, fully Christian Democratic pontiff."[1] The Catholic world provided the DC with its associated cadres, assured it its electoral base, and legitimized the term "Christian" democrat with its authority.

From the hierarchy to the Catholic world, to the unitary Catholic Party, the articulation was smooth. The first serious break in this well-oiled mechanism occurred in 1974, with the referendum on divorce. The Catholic world divided between a "yes" and a "no" vote, with the consequent defeat of the DC and, behind it, of the hierarchy. Following the referendum there were two years of highly polarized administrative and political elections with the DC and the PCI (Italian Communist Party) running neck and neck, but with the Catholic world—both its intellectuals and and its cadres—now more attracted than repelled by what in 1948 had unequivocally been perceived as the enemy. At the end of this period, in November, 1976, in Rome the Italian Church held its first *stati generali*, on the topic of "Evangelization and Human Promotion." The episcopate was visibly divided, Pope Paul VI himself appeared uncertain, and the exclusive authority given to the DC was revoked, with a high-level ecclesiastical assembly thus recognizing Italian Catholics' right of full citizenship for the first time. This acknowledgement was only in theory, however, because in practice, the bishops continued to direct the faithful along a single path.

Ruini Appears at Loreto

In the following *stati generali* of the Italian Church at Loreto in April, 1985,[2] the passage from theory to practice seemed close to becoming reality. Leading the sessions were two cardinals whose backgrounds were quite different from that which up until then had marked Italian Catholicism: the Jesuit biblical scholar Carlo Maria Martini and the Carmelite mystic Anastasio Ballestrero. Among the lay leaders, the historian Alberto Monticone, president of Catholic Action, stood out as a proponent of the "religious choice:" the return of the Church to a genuine evangelical function with the restitution of political choices to lay Catholics, giving them their own autonomous responsibility. Holding firm to the traditional image of the Catholic world was *Comunione e Liberazione* (CL), the combative movement founded by don Luigi Giussani.

When John Paul II arrived at Loreto, however, he chilled a large part of his audience with a speech which vigorously reaffirmed the "leading" role of the Italian Church in the public world, the unrenounceable political unity of Catholics, and the imperative of saving the nation though a Church that was transformed into a "social force."

Relying on the previous silence of the new pope on Italian affairs, the ecclesiastial elite governing the meetings had calculated that a step outside the previous model was practicable. It was precisely at Loreto, however, that Pope Karol Wojtyla decided to break his silence and use his authority to bring the public role of the Italian Church back onto its traditional course. The directors of the Episcopal Conference were soon reshuffled. Since then, the Pope has placed his own cardinal vicar in the presidency of the the bishops: first Ugo Poletti, with Camillo Ruini as the secretary of the group, and then, from 1991 on, Ruini himself was elevated to the vicariate, becoming, in fact, the main political player of the Italian Church.

Curiously, as with the turning point of 1929, this reordering also had its origin in a concordat: to be exact the new agreement signed by Italy and the Holy See in 1984, just a year before the Loreto meetings. A notable aspect of this new concordat was the assignment to the episcopal conference of a direct and central role in relations with the state and society. This role was further strengthened by the concomitant attribution to the Italian Episcopal Conference of exclusive control over all the revenue (hundreds of billions of lire a year) yielded by the new contribution system of the *otto per mille* (0.8 percent of the value of Italian tax returns could be ceded to the Catholic Church) plus other tax-deductible donations.

On the strength of these new powers, Ruini, who from 1986 had already figured as the real manager of these mechanisms, launched a pastoral line with strong political connotations. If the Church's objective was to save the nation, and if its previously used instruments (the Catholic world, the Catholic Party) had become weak, it was the Church's job to assume this task itself, realigning the divided Catholic world and revitalizing the DC.

From a managerial perspective, Ruini's period in office after Loreto was undoubtedly effective. The Catholic associations were rapidly led back to the path of docile obedience to the CEI, at the price of obscuring any original characteristics they may have had. Opposing positions, beginning with those of Catholic Action and CL, were successfully diluted. The daily newspaper *Avvenire,* which had passed to the ownership of the CEI, became the unofficial organ of the CEI's presidency. As for the DC, it now found its ecclesiastical reference points directly in the bishops, primarily in the top levels of the CEI, no longer relying on the mediation of the Catholic world.

The Unequal Struggle

In 1989, with the fall of the communist system, the great enemy which had originally propelled the political unity of the Catholics in Italy was gone. From this point on the enterprises of Cardinal Ruini may be described as an unequal struggle for the continuance of a Catholic Party which was falling to its doom.

The matter of the missing enemy is the first element of this unequal struggle. Francesco Cossiga, Catholic President of the Republic, was the authoritative voice who declared the reason for the unity of Catholics in politics to be defunct with the fall of communism. Ruini felt duty-bound to answer him in the permanent committee of the CEI on September 23, 1991: "Our silence would have been interpreted as implicit agreement."[3] The reasons that Catholics must stay united, Ruini was to repeat often from then on, is a national one. The unity of the DC is a necessary condition for holding it together and thus ensuring the nation's stability. To reinforce this thesis of the crucial importance of the Christian Democratic Party as the cornerstone of the nation, John Paul II himself entered the fray in 1993 and 1994, demonstrating the full agreement between the Pope and his vicar first with his letter to Italian bishops on the "Responsibility of Catholics when Faced with the Challenge of the Present Historical Moment,"[4] and then again with the solemn proclamation of a "great prayer" for Italy.

In rapid succession from 1992 on, however, other elements broke onto the scene, making the difficult struggle of the ecclesiastical executive in defense of the single Catholic party a losing battle. The first of these was the success of a new party, the *Lega* (Northern League) with the concomitant collapse of the Christian Democratic vote in the Lombardy and Veneto regions, the heart of Catholic Italy from which had developed the historical roots of the Catholic world of the 18th and 19th centuries. The second was ex-Christian Democrat Leoluca Orlando's formation of a new party of Catholic background to the left of the DC. Called the *Rete* (Network), the party had the goal of establishing on a national level the progressive alliance which Orlando had tested in Palermo. The third was the birth of Mario Segni's movement, *Popolari per la riforma*, which sought a reform of the Italian political system on majoritarian and presidentialist lines and the construction of a cross-party alliance to lead the country. It was this third element which most disturbed the ecclesiastical leadership. At least in the initial phase, Segni was still a Christian Democrat, but his design was seen as radically changing the future role of the Catholic Party. "He ha[d] placed the problem of the succession to the DC" in question.[5]

Finally there was the explosion of *Tangentopoli*, with the judicial inquests which uncovered the illegal side of political dealings in Italy, and the fall of the first political leaders as a result of the investigations. The response of the DC and the hierarchy to this succession of blows was to reinforce the symbolic and political ties between the two. Mino Martinazzoli, a man whose personal path was suited to the needs of the time, ascended to the leadership of the party. Symbolic figures from the Catholic arena, even from groups outside the DC, were brought onto his staff, among them, Rocco Buttiglione, who went on to succeed him in 1994. Personalities from militant Catholicism were chosen to lead the local DC branches and they were given an explicitly purificatory mandate. The DC asked the Church for a new legitimization and new concepts of Catholicism on which to model itself. The hierarchy offered its resources to the party in an ever more exclusive manner. *Carta 93*, a coalition of the most faithful Catholic intellectuals, was formed with a transparently ecclesiastical investiture. Its aim was to collect members of the Catholic world who had been tempted by other alliances and institutional reforms, not only around, by also inside, the DC, and in fact, the Carta 93 members soon joined the parties en masse.

The heads of the CEI have been reticent on the subject of *Tangentopoli*. In 1991, before the corruption scandal was uncovered, they had published a document titled "Educating on legality."[6] But when the storm hit, they did not add much other than the recognition of omissions and personal weaknesses, which were attributed not to a system in which the Church, too, had been a bad teacher, but to individual sinners of whom penance was asked and to whom indulgence was offered. Ruini spent much more energy in isolating Segni and keeping the Catholic world from giving its support to the crucial referendum looming in 1993. The President of the CEI associated the virtuous reform of the DC with the refusal to embrace the redesign of democratic institutions in Italy. Segni, who took this leadership upon himself, was not only forced to leave the DC, but also to find himself become the target of the ecclesiastical press and the principal stars of the Catholic world, who accused him of having "the hidden intention of breaking up the political unity of Catholics."[7]

The Last Catholic Party

In fact, Segni's referendum on April 18, 1993, revealed a huge major-ity in favor of a majority system. The DC finally supported the "yes" vote just four months before polling and then only on the sly. Promising to resist the change at the point where the new electoral law was to be written, it succeeded, with the passing of the hybrid bill (with 25 percent of parliamentary seats still elected through proportional allocation), authored principally by Sergio Mattarella, a man from the Christian Democratic Left. The upsets which the Catholic Party suffered in the local elections of June, however, (while Segni's alliances with the Left triumphed) forced it to accelerate its reorganization to the point of chang-ing its name: from Christian Democracy to the Italian Popular Party (PPI).

The change took place between July, 1993 and January, 1994. And despite its proclaimed lay nature and the Sturzian name with which it was adorned, the new *Partito Popolare* was born effectively under the leadership of in the President of the CEI, who during the entire transition acted to form "a clerical-democratic party much more similar to *Carta 93* than to the old DC."[8] The operation had its price: first, on the Left, the *Movimento dei Cristiani Sociali* of Ermanno Gorrieri broke away from the old party; then, on the Right the *Centro Cristiano Democratico* of Pier Ferdinando Casini and Clemente Mastella split off. But Ruini did not revoke the commandment urging Catholics to unite in one single party, even with the semantic sweetening that led to formulas such as "unify-ing tension" and "unitary cadre." In this, there is an implicit and per-sistent rejection of the bipolar logic begun with the new voting system. In fact, the *Partito Popolare* approached neither one of the two coalitions which were in the process of forming for the approaching elections. The

PPI remained immobile at the Center with Segni, who had been defeated in his intention of acting as the balancing point between the Center and the Left. Thus the identity crises of *Carta 93*, of Martinazzoli, and of Cardinal Ruini widened the space on the right so that the outsider, Silvio Berlusconi, could rapidly gain ground with his brand-new party, *Forza Italia.*

The elections of March 27, 1994, partially punished the *Partito Popolare.* Together with Segni's forces, it scraped up only forty-six seats in the House of Deputies, almost all through the proportional vote, compared to a total of 366 for the Right. The political overexposure of the CEI during the last phase of the DC and the birth of the PPI caused many bishops and a large part of associated Catholic groups to view the electoral defeat of the popolari as a defeat for the Church itself. But Cardinal Ruini did not renounce the Church's political posture; in fact, beginning in the spring of 1994, he intensified his interventions even further, altering them to fit the new political framework resulting from the elections.

Ruini formulated his post-electoral line in both the plenary session of the CEI which opened on May 16[9] and then again in a speech in memory of Alcide De Gasperi on August 19[10], entrusting to *Avvenire* the task of reiterating the Church's line at daily intervals. It reported that "great changes" had taken place, but also that the situation was "still a long way from being settled." Continuity, in this view, would prevail over change. Berlusconi was the heir to the DC since he had taken most of their votes and manifested concrete "agreement" with Catholic feeling and the needs of the Church. It would, therefore, be on the Center-Right that political Catholicism would fit in and must find its "leading role" again.

To the *Partito Popolare*, which had been left headless by the resignation of Martinazzoli, the president of the CEI issued an invitation to "close the gap which has formed between the party management and its potential electorate." The implicit imperative was a firm "no" to an alliance between PPI and PDS, which became explicit in a November 25 editorial in *Avvenire.* When Rocco Buttiglione, who was from a cultural tradition quite different from that of the Left, was elected to the leadership of the *popolari* in the summer of 1994, the Catholic party's position at the moderate pole seemed likely.

Ruini, however, stopped demanding the political unity from Catholics which he had insisted on until the elections of March 27th. He failed to give reasons for his sudden silence, but it was the progressive crumbling of what had been the Catholic Party which made any further insistence unrealistic. Moreover, there was a growing difference between Ruini's signals and those of the exponents of the *Partito Popolare* who were directly descended from the Christian Democratic Left. Ruini knew that

the passage of Buttiglione's PPI to the Center-Right, which he had supported, could induce defections in the opposite direction. Instead of seeking the political unity of all Catholics, the President of the CEI limited
himself to asking the *popolari* (*Avvenire* talked of little else) to remain
united. In this way Ruini gambled on limiting the risk of schisms to a
few isolated defections.

Also complicating the politics of the CEI's president was the return to
the public arena of the monk, Giuseppe Dossetti.[11] In his youth, Dossetti
had been head of the opposition to De Gasperi in the DC, and he currently showed an intellectual affinity with the archbishop of Milan, Carlo
Maria Martini, in his reading of recent political events. These clerics
shared a dark perspective on the current situation, evoked by Dossetti
with his image of the "night" and by Martini with an image of "fog."
For Dossetti, this implied the need for a defense of the Constitution: the
last bulwark against the turbulence introducedfirst by Segni's referendum and rendered even more menacing by the victory of Berlusconi
and the culture of "idolatry" which he personified. For Dossetti, Catholics involved in politics must directly rebut the idolatry which had
triumphed with the Right. Such a choice for the opposition, "must be
global and non-negotiable." Martini reiterated these arguments in a
homily on June 2, 1994 at the National Eucharistic Congress in Siena.[12]

The distance between this perspective and Cardinal Ruini's pragmatic
approach is clear. The President of the CEI alluded to this distance at the
May assembly of the national episcopate, when he restated his view that
constitutional rights were not seriously at risk, and in his August speech
in memory of De Gasperi, when he denounced "the catastrophic interpretation of the modern western world which has constituted the common background of a large part of Catholic thought and which continues
here and there."

Disintegration

The year 1995 opened with the transition from the Berlusconi government headed by Lamberto Dini. It was also marked by the rapid unfolding of diverse positions in the Catholic and ecclesiastical fields.

With *Avvenire* faithfully reflecting his thoughts, Cardinal Ruini decisively followed the line he had imposed after the elections. "For the
coherence which we owe to the electorate,"[13] he again vetoed an alliance
between the *Partito Popolare*, the *Lega*, and the Left. He repeated that the
future of the PPI lies with its Catholic grassroots, and cited the results
of a postelectoral survey "according to which, out of one hundred
Italians who defined themselves as practicing Catholics, only 17.5 per-

cent would vote for the *Partito Popolare*, while 30 percent would opt for *Forza Italia*, 11.5 percent for *Alleanza Nazionale*, 11 percent for the PDS, 7.5 percent for the *Lega*, and 6 percent for the *Patto Segni.*" Ruini also argued with Catholic politicians and intellectuals who refused to go after this moderate electoral base: "While we extol the basic values, others were raiding the base of the country, which was superficially thought to be already ours."[14]

These arguments had no effect, however, judging by the course of events. On January 14, in Rome, the intellectuals and politicians who had been the object of Ruini's reprobation gathered at the Angelicum: exponents from the left of the PPI, *Carta 93*, and *Città dell'uomo*, a group very close to Dossetti. On January 21, in Milan, Dossetti again set forth his proposals for the defense of the Constitution and proportionalism for an audience of Catholic and lay jurists and most of those who had taken part in the Angelicum meeting. On February 2, the *Popolari* president, Giovanni Bianchi, and group heads Beniamino Andreatta and Nicola Mancino, launched the candidacy of Professor Romano Prodi for Prime Minister of the Center-Left pole—without informing the party secretary Buttiglione. The following day, Prodi, with the go-ahead of the PDS, made his candidacy official.

Catholic, Bolognese, former president of IRI, the largest Italian public holding company, on good terms with both Dossetti and Ruini, and a life-long unofficial Christian Democrat, Prodi was a person of many resources. After Martinazzoli's exit from the scene, Cardinal Ruini had in fact asked Prodi to become a candidate to lead the PPI, but Prodi had answered that he did not want "to accept being the leader overseeing the schism" of the party, which he saw as both near and inevitable, and that he thought it by now "impossible to save the PPI from within."[15] But now, with his candidacy for Prime Minister of the Center-Left, Prodi had actually accelerated the much feared schism, as well as hindering Ruini's plan of taking a large part of the PPI to his appointment with the Center-Right.

The CEI president's disappointment was clearly visible from the pages which *Avvenire* dedicated to the event. *L'Osservatore romano*, the newspaper of the Holy See which reflects the position of the Vatican leadership on Italian affairs, also offered a negative judgment of Prodi's initiative and that of the *popolari* who supported him. But the ecclesiastic delegitimization which had been unleashed against Segni was not employed against Prodi. Paradoxically, Ruini feared that the Christian Democratic nucleus of the PPI, which he himself had forged the year before, might flee from him with Prodi.

Although Ruini was concerned with saving the unity of his creature at the Center of the political spectrum, which he saw as under siege from

Prodi's operation, events did not conform to his expectations. It was neither Prodi, nor his followers, but rather Buttiglione, who caused the division in the party. Just as he had accelerated the fall of the Berlusconi government at the end of 1994, forcing the pace and methods with respect to those Cardinal Ruini would have preferred, this time too the secretary of the PPI forced a showdown in the party which brought it to the breaking point. The dissent arose quickly. On March 8 Buttiglione made an electoral agreement with the Center-Right alliance. On the ninth he called a national meeting of the party, and on the eleventh the members present forced him into the minority by a small margin of votes which were then promptly contested by the losers. The Left demanded his resignation as leader, but he refused. What followed was a bitter dispute over the division of the spoils.

Electing Gerardo Bianco as its leader, the left of the party kept the name of *Partito Popolare*. Buttiglione's Right, christened the *Cristiani Democratici Uniti* (CDU, the United Christian Democrats), retained the symbol of the crossed shield. The party headquarters in Piazza del Gesù was divided, along with the other assets. The daily newspaper, *Il Popolo*, went to the PPI. The periodical, *La Discussione*, which was later turned into a daily, went to the CDU. The PPI entered the *Ulivo* (the Olive Tree), the Center-Left alliance headed by Prodi. The CDU joined the Center-Right alliance, together with its cousin, the CCD, also ex-Christian Democrats.

For some time now, the unity of Catholics in politics had ceased to exist. In fact, it never had existed—not even when the DC was far and away the leading Italian Party. But with this final schism, the last semblance of a unitary Catholic Party had disappeared. Until now, although lacking its former size, Martinazzoli's PPI had been able to claim centrality. But now, even this had disappeared.[16]

After the Flood

At the end of March, in the first regular meeting of the CEI after the schism, Cardinal Ruini took stock:

> Recent painful events have led to a further grave fracture in the political grouping which has Christian inspiration as its reference point. Thus the process which in the past few years has marked the decline of Italian Catholics' organized, united participation in the political world has advanced and seems to have practically reached its conclusion. This has certainly not come about because of our lack of interest, but instead results from a series of factors which have acted jointly to cause it.

Among these factors, the president of the CEI lamented "the spread, even in ecclesiastical circles, of inattention to, or even rejection of the social teaching of the Church and the political commitment which derived from i.." And he drew this conclusion:

> With the progressive decline of the organized Catholic unity in politics, the objective of not confusing Church and politics apparently became easier to fulfill while in reality it is not automatically assured. It is, in fact, still necessary to avoid initiatives or pronouncements by the clergy and the various other ecclesiastical groups which represent involvement with any political side.

Ruini's motivation, in the name of a sort of ecclesiastical *par condicio* (equal rights to publicity for all parties), was to block the likely pronouncements in support of Prodi both by priests and bishops and by such Catholic associations as ACI, ACLI, and Caritas.

Ruini also urged Catholics involved in politics to "draw back from that logic, neither noble nor far-sighted, by which he who is objectively closest to me becomes my first adversary."

This appeal alluded to the ideological disintegration that had occurred during the recent party split. In effect, the PPI had not divided itself between liberals and statists, between conservatives and progressives. Rather, the demarcation line had been the cultural, genealogical divide which had run through the Catholic world since the end of the war. On the one side were the legitimate sons, from the extreme progressive Rosi Bindi to the ultra-moderate Emilio Colombo, along with the Dossettian left, faithful Christian Democrats, Catholic Action, and *Carta 93*. On the other were the outsiders, most notably Buttiglione, who lacked any Christian Democratic past and was not a disciple of Jacques Maritain or Dossetti, but rather of the anti-modernist philosopher, Augusto Del Noce.The incompatibility between the two branches was irreconcilable, almost genetic. Buttiglione highlighted this in an interview in *Avvenire*: There is a very modern political figure who represents a good part of the managerial elite of lay Catholicism. He is intrinsically anti-liberal and is instead attracted by the utopian culture of the Left. In one sense he is the Catholic version of that utopian culture. He desires an alliance with the ex-Communists to build a new Left in Italy. On the other hand, he is absolutely opposed to considering a relationship with the Right. It is on the Right, however, that "the true Catholic base, the millions and millions of Italian citizens who go to Church" is situated, he claimed.[17]

There is an undoubted affinity between Buttiglione's vision and that of Ruini. Proof of this is the considerable attention paid by the president of the CEI during these months to "many very qualified representatives of lay culture" of the liberal type, and to all that which may "bring down or at least lower the fences which have divided Catholics and secularists in Italy for too long." *Avvenire*, with special treatment of the liberal, lay political scientist, Ernesto Galli della Loggia, and *L'Osservatore romano*, which has the moderate Catholic historian, Giorgio Rumi, on its editorial staff, faithfully reflected the sensibility of Ruini and the Vatican leadership. Della Loggia and Rumi, along with Ferdinando Adornato, have, from the beginning of 1995, jointly directed a monthly, *Liberal*, which has as its program (as can be read from its motto) "a meeting place for Catholics and those of a secular orientation."

At the plenary assembly of May 22,[18] Ruini repeated that "the experience of an organized, unitary presence in the political world is practically at an end." He reaffirmed his admonition "not to confuse the Church and politics." Even Pope John Paul II, who had a year before used all of his authority in demanding political unity from Catholics as the cement of national unity, remained silent. Instead, both Ruini and the Pope insisted on the necessity of "influencing" if not politics in the strict sense, then "the general orientations of the culture or cultures in which we live." In the texts and speeches of the assembly, the new proposal is called, variously, the "pastoral project," or "cultural project," or "the elaboration of a new Christian-oriented cultural perspective." This terminological wavering revealed an uncertainty and a lack of content. Aspirations to the Gramscian goal of taking possession of the levers of cultural power (school, press, and media) leaked out via the voice of the Bishop of Vicenza, Pietro Nonis. With the Catholic party and the Catholic world having had their day, Ruini proposed an increased role for the Italian Church as "a great social force"—in line with the one outlined by the Pope at Loreto and in his January 6, 1994 letter to the bishops. The president of the CEI postponed giving substance to the newly drafted project to the ecclesiastic convention planned in Palermo for the end of November, the third edition of the *stati generali* of the Italian Church.

In the political field, ecclesiastical leaders remained "equidistant" from the various fragments moving in the wake of the old DC. The director of *Avvenire* explained this as a "critical detachment, freedom to observe and evaluate."[19] In practice, in both the CEI newspaper and in that of the Holy See, this equidistance was translated into a severe critical stance toward the Prodi operation. With the Palermo convention in view, this generated a gentle polemic-at-a-distance, with significant Catholic voices making themselves heard. As Jesuit Bartolomeo Sorge argued, "the Church must certainly take care not to support one or another political faction; but being outside the struggle between parties does not mean being neutral or equidistant in the face of ethical conceptions and political cultures which depart from the Christian Social vision." And he pointed out that "on an objective level" between the two opposing political cultures in the country, "one neoliberal and one popular and solidarist, Democratic Catholics" cannot but opt for the latter, the only one in line with the Constitution and the social teaching of the Church.[20]

Some of the scholars gravitating around the Catholic University of Milan also joined the fray. In a weighty document, they acknowledged that:

> With the decline of a certain kind of political exposure by the Church, the watchwords of neutrality or equidistance with respect to political forces and alliances have taken its place. We interpret such a distinction and autonomy as a boon for the Church and for Italian Democracy. Not, however, to the point of feeding the propensity toward a sort of full-scale indifference.[21]

The choices which the document indicates as obligatory for Catholics include a vigorous defense of the Constitution, and, overall, restate in the form of a political program the comments made for more than a year by the monk, Dossetti. Among the signatories of the text were two ex-presidents of Catholic Action and some of the founders of *Carta 93* and *Città dell'uomo*, Alberto Monticone, Raffaele Cananzi, Enrico Berti, Franco Monaco, and Luigi Pizzolato. The very same people whom Ruini had recruited to oppose the Segni menace and create the new *Partito Popolare*, the extreme version of the unitary Catholic party, now found themselves both in disagreement with the president of the CEI and coolly received by the PPI, which had survived the division.

Notwithstanding the fact that the party's breakup had the Prodi question as its detonator, the agreement between Prodi and the heads of the PPI had soon revealed itself to be anything but solid.

The new secretary Bianco, along with Franco Marini and Ciriaco De Mita, who had been reinstated to the effective leadership of the party, showed immediate resistance both to the two-party logic personified by Prodi (and by Segni, who remained unforgiven) and to a rapid recourse to elections.

At the PPI congress at the beginning of the summer, the widespread conviction developed, well expressed by De Mita, that the experience of the DC as a "mass popular party" was not over and that a return to this party form would occur in the not too distant future. But this implied that, with its potential as a large party, the PPI had "no need of the enlightened guidance of some of the leaders of the small groups." Thus, a possible alliance with the Center-Left could be, at most, provisional and not binding or stable, as in a full-fledged two-party system.[22]

In Search of New Languages

Thus Ruini paid close attention to these new expectations of the rebirth of a large center party which would no longer be Catholic but made up of Catholics and, hopefully, secular liberals. At the same time he accentuated his detachment from that Catholic world, composed of voluntary associations and circles of intellectuals, which he judged to have fallen prey to Dossettian utopias, and believed to be ever less compatible with his expectations and plans.

At the *stati generali*, held in Palermo on November 20-24,[23] this abandonment of the Catholic world was clear. The leaders and cadres of the associations were physically present but kept at the margins of the operation of the meeting, just as they had already been barred from the preparatory phase. Catholic Action, ACLI, and *Comunione e Liberazione*, which ten years before at Loreto had held the floor and battled noisily, had all disappearred from sight. Even Caritas had been eclipsed, despite the fact that the convention was called "The Gospel of Charity for a New Society in Italy." Important speeches were entrusted to Don Piero Coda, a theologian disciple of Luigi Pareyson, belonging to the *focolari* movement; to Franco Garelli, a sociologist close to a movement of family spirituality, *l'equipe Nôtre Dame*; and to Andrea Riccardi, the founder of the community of Sant'Egidio. These assignments, however, did not signify any promotion of these movements in the overall map of the Catholic world. The choices were of individuals instrumental to the plans of Cardinal Ruini, the only real power behind the conference.

This is proved by two other choices, which were, indeed, the most politically significant of the conference. The President of the CEI named Giorgio Rumi as coordinator of the political arena, while, to the post of lay spokesperson, the only office of the entire conference dedicated to dialogue, he named Ernesto Galli della Loggia (with Massimo Cacciari and Saverio Vertone). These choices represented the management of *Liberal*, almost to a man.

As at Loreto, the Pope again gave the keynote address to the Palermo meeting, but this time without a trace of opposition to his announced line. John Paul II outlined a murky diagnosis of the ills of the Italian nation, but he no longer demanded a path of political unity from Catholics. This time, he said:

> The Church must not and does not intend to involve itself in any choice of political or party alliance, just as it does not express a preference for any particular institutional or constitutional solution as long as it is respectful of genuine democracy. But this has nothing to do with a Catholic cultural *diaspora*, with their belief that every idea or vision of the world

is compatible with faith, or with their facile adhesion to opposing social and political forces, or [with the fact] that they do not pay sufficient attention to the principles of the Church's social doctrine concerning the person and the respect for human life, the family, educational freedom, solidarity, or the promotion of justice and peace.

John Paul II also congratulated the CEI for putting in operation a Christian-oriented "cultural project or perspective." These were the watchwords which Ruini had coined a year before, when he had stopped talking of the political unity of Catholics. The agreement betweent the Pope and his Vicar was so strong that Ruini, in his concluding speech to the conference, added nothing of substance to what had already been said by the head of the Church. The key element of the project was to unite the Catholic diaspora. Since this goal could no longer be reached through political means, "cultural" terrain was selected as the grounds on which this unity was to be built. Meanwhile, in the political field the Pope placed so many limitations on the legitimacy of the adherence of Catholics to other forces, but especially for those of the left, as to make them all problematic and provisional.

Again at Palermo, John Paul II asked Catholics, though they may be committed to different parties, to join in a "community of common sense." Ruini closed the meeting by announcing the establishment of means for encouraging ongoing dialogue. And after the conference he was quick to put this into practice, opening the process to secular liberals as well. After comments from the Palermo meeting by Galli della Loggia and Gianni Vattimo appeared in the *Corriere della Sera* and *La Stampa*, *Avvenire* promptly placed its page reserved for political and cultural debate, titled *La Piazzetta*,[24] at their disposal.

Also as a result of an initiative traceable to the president of the CEI, on December 18, at the Roman convent of Santa Brigida, the leaders of the five Christian parliamentary groups gathered "to give life to a cross-cutting common front to defend Catholic values."[25] Included in this group were Bianco for the PPI, Buttiglione for the CDU, Casini for the CCD, Alberto Michelini for the Liberal Catholics, and Pierre Carniti for the Social Christians, plus Carlo Casini, president of the Movement for Life.

Cardinal Ruini, however, was less disposed to opening an explicit dialogue within the Church, especially at its upper hierarchical echelons. In Palermo, the Italian bishops, although almost all present, stayed quiet. The defeat, with the end of the Catholic Party, of the line first imposed at Loreto and strenuously followed to the last, had not been subjected to any public critical analysis, despite the fact that it was known that the policy had not been positively viewed by all.

Not until December 6, the eve of Sant'Ambrogio, patron saint of Milan, was the first authoritative, dissonant voice heard, in a homily by Cardinal Martini. The Archbishop of Milan recalled the urgency of returning to "that evangelical and prophetic choice once called religious choice;" that is, to the choice defeated at Loreto by the Pope and opposed in the following decade by the President of the CEI. He then took aim at Ruini's latest watchword, the "cultural project," reducing it to a simple verbal variant of the above-mentioned religious choice. Martini continued: "At risk, in the political choices that lie ahead of us, is not the survival of the Church as such (another Ruinian theme), but 'that of a shared civil ethos which lies at the foundation of every democratic society'." As for the Church's participation in the political arena, he said:

> This is not the time for indifference, for silence, nor even for detached neutrality or tranquil equidistance. It is not permissible to think that one may choose indifferently between one thing or another depending merely on the advantages which each offers at the moment. This is a time in which it is necessary to help discern the moral quality inherent not only in political choices but also in the manner in which they are made and in the conception of political action which they imply.

Then Martini brought his "common sense" to bear, in a harsh accusation against *decisionismo*, surveys, plebescites, utilitarian liberalism, and politics as spectacle, in essence against the whole panoply of features which, in the words of Dossetti, denote the "idolatry" of the Berlusconian right.

On the opposite political side, Cardinal Martini articulated a broad theory of good government in matters on which there are differences but, which are, for Catholics, crucial, such as the care of the unborn. In the eyes of Pope John Paul II and Ruini this forms the typical stumbling block which sets off the *non possumus* [we cannot] regarding an alliance between Catholics and the Left in Italy. For Martini, instead:

> We find ourselves in a pluralistic and complex situation in which what we consider as a moral good may not always be immediately translated into law....It is not enough to proclaim the primary value of life in its entirety without also seeking the shared political paths which foster the love for life by creating social conditions favorable to young couples, to the condition of women, to the politics of the household, and to the reduction of the financial penalties on those who wish to enrich society with new life.

The newspaper which discussed the Archbishop of Milan's address in its entirety was neither *Avvenire*, which in its national edition did not dedicate even one line to it, nor even *L'Osservatore romano*, but rather *L'Unità*,[26] the PDS daily newspaper. This deafening silence of the ecclesiastical press spoke volumes. To reply, Cardinal Ruini wrote on Christmas Eve in the *Corriere della Sera*. He began by quoting Galli della Loggia and his own 1994 speech in memory of De Gasperi, and repeated his wish for the demolition of the "historical fence" that separated Catholics and secularists, and his hopes for places for dialogue between the two. He faulted the "limits of the Catholic cultural area" (in other words, the religious choice reproposed by Martini) for having "weighed heavily in the crisis of the DC." He again defined it as "improper and dangerous to burden either one or another choice of political alliance with a moral obligation." This was a polemic aimed against all those, from Dossetti to Sorge, to *Città dell'uomo*, to the Archbishop of Milan, who judge the "utilitarian neoliberalism" of the Right morally unacceptable for Christians. And again arguing with Martini, he asserted the correctness of proposing in Parliament, even in the absence of unanimous agreement, the "Catholic contents" of politics, from the safeguarding of the unborn to private schools. In proposing them, we "cannot be accused of fanaticism," wrote Ruini. "Democratic dialectic thrives, in fact, on disagreement no less than on agreement." The Church "must not renounce the pretense of truth inherent in Christian faith."

Thus at the end of 1995, the Italian Church no longer had its Catholic Party. It did not even have its disciplined and committed Catholic world. It had not, however, lost its political language, or rather its languages, almost all spoken only from on high. The languages of Cardinals Ruini and Martini are as authoritative as they are conflicting. Cardinal Ruini, the ecclesiastic with the devil of politics in his blood, dreams of an Italian duplicate of the German CDU, Cardinal Martini of something completely different. But tomorrow? Just as the end of the Catholic party snuck up on the hierarchy of the Church like a thief in the night, the same thing could happen to its current political language and projects.

Translated by Timothy Cooper and Susan Kertzer

Notes

1. F. Margiotta Broglio, "La laicità in questione", *Il Regno*, n. 22, 1995. To find the ecclesiastical texts cited in this chapter, see the documentary appendix of the biweekly, *Il Regno*, published by the Dehonians of Bologna.

2. Italian episcopal conference, *Christian reconciliation and the community of men. Proceedings of the 2° Convegno ecclesiale. Loreto April 9-13, 1985*, (Roma: editrice A.V.E., 1985).

3. Ruini's contribution in *L'Osservatore Romano*, September 30, 1991.

4. Full text of the papal letter, made public on January 10, 1994, in *Il Regno*, n. 3, 1994.

5. G.F. Brunelli, "Chiesa, società e politica: i cattolici e le prospettive del paese", in *Chiesa in Italia 1992*, (Bologna: Edizioni Dehoniane, 1993), p. 106.

6. Full text in *Il Regno*, n. 21, 1991.

7. Editorial of Dino Boffo in *Avvenire*, December 29, 1992.

8. G.F. Brunelli, "Nel tramonto della DC: chiesa e unità nazionale", in *Chiesa in Italia 1993*, (Bologna: Edizioni Dehoniane, 1994), p. 103.

9. Relative documentation in *Il Regno*, n.13, 1994.

10. Full text in *Il Regno*, n. 15, 1994.

11. His contributions between spring 1994 and spring 1995 in G. Dossetti, *I valori della Costituzione*, (Reggio Emilia: Edizioni S. Lorenzo, 1995).

12. Full text of the homily in *La Discussione*, June 11, 1994.

13. D. Boffo, *Avvenire*, November 25, 1994.

14. *Avvenire*, December 18, 1995.

15. Affirmed by Romano Prodi in an interview in *Il Regno*, n. 8, 1995.

16. Ruini's contribution in *Avvenire*, March 28, 1995.

17. *Avvenire*, March 26, 1995.

18. The main texts of the CEI assembly in *Il Regno*, n. 13, 1995.

19. *Avvenire*, July 20, 1995.

20. B. Sorge, "Ma ci sono partiti di 'veri' e di 'falsi' cattolici?", in *Famiglia Cristiana*, n. 26, 1995.

21. *Avvenire*, October 27, 1995.

22. G.F. Brunelli, "Coalizione democratica: i rischi della riduzione", in *Il Regno*, n. 14, 1995.

23. Relative texts in *Il Regno*, n. 21, 1995.

24. Dino Boffo, *Avvenire*, November 28, 1995.

25. *Avvenire*, December 19, 1995.

26. *L'Unità*, December 8, 1995.

Documentary Appendix

compiled by Marzia Zannini

The documentary appendix that completes this edition of *Italian Politics* continues the traditional data series on Italian political and social life.

The data are organized into three sections and offer a diversified panorama. The main sections supply a long-term background for the events illustrated in the volume. The first section (tables A1 to A7) refers to population, labor force, crime and national economical statistics, during the last ten years. This heterogeneous sections shows the trend of the most significant indicators of the social and economical tissue.

The second section is the central one (tables B1 to B8). It provides the results of the main electoral events, which were numerous and important in 1995. The regional elections of April 23 were carried out under new electoral laws; on June 11, twelve referenda on crucial themes were held. Regional elections results are followed by provincial and communal returns. Both absolute and percentage figures are reported.

The third part of the appendix reports data on political parties. As usual, information on both membership and the budget are presented.

TABLE A1   Resident Population by Age Group and by Sex (in Thousands)[a].

	Age Groups			
	0-14	15-64	65 and over	Total Population
	Both Sexes			
1985	11,177	38,632	7,270	57,080
1986	10,877	38,854	7,470	57,202
1987	10,541	39,085	7,664	57,290
1988	10,218	39,293	7,887	57,399
1989	9,924	39,467	8,112	57,504
1990	9,620	39,620	8,335	57,576
1991	9,385	39,804	8,558	57,746
1992	8,846	39,164	8,950	56,960
1993	8,725	39,210	8,352	56,287
1994[b]	8,620	39,247	9,401	57,268
	Men Only			
1985	5,732	19,080	2,927	27,740
1986	5,578	19,209	3,003	27,791
1987	5,408	19,348	3,076	27,833
1988	5,245	19,482	3,162	27,889
1989	5,096	19,586	3,255	27,938
1990	4,941	19,678	3,349	27,968
1991	4,825	19,802	3,445	28,072
1992	4,547	19,472	3,635	27,654
1993	4,468	19,508	3,507	27,483
1994[b]	4,415	19,528	3,848	27,791

[a] Rounded figures.
[b] Istat, *Rilevazione delle forze di lavoro*, (Rome, 1995)

Source: Istat, *Popolazione e movimento anagrafico dei comuni*, (Rome, 1985-1994).

TABLE A2   Present Population by Position on the Labor Market (in Thousand)

| | Employed | Labor Forces | | | Total |
| | | Seeking Job | | | |
		Unemployed	Seeking First Job	Other People Seeking Job	
		Both Sexes			
1985	20,742	468	1,215	698	23,123
1986	20,856	501	1,296	814	23,467
1987	20,836	547	1,354	932	23,669
1988	21,103	537	1,412	937	23,989
1989	21,004	507	1,405	954	23,870
1990	21,396	483	1,357	912	24,148
1991	21,592	469	1,285	898	24,244
1992	21,459	551	1,370	878	24,258
1993	20,466	845	1,005	485	22,801
1994	20,119	983	1,048	529	22,679
		Men Only			
1985	13,986	269	580	174	15,009
1986	13,953	289	617	209	15,068
1987	13,845	313	665	251	15,074
1988	13,990	305	687	248	15,230
1989	13,851	286	676	257	15,070
1990	14,015	264	667	246	15,192
1991	14,102	256	645	241	15,244
1992	13,945	297	692	238	15,172
1993[a]	13,332	490	518	90	14,430
1994	13,057	593	552	105	14,307

[a] Starting from 1993 new definitions of «active population» and «people seeking job» have been introduced. The definitions now apply to people who are at least 15 years old, whereas the prior definitions applied to 14-years-olds as well. In particular people who lose their job for reasons different from dismissal (resignation or end of temporary employement) are excluded from «other people seeking job».

Source: Istat, *Annuario statistico italiano*, (Rome, 1986-1995).

TABLE A3 Labor Conflicts: Number and Impact of Contractual and Non-Contractual (i.e. Political) Disputes (in Thousands)

	Conflicts	Participants	Number of Hours Lost
		Contractual Disputes	
1985	1,166	1,224	11,036
1986	1,462	2,940	36,742
1987	1,146	1,473	20,147
1988	1,767	1,609	17,086
1989	1,295	2,108	21,001
1990	1,094	1,634	36,269
1991	784	750	11,573
1992	895	621	5,605
1993	1,047	848	8,796
1994	858	745	7,651
		Non-Contractual Disputes	
1985	5	3,619	15,779
1986	7	667	2,764
1987	3	2,800	12,093
1988	2	1,103	6,120
1989	2	2,344	10,052
1990	-	-	-
1991	7	2,202	9,322
1992	8	2,557	13,905
1993	7	3,536	15,084
1994	3	1,868	15,967

Source: Istat, Annuario statistico italiano, (Rome, 1986-1995).

TABLE A4   Births and Marriages

	Births		Marriages			
	Total Births	% Variation	Total Marriages	% Variation	Religious	% Variation
1985	577,345	-1.79	298,523	-0.79	256,911	-1.04
1986	555,445	-3.79	297,540	-0.33	255,407	-0.59
1987	551,539	-0.70	306,264	2.93	261,847	2.52
1988	569,698	3.29	318,296	3.93	266,534	1.79
1989	560,688	-1.58	321,272	0.93	267,617	0.41
1990	569,255	1.53	319,711	-0.49	266,084	-0.57
1991	562,787	-1.14	312,061	-2.39	257,555	-3.21
1992	575,216	2.21	312,348	0.09	255,355	-0.85
1993	552,587	-3.93	302,230	-3.24	248,111	-2.84
1994	536,665	-2.88	285,112	-5.66	230,573	-7.07

Source: Istat, *Annuario statistico italiano,* (Rome, 1986-1995).

TABLE A5 Classification of Officially Recorded Crimes [a]

	Against Persons	Against the Family or Morality	Against Property	Against the Economy or Public Trust	Against the State	Other	Total
1985	125,940	13,559	1,369,325	385,691	37,831	68,090	2,000,436
1986	125,192	14,118	1,355,507	410,934	41,734	82,688	2,030,173
1987	138,272	14,826	1,507,040	394,360	47,093	103,395	2,204,986
1988	136,685	14,228	1,529,876	416,387	46,158	90,597	2,233,931
1989	125,769	13,073	1,573,805	422,166	41,968	97,314	2,274,095
1990	103,039	7,363	1,575,016	223,740	21,550	67,366	1,998,074
1991	121,881	10,256	2,255,918	326,584	35,590	66,834	2,817,063
1992	202,149	11,552	2,032,579	378,331	43,297	72,983	2,740,891
1993	183,072	12,694	1,980,831	373,155	54,034	76,182	2,679,968
1994	194,007	13,731	2,059,869	387,791	59,690	77,654	2,792,742

[a] For 1990 and susequent years, the data are no longer fully comparable with those for earlier years. For criminal accusations against a person already subjected to investigations, the new Code of Criminal Procedure (Article 405) identifies the start of judicial action as the moment at which the person is formally charged with a crime. Unlike previous years, then, the statistics no longer include cases closed without trial for lack of evidence or other causes. In comparing 1990 and 1991 data, it should be kept in mind that organizational difficulties linked to the implementation of the new Code have caused delays in judicial action and in the transmittal of information to ISTAT. Thus, for most classifications above, the ISTAT data register decreases in 1990 and then increases in 1991.

Source: Istat, *Annuario statistico italiano*, (Rome, 1986-1995).

TABLE A6   Gross Domestic Product (in Market Prices) and the Consumer Price
Index: Yearly Values and Percentage Variations Figures Over the Previous Year

	Gross Domestic Product				Consumer Price Index (1990=100)	
	In Current Prices [a]	% Variation	In 1985 Prices	% Variation	Index	% Variation
1985	810,580	11.69	810,580	2.60	75.90	9.21
1986	899,903	11.02	834,262	2.92	80.30	5.80
1987	983,803	9.32	860,422	3.14	84.10	4.73
1988	1,091,837	10.98	895,397	4.06	88.40	5.11
1989	1,193,462	9.31	921,714	2.94	93.90	6.22
1990	1,312,066	9.94	941,387	2.13	100.00	6.50
1991	1,426,580	8.73	953,181	1.25	106.30	6.30
1992	1,507,190	5.65	962,037	0.93	111.70	5.08
1993	1,560,114	3.51	953,446	-0.89	116.70	4.48
1994 [b]	1,641,105	5.19	968,986	1.63	120.50	3.26

[a] In billions of lire.
[b] Istat, *Conti economici nazionali*, (Rome, 1995).

Source: Istat, *Annuario statistico italiano*, (Rome, 1985-1996).

TABLE A7   National Debt and Annual Budgetary Deficit, in Absolute Terms and as a Percentage of the Gross Domestic Product

	National Debt			Budget Deficit		
	Absolute Figures [a]	% Variation	% of GDP	Absolute Figures [a]	% Variation	% of GDP
1985	683,044	21.65	84.27	107,702	39.69	13.29
1986	793,583	16.18	88.19	116,826	8.47	12.98
1987	910,542	14.74	92.55	128,226	9.76	13.03
1988[b]	1,035,812	13.76	94.87	124,986	-2.53	11.45
1989	1,168,361	12.80	97.90	119,466	-4.42	10.01
1990	1,318,936	12.89	100.52	122,471	2.52	9.33
1991	1,485,742	12.65	103.94	118,620	-3.14	8.30
1992	1,675,276	12.76	111.36	107,189	-9.64	7.13
1993	1,862,937	11.20	119.41	149,128	39.13	9.56
1994[c]	1,815,729	-2.53	110.64	147,864	-0.85	9.01

[a] In billions of lire.

[b] Some methodological innovations in banking statistics determine a discontinuity in the data series. starting from December 31, 1988.

[c] Istat, «Bollettino mensile di statistica», (Roma, 1994).

Source: Banca d'Italia, *Relazione annuale*, (Rome, 1994).

TABLE B1 Regional Elections, April 23. Regional and National Returns (Absolute Number of Votes Cast).

Lists	Piemonte	Lombardia	Veneto	Liguria	Emilia Romagna	Toscana	Umbria	Marche
Forza Italia-Polo Pop.	588,171	1,455,706	606,977	234,151	467,863	409,266	93,841	164,829
Alleanza Nazionale (c)	247,103	496,939	271,835	107,557	264,367	281,298	84,065	129,220
Centro Cristiano Democratico	65,099	110,058	90,285	25,447	59,898	53,291	11,124	26,756
Lega Nord	217,194	879,139	422,410	62,755	86,400	15,049	-	4,252
Lega Italia Federale	-	-	-	-	-	-	-	-
PDS	478,615	821,280	416,799	290,829	1,106,929	874,463	199,779	283,429
Rifondazione Comunista	203,842	381,221	126,594	76,507	196,274	237,405	56,894	86,293
Green Federation	59,238	154,624	102,156	28,101	82,178	57,666	9,884	24,632
Progressisti	-	-	-	-	-	-	6,103	-
Popolari	136,664	321,314	271,423	54,843	144,398	-	-	51,057
Patto Democratici	76,592	146,293	109,778	34,127	96,042	-	19,874	38,695
Popolari Democratici	8,507	11,146	-	-	-	-	-	-
Part. Pens.	35,162	71,608	-	14,858	-	-	-	-
Popolari - Patto Dem.(b)	-	-	-	-	-	135,895	-	-
PRI	-	-	11,686	-	34,802	16,395	-	16,866
PRI- Fed. Laburista (d)	-	-	-	-	-	-	-	-
Fed. Laburista	-	18,682	-	4,345	-	30,204	10,451	4,648
Pannella-Riformatori	35,899	90,445	29,254	14,226	33,995	28,295	4,368	7,344
Fronte Autonomista	2,703	5,596	-	2,396	-	-	-	-
Mov. Soc. Tricolore	-	-	-	-	-	-	-	4,397
Green Green	31,145	-	-	-	-	-	-	-
Other Green lists	-	-	-	-	-	-	-	-
Others (a)	16,356	14,518	73,342	9,827	-	-	21,458	-
Total valid votes	2,202,290	4,978,569	2,532,539	959,969	2,573,146	2,139,227	517,841	842,418
Entitled to vote	3,682,963	7,506,052	3,769,114	1,479,131	3,412,766	3,032,797	706,444	1,241,554
Voters	3,056,372	6,321,953	3,213,604	1,177,279	3,012,713	2,583,567	604,749	1,050,054
% of voters/entitled to vote	83.0	84.2	85.3	79.6	88.3	85.2	85.6	84.6
Invalid votes	377,857	487,842	260,762	128,318	194,170	221,997	50,972	109,057
% of invalid votes/voters	12.4	7.7	8.1	10.9	6.4	8.6	8.4	10.4
Regional list votes only	476,225	855,542	420,303	88,992	245,397	222,343	35,936	98,579
% of regional list votes/voters	15.6	13.5	13.1	7.6	8.1	8.6	5.9	9.4

(continues)

TABLE B1 *(continued)*

Lists	Lazio	Abruzzo	Molise	Campania	Puglia	Basilicata	Calabria	National Total
Forza Italia-Polo Pop.	530,860	141,685	37,132	503,042	404,417	55,193	182,127	5,875,260
Alleanza Nazionale (c)	687,061	128,539	32,603	487,291	398,597	38,738	151,234	3,806,447
Centro Cristiano Democratico	117,329	53,745	21,380	259,380	109,888	16,635	83,707	1,104,022
Lega Nord	-	-	-	-	-	-	-	1,687,199
Lega Italia Federale	13,516	-	-	8,849	6,841	-	4,173	33,379
PDS	763,077	173,726	38,102	521,135	432,171	70,111	-	6,470,445
Rifondazione Comunista	258,336	65,668	13,259	246,170	158,446	17,144	80,851	2,204,904
Green Federation	100,211	20,886	2,919	78,277	51,607	8,333	-	780,712
Progressisti	-	-	-	-	-	-	205,734	211,837
Popolari	-	62,597	20,759	220,557	152,284	51,885	92,728	1,580,509
Patto Democratici	-	48,395	17,479	147,948	112,776	16,393	46,916	911,308
Popolari Democratici	-	-	-	-	-	-	-	19,653
Part. Pens.	-	-	-	-	-	-	-	121,628
Popolari - Patto Dem.(b)	167,518	-	-	-	-	-	-	303,413
PRI	31,355	-	-	30,524	-	-	34,865	130,005
PRI- Fed. Laburista (d)	-	-	-	-	42,494	-	-	88,982
Fed. Laburista	-	-	-	-	-	25,892	-	94,222
Pannella-Riformatori	35,536	14,689	-	27,460	28,790	1,900	5,048	357,249
Fronte Autonomista	-	-	-	-	-	-	-	10,695
Mov. Soc. Tricolore	37,869	10,000	-	33,633	10,879	1,814	8,609	107,201
Green Green	-	-	-	-	-	-	-	31,145
Other Green lists	13,259	-	-	-	-	-	-	13,259
Others (a)	45,608	-	5,611	101,840	43,670	17,639	29,973	379,842
Total valid votes	2,801,535	719,930	189,244	2,666,106	1,952,860	321,677	925,965	26,323,316
Entitled to vote	4,409,404	1,156,448	318,775	4,612,101	3,330,735	521,403	1,771,144	40,950,831
Voters	3,584,259	887,157	230,127	3,408,003	2,520,633	409,663	1,215,072	33,275,205
% of voters/entitled to vote	81.3	76.7	72.2	73.9	75.7	78.6	68.6	81.3
Invalid votes	271,363	118,883	25,842	427,397	363,526	57,267	164,309	3,259,563
% of invalid votes/voters	7.6	13.4	11.2	12.5	14.4	14.0	13.5	9.8
Regional list votes only	511,361	48,344	15,041	314,500	204,247	30,719	124,798	3,692,326
% of regional list votes/voters	14.3	5.4	6.5	9.2	8.1	7.5	10.3	11.1

(a) "Others" includes the local lists.
(b) In Toscana Liberal participates at the coalition.
(c) Alleanza Nazionale in Umbria was in a coalition with two local lists.
(d) Socialdemocratici are included.

TABLE B2 Regional Elections, April 23. Regional and National Returns (Percentage Number of Valid Votes Cast).

Lists	Piemonte	Lombardia	Veneto	Liguria	Emilia Romagna	Toscana	Umbria	Marche
Forza Italia-Polo Pop.	26.7	29.2	24.0	24.4	18.2	19.1	18.1	19.6
Alleanza Nazionale (c)	11.2	10.0	10.7	11.2	10.3	13.1	16.2	15.3
Centro Cristiano Democratico	3.0	2.2	3.6	2.7	2.3	2.5	2.1	3.2
Lega Nord	9.9	17.7	16.7	6.5	3.4	0.7	-	0.5
Lega Italia Federale	-	-	-	-	-	-	-	-
PDS	21.7	16.5	16.5	30.3	43.0	40.9	38.6	33.6
Rifondazione Comunista	9.3	7.7	5.0	8.0	7.6	11.1	11.0	10.2
Green Federation	2.7	3.1	4.0	2.9	3.2	2.7	1.9	2.9
Progressisti	-	-	-	-	-	-	1.2	-
Popolari	6.2	6.5	10.7	5.7	5.6	-	-	6.1
Patto Democratici	3.5	2.9	4.3	3.6	3.7	-	3.8	4.6
Popolari Democratici	0.4	0.2	-	-	-	-	-	-
Part. Pens.	1.6	1.4	-	1.5	-	-	-	-
Popolari - Patto Dem.(b)	-	-	-	-	-	6.4	-	-
PRI								
PRI- Fed. Laburista (d)	-	-	0.5	-	1.4	-	-	-
Fed. Laburista	-	0.4	-	0.5	-	1.4	2.0	0.6
Pannella-Riformatori	1.6	1.8	1.2	1.5	1.3	1.3	0.8	0.9
Fronte Autonomista	0.1	0.1	-	0.2	-	-	-	-
Mov. Soc. Tricolore	-	-	-	-	-	-	-	0.5
Green Green	1.4	-	-	-	-	-	-	-
Other Green Lists	-	-	-	-	-	-	-	-
Others (a)	0.7	0.3	2.9	1.0	-	-	4.1	-
Total valid votes	100.0	100.0	100.0	100.0	100.0	100.0	100.0	100.0

(continues)

252

TABLE B2 *(continued)*

Lists	Lazio	Abruzzo	Molise	Campania	Puglia	Basilicata	Calabria	National Total
Forza Italia-Polo Pop.	18.9	19.7	19.6	18.9	20.7	17.2	19.7	22.3
Alleanza Nazionale (c)	24.5	17.9	17.2	18.3	20.4	12.0	16.3	14.5
Centro Cristiano Democratico	4.2	7.5	11.3	9.7	5.6	5.2	9.0	4.2
Lega Nord	-	-	-	-	-	-	-	6.4
Lega Italia Federale	0.5	-	-	0.3	0.4	-	0.5	0.1
PDS	27.2	24.1	20.1	19.5	22.1	21.8	-	24.6
Rifondazione Comunista	9.2	9.1	7.0	9.2	8.1	5.3	8.7	8.4
Green Federation	3.6	2.9	1.5	2.9	2.6	2.6	-	3.0
Progressisti	-	-	-	-	-	-	22.2	0.8
Popolari	-	8.7	11.0	8.3	7.8	16.1	10.0	6.0
Patto Democratici	-	6.7	9.2	5.5	5.8	5.1	5.1	3.5
Popolari Democratici	-	-	-	-	-	-	-	0.0
Part. Pens.	-	-	-	-	-	-	-	0.5
Popolari - Patto Dem.(b)	6.0	-	-	-	-	-	-	1.2
PRI	1.1	-	-	1.1	2.2	-	3.8	0.5
PRI- Fed. Laburista (d)	-	-	-	-	-	-	-	0.3
Fed. Laburista	-	-	-	-	-	8.0	-	0.4
Pannella-Riformatori	1.3	2.0	-	1.0	1.5	0.6	0.5	1.4
Fronte Autonomista	-	-	-	-	-	-	-	0.0
Mov. Soc.Tricolore	1.4	1.4	-	1.3	0.6	0.6	0.9	0.4
Green Green	-	-	-	-	-	-	-	0.1
Other Green lists	0.5	-	-	-	-	-	-	0.1
Others (a)	1.6	-	3.0	3.8	2.2	5.5	3.2	1.4
Total valid votes	100.0	100.0	100.0	100.0	100.0	100.0	100.0	100.0

(ª) "Others" includes the local lists.
(ᵇ) In Toscana Liberal participates at the coalition.
(ᶜ) Alleanza nazionale in Umbria was in a coalition with two local lists.
(ᵈ) Socialdemocratici are included.

Source: Calculated from data provided by Ministero dell'Interno- Direzione centrale per i servizi elettorali.

TABLE B3   Provincial Election, April 23. Summary of National Returns.

Lists	Valid Votes	%	Seats
Forza Italia	1,692,617	6.3	112
Forza Italia-Polo Pop.	2,628,544	9.8	143
Forza Italia-CCD	41,164	0.2	5
Forza Italia-PPI	63,668	0.2	6
FI-Fed.FLD-Lib.	36,296	0.1	4
Alleanza Nazionale	3,392,258	12.7	205
Centro Cristiano Democratico	832,164	3.1	44
FI-PP-CCD-AN-Altre	742,791	2.8	66
AN-U. Umbria-CPA	91,825	0.3	9
Unione di Centro	17,419	0.0	-
Lega Nord	1,775,432	6.7	120
Lega Italia Federale	17,499	0.0	-
Lega Nord-GAP-PSR	2,580	0.0	-
Federalisti	3,388	0.0	-
PDS	5,855,142	21.9	605
PDS-altre	88,433	0.3	5
Rifondazione Comunista	2,289,848	8.6	82
Green Federation	747,969	2.8	42
Progressisti	160,153	0.6	30
P. Popolare Italiano	815,284	3.1	58
Popolari	1,646,595	6.2	180
Patto dei Democratici	1,043,610	3.9	93
Popolari-Patto Dem.	91,228	0.3	21
Popolari-Socialdemocr.	11,475	0.0	1
Pop.-Patto D.-Lib-Lega Nord	36,203	0.1	2
Popolari-Soc. It. Dem.	10,270	0.0	1
PRI	99,587	0.4	3
Fed. Laburista	143,113	0.5	8
Socialdemocrazia	36,899	0.1	1
Soc.P Lad Tri-Altre	82,317	0.3	4
Crist. Soc-F. Laburisti	3,705	0.0	-
So.l.e	1,770	0.0	-
La Rete -Mov. Dem.	3,661	0.0	-
Pannella-Riformatori	369,224	1.4	-
Center-Left Mixed	112,143	0.4	5
Center Mixed	64,320	0.2	7
Center-Right Mixed	98,296	0.4	10
Mov. Soc. Tricolore	139,534	0.5	-
Piemonte Naz. Europea	22,858	0.0	-
Fronte Autonomista	3,964	0.0	-
Nuova It.Aut. Veneta	98,113	0.4	8
Psr-Sin.Lib	42,992	0.2	-
Other Green Lists	77,261	0.3	-
Other League	58,320	0.2	1
Autonomist Lists	181,978	0.7	15
Civic Lists	225,338	0.8	12
Others	696,701	2.6	87
Total	26,695,949	100.0	1,995

A total of 2,217 seats were assigned; 222 seats are reserved for lists the mayoral candidates of which were not elected.

Entitled to vote	37,288,032
Voters	30,301,667
% of voters/entitled to vote	81.3
Invalid votes	3,605,718
% of invalid votes /voters	11.9
of which blank ballots	1,375,345
% of blank ballots/invalid votes	38.1

Source: Calculated from data provided by Ministero dell'Interno- Direzione centrale per i servizi elettorali.

TABLE B4   Municipal Elections, April 23, 1995: 278 Municipalities with over 15,000 Inhabitants. Summary of National Returns

Lists	Valid Votes	%	Seats
Forza Italia	310,764	4.9	284
Alleanza Nazionale	609,925	9.6	429
Centro Crist. Dem.	157,311	2.5	115
FI-PP-CCD-An-altre	537,797	8.5	372
Unione di Centro	7,621	0.1	4
Lega Nord	218,240	3.5	189
Lega Italia Federale	1,881	0.0	0
Lega Nord-altre	7876	0.1	13
Federalisti	279	0.0	0
PDS	1,349,558	21.3	1,545
PDS-altre	5,384	0.0	14
Rifondaz. Comunista	444,978	7.0	275
Rifondaz. Comunista-altre	9,588	0.2	11
Green Federation	149,590	2.4	99
Progressisti	60,162	1.0	100
P. Popolare Italiano	187,814	3.0	146
Popolari	246,199	3.9	284
Patto Democratici	189,497	3.0	169
LN-Patto D-Pop-altre	22,408	0.4	17
Popolari- Patto Dem.	18,139	0.3	18
PRI	26,963	0.4	16
Fed. Laburista	26,985	0.4	15
Cristiano Sociali	5,684	0.0	8
Socialdemocrazia	2,457	0.0	2
So.le	1,080	0.0	0
La Rete-Mov. Dem.	891	0.0	1
Pannella-Riformatori	37,324	0.6	0
Left Mixed	88,802	1.4	152
Center-Left Mixed	464,326	7.3	602
Center Mixed	397,379	6.3	479
Center-Right Mixed	294,580	4.7	237
Right Mixed	3,254	0.0	1
Mov. Soc. Tricolore	7,017	0.1	0
Piemonte Naz. Europea	148	0.0	0
PSR-Sin. lib.	3,232	0.0	0
Other Green Lists	1,752	0.0	1
Autonomist Lists	15,602	0.2	12
Civic Lists	371,682	5.9	255
Others	37,250	0.6	24
Total	6,321,419	100.0	5,889

A total of 6,752 seats were assigned; 863seats are reserved for lists of which the mayoral candidates were not elected.

Entitled to vote	8,490,683
Voters	7,211,082
% of voters/entitled to vote	84.9
Invalid votes	889,657
% of invalid votes/voters	12.3
of which blank ballots	173,051
% of blank ballots/invalid votes	14.5
Mayor votes only	405,425
% of Mayor votes only	5.6

Source: Calculated from data provided by Ministero dell'Interno- Direzione centrale per i servizi elettorali.

TABLE B5   Municipal Elections, April 23, 1995: 4,841 Municipalities with up to 15,000 Inhabitants. Summary of National Returns.

Lists	Valid Votes	%	Seats
Forza Italia	1,467	0.0	5
Alleanza Nazionale	81,820	0.9	277
Centro Crist. Dem.	17,589	0.2	109
FI-PP-CCD-AN-altre	54,006	0.6	193
Unione di Centro	164	0.0	9
Lega Nord	224,387	2.4	751
Lega Italia Federale	20	0.0	-
Lega Nord-altre	111,311	1.2	425
Federalisti	92	0.0	4
PDS	67,319	0.7	342
PDS-altre	9,069	0.0	60
Rifondaz. Comunista	125,682	1.4	321
Rifondaz. Comunista-altre	3,033	0.0	6
PDS-Rif. Comunista	3,998	0.0	6
Green Federation	2,728	0.0	5
Progressisti	112,508	1.2	565
P. Popolare Italiano	91,278	1.0	597
Popolari	88,848	1.0	646
Patto Democratici	7,775	0.0	32
LN-Patto D-Pop-altre	36,657	0.4	142
PRI	2,931	0.0	5
Fed. Laburista	805	0.0	2
Pannella-Riformatori	263	0.0	-
Left Mixed	400,066	4.3	2,889
Center-Left Mixed	2,830,727	30.7	18,925
Center	1,911,371	20.7	16,094
Center-Right Mixed	1,124,241	12.2	5,844
Right Mixed	16,139	0.2	96
Mov. Soc. Tricolore	1,062	0.0	1
Piemonte Naz. Europea	660	0.0	5
Other Green Lists	27	0.0	8
Other Leagues	15	0.0	4
Autonomist Lists	2,386	0.0	23
Civic Lists	1,879,250	20.4	16,035
Others	1,881	0.0	10
Total	9,211,575	100.0	64,436

424 seats were not assigned.

Entitled to vote	11,688,468
Voters	9,892,783
% of voters/entitled to vote	84.6
Invalid votes	681,208
% of invalid votes/voters	6.9
of which blank ballots	385,256
% of blank ballots/invalid votes	56.6

Source: Calculated from data provided by Ministero dell'Interno- Direzione centrale per i servizi elettorali.

TABLE B6   Municipal Elections, November 19,1995: 25 Municipalities with over 15,000 Inhabitants. Summary of National Returns.

Lists	Valid Votes	%	Seats
Forza Italia	53,083	11.4	75
Alleanza Nazionale	52,085	11.2	61
Centro Crist. Dem.	27,822	6.0	26
Lega Nord	12,557	2.7	7
Lega Italia Federale	291	0.0	-
Federalisti	231	0.0	-
PDS	59,786	12.9	92
Rifond. Comunista	22,681	4.9	27
Green Federation	7,183	1.5	5
CDU	29,459	6.3	52
PPI (Pop.)	36,816	7.9	49
Patto Democratici	15,663	3.4	14
PRI	6,250	1.3	5
Fed. Laburista	5,833	1.3	3
So.l.e	1,613	0.3	1
La Rete-Mov. Dem	680	0.1	-
Left Mixed	11,768	2.5	18
Center-Left Mixed	43,793	9.4	72
Center Mixed	44,641	9.6	41
Center-Right Mixed	10,589	2.3	10
Right Mixed	405	0.0	-
Mov. Soc. Tricolore	2,883	0.6	1
Civic Lists	18,103	3.9	7
Others	1,028	0.2	-
Total	465,243	100.0	566

A total of 630 seats were assigned; 64 seats are reserved for lists the mayoral candidates of which were not elected.

Entitled to vote	677,316
Voters	519,884
% of voters/entitled to vote	76.8
Invalid votes	25,665
% of invalid votes/voters	4.9
of which blank ballots	5,784
% of blank ballots/invalid votes	6.4
Mayor votes only	28,976
% of Mayor votes	5.6

Source: Calculated from data provided by Ministero dell'Interno- Direzione centrale per i servizi elettorali.

TABLE B7 Municipal Elections, November 19, 1995: 108 Municipalities with up to 15,000 Inhabitants. Summary of National Returns.

Lists	Valid Votes	%	Seats
Forza Italia	2,504	0.9	10
Alleanza Nazionale	2,771	1.0	18
Lega Nord	5,936	2.2	40
PDS	2,886	1.1	18
Rifond. Comunista	5,477	2.0	15
CDU	1,675	0.6	6
PPI (Pop.)	2,953	1.1	23
Socialdemocrazia	1,212	0.4	2
Left Mixed	10,427	3.8	53
Center-Left Mixed	83,814	30.7	485
Center Mixed	40,479	14.8	291
Center-Right Mixed	61,638	22.5	249
Other Leagues	123	0.0	-
Autonomist Lists	81	0.0	5
Civic Lists	51,435	18.8	316
Others	22	0.0	1
Total	273,433	100.0	1,532

32 seats were not assigned because of not valid elections in 2 Municipalities.

Entitled to vote	374,209
Voters	285,752
% of voters/entitled to vote	76.4
Invalid votes	12,319
% of invalid votes/voters	4.3
of which blank ballots	4,310
% of blank ballots/invalid votes	5.6

Source: Calculated from data provided by Ministero dell'Interno- Direzione centrale per i servizi elettorali.

TABLE B8-1 Popular Referendum June 11, 1995 n.1: "Abolish Restrictions on Union Accorded Negotiating Rights". Regional and National Returns.

	Valle D'Aosta	Piemonte	Lombardia	Liguria	Trentino A.A.	Veneto	Friuli V.G.	Emilia Romagna	Toscana	Umbria
Entitled to vote	100,944	3,683,821	7,509,878	1,477,911	752,150	3,771,080	1,081,243	3,413,315	3,032,757	706,841
Voters	55,638	2,302,769	4,976,013	901,243	443,253	2,503,669	625,228	2,359,374	1,928,317	435,505
% voters	55.1	62.5	66.3	61.0	58.9	66.4	57.8	69.1	63.6	61.6
"Yes" votes	24,501	1,030,396	2,415,628	398,406	178,636	1,170.047	304,766	851,903	766,149	180,388
%	51.6	50.0	53.0	48.9	45.9	51.0	53.3	39.5	44.0	46.4
"No" votes	22,959	1,031,611	2,143,358	416,497	210,406	1,122,056	267,061	1,306,856	973,304	208,294
%	48.4	50.0	47.0	51.1	54.1	49.0	46.7	60.5	56.0	53.6
Total valid votes	47,460	2,062,007	4,558,986	814,903	389,042	2,292,103	571,827	2,158,759	1,739,453	388,682
Invalid votes	8,178	240,716	416,396	86,323	54,206	211,201	53,369	200,248	188,795	46,816
% of invalid votes/voters	14.7	10.5	8.4	9.6	12.2	8.4	8.5	8.5	9.8	10.7
of which blank ballots	6,945	192,694	346,701	70,877	47,593	167,626	42,707	167,494	156,957	37,469
% of blank ballots/invalid votes	84.9	80.1	83.3	80.0	87.8	79.4	82.1	83.6	83.1	80.0

	Marche	Lazio	Abruzzo	Molise	Campania	Puglia	Basilicata	Calabria	Sicilia	Sardegna	Total Italy
Entitled to vote	1,242,148	4,414,698	1,157,881	319,004	4,616,981	3,335,480	521,790	1,772,684	4,338,240	1,381,882	48,630,728
Voters	765,112	2,587,153	589,333	125,897	1,950,442	1,493,995	200,518	659,217	2,106,482	685,890	27,695,048
% voters	61.6	58.6	50.9	39.5	42.2	44.8	38.4	42.8	48.6	49.6	56.9
"Yes" votes	309,645	1,310,407	263,297	54,139	816,053	645,120	79,153	272,558	909,636	316,205	12,297,033
%	45.9	56.0	52.4	51.9	48.6	51.3	47.6	51.0	52.8	52.2	50.0
"No" votes	364,508	1,030,425	238,847	50,117	862,196	611,465	87,110	261,862	812,517	289,305	12,310,754
%	54.1	44.0	47.6	48.1	51.4	48.7	52.4	49.0	47.2	47.8	50.0
Total valid votes	674,153	2,340,832	502,144	104,256	1,678,249	1,256,585	166,263	534,420	1,722,153	605,510	24,607,787
Invalid votes	90,908	245,530	87,185	21,558	272,000	237,384	34,248	124,348	383,416	80,314	3,083,139
% of invalid votes/voters	11.9	9.5	14.8	17.1	13.9	15.9	17.1	18.9	18.2	11.7	11.1
of which blank ballots	75,007	121,076	71,139	18,208	228,505	200,494	27,836	101,651	292,737	59,493	2,433,279
% of blank ballots/invalid votes	82.6	49.3	81.6	84.5	84.0	84.5	81.3	81.7	76.3	74.1	78.9

Source: Calculated from data provided by Ministero dell'Interno- Direzione centrale per i servizi elettorali.

*"The sum of valid votes" and "invalid votes" sometime differs from voters because of a negligible amount of contested votes.

TABLE B8-2 Popular Referendum June 11, 1995 n.2: "Reduce Restrictions on Union Accorded Negotiating Rights". Regional and National Returns.

	Valle D'Aosta	Piemonte	Lombardia	Liguria	Trentino A.A.	Veneto	Friuli V.G.	Emilia Romagna	Toscana	Umbria
Entitled to vote	100,944	3,683,821	7,509,878	1,477,911	752,150	3,771,080	1,081,243	3,413,315	3,032,757	706,841
Voters	55,648	2,301,503	4,973,427	900,411	443,139	2,500,350	624,315	2,357,111	1,925,441	435,149
% voters	55.1	62.5	66.2	60.9	58.9	66.3	57.7	69.1	63.5	61.6
"Yes" votes	26,370	1,181,188	2,882,971	568,309	196,103	1,318,853	337,914	1,476,144	1,199,299	251,484
%	56.5	57.9	63.8	70.5	51.0	58.1	59.8	69.0	69.7	65.3
"No" votes	20,332	859,524	1,634,531	237,712	188,402	949,999	227,473	664,299	522,019	133,346
%	43.5	42.1	36.2	29.5	49.0	41.9	40.2	31.0	30.3	34.7
Total valid votes	46,702	2,040,712	4,517,502	806,021	384,505	2,268,852	565,387	2,140,443	1,721,318	384,830
Invalid votes	8,946	260,628	455,416	94,385	58,632	231,134	58,904	216,638	204,026	50,290
% of invalid votes/voters	16.1	11.3	9.2	10.5	13.2	9.2	9.4	9.2	10.6	11.6
of which blank ballots	7,742	211,823	383,359	78,467	52,319	172,165	48,753	181,123	173,309	41,055%
of blank ballots/invalid votes	86.5	81.3	84.2	83.1	89.2	74.5	82.8	83.6	84.9	81.6

	Marche	Lazio	Abruzzo	Molise	Campania	Puglia	Basilicata	Calabria	Sicilia	Sardegna	Total Italy
Entitled to vote	1,242,148	4,414,698	1,157,881	319,004	4,616,981	3,335,480	521,790	1,772,684	4,338,240	1,381,882	48,630,728
Voters	764,552	2,585,233	588,739	125,760	1,951,253	1,491,772	200,257	658,535	2,106,002	685,444	27,674,041
% voters	61.6	58.6	50.8	39.4	42.3	44.7	38.4	37.1	48.5	49.6	56.9
"Yes" votes	415,143	1,548,976	303,042	59,344	931,225	701,458	90,056	295,294	958,154	364,485	15,105,812
%	62.3	66.8	61.2	57.9	56.2	56.9	55.2	56.2	56.4	61.0	62.1
"No" votes	250,889	769,241	192,389	43,155	724,734	530,352	73,150	230,335	741,501	232,688	9,226,071
%	37.7	33.2	38.8	42.1	43.8	43.1	44.8	43.8	43.6	39.0	37.9
Total valid votes	666,032	2,318,217	495,431	102,499	1,655,959	1,231,810	163,206	525,629	1,699,655	597,173	24,331,883
Invalid votes	98,518	266,118	93,304	23,135	295,233	259,955	37,050	132,528	405,487	88,226	3,338,553
% of invalid votes/voters	12.9	10.3	15.8	18.4	15.1	17.4	18.5	20.1	19.3	12.9	12.1
of which blank ballots	83,116	135,333	78,667	19,881	250,748	223,918	30,639	110,685	318,652	73,519	2,675,273
of blank ballots/invalid votes	84.4	50.9	84.3	85.9	84.9	86.1	82.7	83.5	78.6	83.3	80.1

Source: Calculated from data provided by Ministero dell'Interno- Direzione centrale per i servizi elettorali.

*"The sum valid votes" of "invalid votes" sometime differs from voters because of a negligible amount of contested votes.

TABLE B8-3 Popular Referendum June 11, 1995 n.3: "Abolish Restrictions on Negotiating Rights in State Sector". Regional and National Returns.

	Valle D'Aosta	Piemonte	Lombardia	Liguria	Trentino A.A.	Veneto	Friuli V.G.	Emilia Romagna	Toscana	Umbria
Entitled to vote	100,944	3,683,821	7,509,878	1,477,911	752,150	3,771,080	1,081,243	3,413,315	3,032,757	706,841
Voters	55,609	2,301,450	4,972,345	900,111	443,195	2,499,995	624,128	2,356,017	1,925,980	435,068
% voters	55.1	62.5	66.2	60.9	58.9	66.3	57.7	69.0	63.5	61.6
"Yes" votes	27,093	1,232,252	2,969,861	584,705	201,623	1,377,358	353,864	1,553,385	1,245,918	259,611
%	58.4	60.7	66.0	72.8	52.1	61.0	62.9	72.8	72.6	67.7
"No" votes	19,274	796,910	1,528,822	218,672	185,258	880,600	208,454	580,023	470,675	123,683
%	41.6	39.3	34.0	27.2	47.9	39.0	37.1	27.2	27.4	32.3
Total valid votes	46,367	2,029,162	4,498,683	803,377	386,881	2,257,958	562,318	2,133,408	1,716,593	383,294
Invalid votes	9,242	272,161	472,729	96,717	56,312	241,708	61,794	222,542	209,320	51,741
% of invalid votes/voters	16.6	11.8	9.5	10.7	12.7	9.7	9.9	9.4	10.9	11.9
of which blank ballots	7,944	221,601	399,356	81,264	49,818	201,515	51,262	191,498	177,981	42,514
% of blank ballots/invalid votes	86.0	81.4	84.5	84.0	88.5	83.4	83.0	86.1	85.0	82.2

	Marche	Lazio	Abruzzo	Molise	Campania	Puglia	Basilicata	Calabria	Sicilia	Sardegna	Total Italy
Entitled to vote	1,242,148	4,414,698	1,157,881	319,004	4,616,981	3,335,480	521,790	1,772,684	4,338,240	1,381,882	48,630,728
Voters	764,129	2,585,041	589,250	125,949	1,950,091	1,491,531	200,241	658,750	2,106,078	685,455	27,670,413
% voters	61.5	58.6	50.9	39.5	42.2	44.7	38.4	37.2	48.5	49.6	56.9
"Yes" votes	431,297	1,608,535	315,177	61,558	972,466	724,267	93,271	305,283	992,604	380,382	15,690,510
%	65.0	69.5	63.9	60.3	58.9	59.1	57.5	58.3	58.6	63.9	64.7
"No" votes	232,161	704,889	178,312	40,527	678,386	500,421	69,029	218,569	700,785	214,910	8,550,360
%	35.0	30.5	36.1	39.7	41.1	40.9	42.5	41.7	41.4	36.1	35.3
Total valid votes	663,458	2,313,424	493,489	102,085	1,650,852	1,224,688	162,300	523,852	1,693,389	595,292	24,240,870
Invalid votes	100,669	270,605	95,744	23,790	299,184	266,835	37,938	134,617	411,912	90,131	3,425,691
% of invalid votes/voters	13.2	10.5	16.2	18.9	15.3	17.9	18.9	20.4	19.6	13.1	12.4
of which blank ballots	85,920	138,490	80,446	20,606	260,696	231,120	31,583	112,693	326,500	75,483	2,788,290
% of blank ballots/invalid votes	85.3	51.2	84.0	86.6	87.1	86.6	83.2	83.7	79.3	83.7	81.4

Source: Calculated from data provided by Ministero dell'Interno- Direzione centrale per i servizi elettorali.

*"The sum valid votes" of "invalid votes" sometime differs from voters because of a negligible amount of contested votes.

TABLE B8-4 Popular Referendum June 11, 1995 n.4: "Repeal Compulsory Residence for Mafia Suspects". Regional and National Returns.

Lista	Valle D'Aosta	Piemonte	Lombardia	Liguria	Trentino A.A.	Veneto	Friuli V.G. A.A.	Emilia Romagna	Toscana	Umbria
Entitled to vote	100,944	3,683,821	7,509,878	1,477,911	752,150	3,771,080	1,081,243	3,413,315	3,032,757	706,841
Voters	55,975	2,308,465	4,985,952	901,118	445,522	2,518,879	626,837	2,360,082	1,927,157	434,890
% voters	55.5	62.7	66.4	61.0	59.2	66.8	58.0	69.1	63.5	61.5
"Yes" votes	35,611	1,406,317	3,254,813	556,295	301,152	1,785,596	405,422	1,434,459	1,110,025	220,245
%	72.8	67.7	72.4	70.0	74.7	77.2	70.9	70.4	67.0	61.5
"No" votes	13,330	671,281	1,242,464	238,731	102,236	526,960	166,729	602,440	547,965	138,079
%	27.2	32.3	27.6	30.0	25.3	22.8	29.1	29.6	33.0	38.5
Total valid votes	48,941	2,077,598	4,497,277	795,026	403,388	2,312,556	572,151	2,036,899	1,657,990	358,324
Invalid votes	7,034	230,848	488,064	106,090	42,127	205,984	54,653	323,180	268,998	76,526
% of invalid votes/voters	12.6	10.0	9.8	11.8	9.5	8.2	8.7	13.7	14.0	17.6
of which blank ballots	5,970	186,328	417,521	89,606	36,250	146,157	44,980	285,610	214,686	65,913
% of blank ballots/invalid votes	84.9	80.7	85.5	84.5	86.0	71.0	82.3	88.4	79.8	86.1

Lista	Marche	Lazio	Abruzzo	Molise	Campania	Puglia	Basilicata	Calabria	Sicilia	Sardegna	Total Italy
Entitled to vote	1,242,148	4,414,698	1,157,881	319,004	4,616,981	3,335,480	521,790	1,772,684	4,338,240	1,381,882	48,630,728
Voters	765,017	2,581,809	589,113	125,845	1,950,457	1,491,565	200,133	659,704	2,106,704	684,518	27,719,742
% voters	61.5	58.5	50.9	39.4	42.2	44.7	38.4	37.2	48.6	49.5	57.0
"Yes" votes	426,656	1,292,181	283,075	57,546	780,515	604,260	80,880	251,249	758,839	329,570	15,374,706
%	65.2	56.6	57.9	56.5	47.2	49.4	50.4	47.8	44.5	55.7	63.7
"No" votes	227,959	988,877	205,947	44,321	872,604	619,672	79,746	274,076	948,082	261,890	8,773,389
%	34.8	43.4	42.1	43.5	52.8	50.6	49.6	52.2	55.5	44.3	36.3
Total valid votes	654,615	2,281,058	489,022	101,867	1,653,119	1,223,932	160,626	525,325	1,706,921	591,460	24,148,095
Invalid votes	110,401	299,692	100,081	23,918	297,210	267,630	39,505	134,026	398,943	93,028	3,567,938
% of invalid votes/voters	14.4	11.6	17.0	19.0	15.2	17.9	19.7	20.3	18.9	13.6	12.9
of which blank ballots	94,710	146,583	84,184	20,681	255,151	232,759	32,946	110,329	316,379	77,881	2,864,624
% of blank ballots/invalid votes	85.8	48.9	84.1	86.5	85.8	87.0	83.4	85.4	79.3	83.7	80.3

Source: Calculated from data provided by Ministero dell'Interno- Direzione centrale per i servizi elettorali.

*"The sum of valid votes" plus "invalid votes" sometime differs from voters because of a negligible amount of contested votes.

TABLE B8-5 Popular Referendum June 11, 1995 n.5: "Privatize State Broadcasting Services". Regional and National Returns.

	Valle D'Aosta	Piemonte	Lombardia	Liguria	Trentino A.A.	Veneto	Friuli V.G.	Emilia Romagna	Toscana	Umbria
Entitled to vote	100,944	3,683,821	7,509,878	1,477,911	752,150	3,771,080	1,081,243	3,413,315	3,032,757	706,841
Voters	56,036	2,314,576	5,005,139	905,475	445,668	2,520,163	629,013	2,369,354	1,940,115	436,895
% voters	55.5	62.8	66.6	61.3	59.3	66.8	58.2	69.4	64.0	61.8
"Yes" votes	29,669	1,211,139	2,871,776	507,742	199,134	1,364,679	330,131	1,452,150	1,054,591	214,546
%	60.5	57.2	61.7	60.9	49.1	58.4	56.5	66.1	59.2	54.3
"No" votes	19,338	906,063	1,783,623	325,574	206,412	971,542	253,835	744,611	728,555	180,922
%	39.5	42.8	38.3	39.1	50.9	41.6	43.5	33.9	40.9	45.7
Total valid votes	49,007	2,117,202	4,655,399	833,316	405,546	2,336,221	583,966	2,196,761	1,782,612	395,468
Invalid votes	7,029	197,361	349,113	72,153	40,119	183,747	45,038	172,590	157,452	41,405
% of invalid votes/voters	12.5	8.5	7.0	8.0	9.0	7.3	7.2	7.3	8.1	9.5
of which blank ballots	6,055	158,661	290,082	59,668	35,150	154,256	36,868	146,207	131,266	33,464
% of blank ballots/invalid votes	86.1	80.4	83.1	82.7	87.6	84.0	81.9	84.7	83.4	80.8

	Marche	Lazio	Abruzzo	Molise	Campania	Puglia	Basilicata	Calabria	Sicilia	Sardegna	Total Italy
Entitled to vote	1,242,148	4,414,698	1,157,881	319,004	4,616,981	3,335,480	521,790	1,772,684	4,338,240	1,381,882	48,630,728
Voters	767,155	2,601,348	589,655	126,157	1,953,869	1,494,390	200,646	659,814	2,108,270	687,071	27,810,809
% voters	61.8	58.9	50.9	39.5	42.3	44.8	38.5	37.2	48.6	49.7	57.2
"Yes" votes	366,506	1,181,024	248,480	49,130	745,791	552,959	76,863	231,303	773,933	306,120	13,767,132
%	53.4	49.6	48.9	46.3	43.9	43.7	45.8	42.6	44.1	49.8	54.9
"No" votes	319,711	1,200,081	259,996	56,944	953,159	711,154	90,796	311,429	979,382	308,141	11,311,268
%	46.6	50.4	51.1	53.7	56.1	56.3	54.2	57.4	55.9	50.2	45.1
Total valid votes	686,217	2,381,105	508,476	106,074	1,698,950	1,264,113	167,659	542,732	1,753,315	614,261	25,078,400
Invalid votes	80,811	219,269	81,176	20,014	254,869	230,268	32,987	116,786	354,234	72,758	2,729,179
% of invalid votes/voters	10.5	8.4	13.8	15.9	13.0	15.4	16.4	17.7	16.8	10.6	9.8
of which blank ballots	68,164	114,839	67,170	17,146	219,918	199,381	27,438	97,222	279,818	60,875	2,203,648
% of blank ballots/invalid votes	84.3	52.4	82.7	85.7	86.3	86.6	83.2	83.2	79.0	83.7	80.7

Source: Calculated from data provided by Ministero dell'Interno- Direzione centrale per i servizi elettorali.

*"The sum valid votes" of "invalid votes" sometime differs from voters because of a negligible amount of contested votes.

TABLE B8-6 Popular Referendum June 11, 1995 n.6: " Abolish Power of Municipalities to Limit Retail Trade. Regional and National Returns.

	Valle D'Aosta	Piemonte	Lombardia	Liguria	Trentino A.A.	Veneto	Friuli V.G.	Emilia Romagna	Toscana	Umbria
Entitled to vote	100,944	3,683,821	7,509,878	1,477,911	752,150	3,771,080	1,081,243	3,413,315	3,032,757	706,841
Voters	55,812	2,307,714	4,983,153	901,711	445,078	2,508,426	626,436	2,360,043	1,932,065	435,784
% voters	55.3	62.6	66.4	61.0	59.2	66.5	57.9	69.1	63.7	61.7
"Yes" votes	20,738	778,797	1,622,330	267,360	139,998	814,132	225,036	619,363	516,942	121,397
%	43.2	37.6	35.7	32.8	35.5	35.5	39.4	28.8	29.7	31.3
"No" votes	27,271	1,294,668	2,925,294	547,944	254,681	1,481,936	346,828	1,527,598	1,224,380	266,592
%	56.8	62.4	64.3	67.2	64.5	64.5	60.6	71.2	70.3	68.7
Total valid votes	48,009	2,073,465	4,547,624	815,304	394,679	2,296,068	571,864	2,146,961	1,741,322	387,989
Invalid votes	7,803	233,435	434,588	86,400	50,395	212,227	54,548	213,067	190,651	47,774
% of invalid votes/voters	14.0	10.1	8.7	9.6	11.3	8.5	8.7	9.0	9.9	11.0
of which blank ballots	6,736	190,652	367,091	72,651	44,535	183,135	45,313	184,258	161,294	39,126
% of blank ballots/invalid votes	86.3	81.7	84.5	84.1	88.4	86.3	83.1	86.5	84.6	81.9

	Marche	Lazio	Abruzzo	Molise	Campania	Puglia	Basilicata	Calabria	Sicilia	Sardegna	Total Italy
Entitled to vote	1,242,148	4,414,698	1,157,881	319,004	4,616,981	3,335,480	521,790	1,772,684	4,338,240	1,381,882	48,630,728
Voters	765,917	2,587,152	589,955	125,929	1,952,320	1,492,878	200,433	658,921	2,106,970	685,821	27,722,518
% voters	61.7	58.6	51.0	39.5	42.3	44.8	38.4	37.2	48.6	49.6	57.0
"Yes" votes	226,564	850,780	193,943	41,133	639,850	463,243	66,031	208,279	700,935	221,758	8,738,609
%	33.6	36.6	38.9	39.8	38.3	37.3	40.2	39.3	40.9	36.8	35.6
"No" votes	447,486	1,470,777	304,940	62,173	1,030,787	777,169	98,370	321,026	1,010,953	380,556	15,801,429
%	66.4	63.4	61.1	60.2	61.7	62.7	59.8	60.7	59.1	63.2	64.4
Total valid votes	674,050	2,321,557	498,883	103,306	1,670,637	1,240,412	164,401	529,305	1,711,888	602,314	24,540,038
Invalid votes	91,867	264,681	91,067	22,557	281,630	252,454	36,028	129,608	394,293	83,458	3,178,531
% of invalid votes/voters	12.0	10.2	15.4	17.9	14.4	16.9	18.0	16.2	18.7	12.2	11.5
of which blank ballots	78,432	133,576	76,724	19,540	243,704	219,880	30,075	107,281	314,008	69,726	2,587,737
% of blank ballots/invalid votes	85.4	50.5	84.3	86.6	86.5	87.1	83.5	82.8	79.6	83.5	81.4

Source: Calculated from data provided by Ministero dell'Interno- Direzione centrale per i servizi elettorali.

*"The sum valid votes" of "invalid votes" sometime differs from voters because of a negligible amount of contested votes.

TABLE B8-7 Popular Referendum June 11, 1995 n.7: "Abolish Union Dues Deduction by Employers". Regional and National Returns.

	Valle D'Aosta	Piemonte	Lombardia	Liguria	Trentino A.A.	Veneto	Friuli V.G.	Emilia Romagna	Toscana	Umbria
Entitled to vote	100,944	3,683,821	7,509,878	1,477,911	752,150	3,771,080	1,081,243	3,413,315	3,032,757	706,841
Voters	55,922	2,309,531	4,992,955	903,813	444,993	2,514,700	627,734	2,364,862	1,935,260	436,459
% voters	55.4	62.7	66.5	61.2	59.2	66.7	58.1	69.3	63.8	61.7
"Yes" votes	28,500	1,224,313	2,740,230	450,458	219,620	1,367,166	352,245	976,896	841,435	198,953
%	59.0	58.7	59.6	54.7	55.7	59.2	60.8	44.9	47.9	50.7
"No" votes	19,833	860,748	1,857,216	373,309	174,751	942,833	226,902	1,201,087	915,247	193,178
%	41.0	41.3	40.4	45.3	44.3	40.8	39.2	55.1	52.1	49.3
Total valid votes	48,333	2,085,061	4,597,446	823,767	394,371	2,309,999	579,147	2,177,983	1,756,682	392,131
Invalid votes	7,589	224,403	395,143	80,043	50,621	204,363	48,581	186,876	178,477	44,328
% of invalid votes/voters	13.6	9.7	7.9	8.9	11.4	8.1	7.7	7.9	9.2	10.2
of which blank ballots	6,550	181,781	333,940	67,159	45,308	173,585	40,048	160,846	151,634	35,920
% of blank ballots/invalid votes	86.3	81.0	84.5	83.9	89.5	84.9	82.4	86.1	85.0	81.0

	Marche	Lazio	Abruzzo	Molise	Campania	Puglia	Basilicata	Calabria	Sicilia	Sardegna	Total Italy
Entitled to vote	1.242.148	4.414.698	1.157.881	319,004	4,616,981	3,335,480	521,790	1,772,684	4,338,240	1,381,882	48,630,728
Voters	766,362	2.594.178	589.248	126,043	1,951,673	1,494,130	200,789	659,460	2,108,025	687,054	27,763,191
% voters	61.7	58.8	50.9	39.5	42.3	44.8	38.5	37.2	48.6	49.7	57.1
"Yes" votes	354.720	1.421.900	287.711	59,209	957,126	720,733	90,773	297,867	1,012,565	347,079	13,949,499
%	52.2	60.3	57.2	56.7	57.0	57.4	54.4	55.5	58.2	56.8	56.2
"No" votes	324,726	937,422	215,039	45,235	722,884	535,596	76,005	239,031	725,943	264,372	10,851,357
%	47.8	39.7	42,8	43.3	43.0	42.6	45.6	44.5	41.8	43.2	43.8
Total valid votes	679,446	2.359.322	502.750	104,444	1,680,010	1,256,329	166,778	536,898	1,738,508	611,451	24,800,856
Invalid votes	86,756	233.991	86.494	21,527	271,627	237,790	34,009	122,063	368,803	75,548	2,959,032
% of invalid votes/voters	11,3	9,0	14,7	17.1	13.9	15.9	16.9	18.5	17.5	11.0	10.7
of which blank ballots	74.028	121.945	71.346	18,674	234,036	205,179	28,194	101,870	288,778	62,900	2,403,721
% of blank ballots/invalid votes	85,3	52,1	82,5	86.7	86.2	86.3	82.9	83.5	78.3	83.3	81.2

Source: Calculated from data provided by Ministero dell'Interno- Direzione centrale per i servizi elettorali.

*"The sum valid votes" of "invalid votes" sometime differs from voters because of a negligible amount of contested votes.

TABLE B8-8 Popular Referendum June 11, 1995 n.8: "Change Mayoral Election Rules in Municipalities with over 15,000 Inhabitants". Regional and National Returns.

	Valle D'Aosta	Piemonte	Lombardia	Liguria	Trentino A.A.	Veneto	Friuli V.G.	Emilia Romagna	Toscana	Umbria
Entitled to vote	100,944	3,683,821	7,509,878	1,477,911	752,150	3,771,080	1,081,243	3,413,315	3,032,757	706,841
Voters	55,751	2,313,041	4,997,372	904,267	444,837	2,512,481	627,558	2,365,768	1,937,583	436,506
% voters	55.2	62.8	66.5	61.2	59.1	66.6	58.0	69.3	63.9	61.8
"Yes" votes	24,000	1,071,376	2,412,173	387,523	186,630	1,191,641	317,622	839,323	718,852	173,304
%	51.9	51.7	52.8	47.4	47.3	51.9	55.6	39.0	41.2	44.7
"No" votes	22,218	1,002,244	2,152,040	429,358	208,252	1,102,548	253,611	1,311,764	1,026,584	214,571
%	48.1	48.3	47.2	52.6	52.7	48.1	44.4	61.0	58.8	55.3
Total valid votes	46,218	2,073,620	4,564,213	816,881	394,882	2,294,189	571,233	2,151,087	1,745,436	387,875
Invalid votes	9,533	239,313	432,592	87,370	49,954	217,881	56,313	214,674	192,081	48,588
% of invalid votes/voters	17.1	10.3	8.7	9.7	11.2	8.7	9.0	9.1	9.9	11.1
of which blank ballots	8,304	195,903	369,821	73,548	44,222	191,133	46,889	186,347	163,477	39,975
% of blank ballots/invalid votes	87.1	81.9	85.5	84.2	88.5	87.7	83.3	86.8	85.1	82.3

	Marche	Lazio	Abruzzo	Molise	Campania	Puglia	Basilicata	Calabria	Sicilia	Sardegna	Total Italy
Entitled to vote	1,242,148	4,414,698	1,157,881	319,004	4,616,981	3,335,480	521,790	1,772,684	4,338,240	1,381,882	48,630,728
Voters	766,676	2,602,134	590,074	126,060	1,954,089	1,494,460	200,773	659,401	2,108,546	686,656	27,784,033
% voters	61.7	58.9	51.0	39.5	42.3	44.8	38.5	37.2	48.6	49.7	57.1
"Yes" votes	310,896	1,228,122	264,818	53,555	812,379	633,367	78,190	266,742	888,284	303,708	12,162,505
%	46.3	52.2	53.2	51.7	48.5	50.8	47.5	50.1	51.6	50.6	49.4
"No" votes	360,521	1,125,850	233,260	50,041	863,136	612,462	86,339	265,612	831,664	296,954	12,449,029
%	53.7	47.8	46.8	48.3	51.5	49.2	52.5	49.9	48.4	49.4	50.6
Total valid votes	671,417	2,353,972	498,078	103,596	1,675,515	1,245,829	164,529	532,354	1,719,948	600,662	24,611,534
Invalid votes	95,257	247,271	91,991	22,392	278,547	248,612	36,242	126,778	387,683	85,920	3,168,992
% of invalid votes/voters	12.4	9.5	15.6	17.8	14.3	16.6	18.1	19.2	18.4	12.5	11.4
of which blank ballots	82,779	128,417	75,627	19,395	238,758	217,015	30,300	105,816	306,231	71,538	2,595,495
% of blank ballots/invalid votes	86.9	51.9	82.2	86.6	85.7	87.3	83.6	83.5	79.0	83.3	81.9

Source: Calculated from data provided by Ministero dell'Interno- Direzione centrale per i servizi elettorali.

*"The sum valid votes" of "invalid votes" sometime differs from voters because of a negligible amount of contested votes.

TABLE B8-9 Popular Referendum June 11, 1995 n.9: "Abolish Power of Local Governments to Limit Businness Hour". Regional and National Returns.

	Valle D'Aosta	Piemonte	Lombardia	Liguria	Trentino A.A.	Veneto	Friuli V.G.	Emilia Romagna	Toscana	Umbria
Entitled to vote	100,944	3,683,821	7,509,878	1,477,911	752,150	3,771,080	1,081,243	3,413,315	3,032,757	706,841
Voters	55,897	2,311,869	4,991,407	902,980	445,463	2,516,799	627,482	2,362,878	1,933,177	436,306
% voters	55.4	62.8	66.5	61.1	59.2	66.7	58.0	69.2	63.7	61.9
"Yes" votes										
%	50.3	41.1	39.1	37.5	39.8	37.0	43.3	30.5	32.4	32.6
"No" votes	24,413	1,247,311	2,817,871	517,693	241,647	1,469,063	329,935	1,514,466	1,194,924	266,779
%	49.7	58.9	60.9	62.5	60.2	63.0	56.7	69.5	67.6	67.4
Total valid votes	49,111	2,116,867	4,625,101	828,722	401,194	2,332,872	581,756	2,178,257	1,768,362	395,608
Invalid votes	6,786	194,668	365,657	74,253	44,265	183,451	45,722	184,600	164,754	40,695
% of invalid votes/voters	12.1	8.4	7.3	8.2	9.9	7.3	7.3	7.8	8.5	9.3
of which blank ballots	5,862	157,890	275,527	62,420	39,234	155,199	37,483	159,362	139,991	32,881
% of blank ballots/invalid votes	86.4	81.1	75.4	84.1	88.6	84.6	82.0	86.3	85.0	80.8

	Marche	Lazio	Abruzzo	Molise	Campania	Puglia	Basilicata	Calabria	Sicilia	Sardegna	Total Italy
Entitled to vote	1,242,148	4,414,698	1,157,881	319,004	4,616,981	3,335,480	521,790	1,772,684	4,338,240	1,381,882	48,630,728
Voters	766,818	2,593,259	591,110	126,082	1,952,647	1,494,587	200,681	658,514	2,108,400	686,127	27,762,483
% voters	61.7	58.7	51.1	39.5	42.3	44.8	38.5	37.1	48.6	49.7	57.1
"Yes" votes	240,903	884,002	203,987	43,193	655,951	466,665	67,447	215,899	714,974	237,721	9,384,490
%	35.0	37.5	39.7	40.6	38.4	36.4	40.0	39.5	40.3	38.6	37.5
"No" votes	447,959	1,472,996	309,198	63,159	1,053,318	814,191	101,148	330,719	1,058,368	378,613	15,653,771
%	65.0	62.5	60.3	59.4	61.6	63.6	60.0	60.5	59.7	61.4	62.5
Total valid votes	688,862	2,356,998	513,185	106,352	1,709,269	1,280,856	168,595	546,618	1,773,342	616,334	25,038,261
Invalid votes	77,956	235,402	77,924	19,665	242,930	213,720	32,084	111,571	334,282	69,756	2,720,141
% of invalid votes/voters	10.2	9.1	13.2	15.6	12.4	14.3	16.0	16.9	15.9	10.2	9.8
of which blank ballots	66,173	113,898	64,599	16,908	206,970	183,815	26,744	93,324	259,024	58,173	2,155,477
% of blank ballots/invalid votes	84.9	48.4	82.9	86.0	85.2	86.0	83.4	83.6	77.5	83.4	79.2

Source: Calculated from data provided by Ministero dell'Interno- Direzione centrale per i servizi elettorali.

*" The sum valid votes" of "invalid votes" sometime differs from voters because of a negligible amount of contested votes.

TABLE B8-10 Popular Referendum June 11, 1995 n.10: "Limit Private Ownership of TV Channels". Regional and National Returns.

	Valle D'Aosta	Piemonte	Lombardia	Liguria	Trentino A.A.	Veneto	Friuli V.G.	Emilia Romagna	Toscana	Umbria	Total Italy
Entitled to vote	100,944	3,683,821	7,509,878	1,477,911	752,150	3,771,080	1,081,243	3,413,315	3,032,757	706,841	48,630,728
Voters	56,908	2,339,448	5,064,392	917,912	451,447	2,547,113	638,467	2,396,365	1,970,315	443,012	28,147,146
% voters	56.4	63.5	67.4	62.1	60.0	67.5	59.0	70.2	65.0	62.7	57.9
"Yes" votes	22,678	964,910	2,042,692	437,206	233,233	1,116,129	256,673	1,306,594	1,049,886	205,331	11,590,539
%	42.3	42.9	41.5	49.2	54.7	45.5	41.5	56.4	55.1	48.2	43.0
"No" votes	30,899	1,286,760	2,877,898	451,366	193,407	1,334,863	361,326	1,011,409	854,894	220,282	15,366,242
%	57.7	57.1	58.5	50.8	45.3	54.5	58.5	43.6	44.9	51.8	57.0
Total valid votes	53,577	2,251,670	4,920,590	888,572	426,640	2,450,992	617,999	2,318,003	1,904,780	425,613	26,956,781
Invalid votes	3,331	87,620	143,368	29,334	24,801	95,788	20,464	78,348	65,377	17,399	1,187,715
% of invalid votes/voters	5.9	3.7	2.8	3.2	5.5	3.8	3.2	3.3	3.3	3.9	4.2
of which blank ballots	2,666	61,501	89,000	20,132	20,311	67,523	14,479	58,887	47,622	11,868	820,482
% of blank ballots/invalid votes	80.0	70.2	62.1	68.6	81.9	70.5	70.8	75.2	72.8	68.2	69.1

	Marche	Lazio	Abruzzo	Molise	Campania	Puglia	Basilicata	Calabria	Sicilia	Sardegna
Entitled to vote	1,242,148	4,414,698	1,157,881	319,004	4,616,981	3,335,480	521,790	1,772,684	4,338,240	1,381,882
Voters	775,841	2,648,363	599,426	127,785	1,969,324	1,513,784	203,101	667,245	2,121,892	695,006
% voters	62.5	60.0	51.8	40.1	42.7	45.4	38.9	37.6	48.9	50.3
"Yes" votes	361,387	1,033,724	217,463	44,530	692,637	477,297	77,395	212,652	569,478	268,644
%	48.9	4.4	38.4	37.9	37.3	33.4	41.8	34.7	29.0	40.3
"No" votes	378,266	1,524,103	349,020	72,977	1,166,210	950,642	107,567	400,189	1,395,974	398,190
%	51.1	59.6	61.6	62.1	62.7	66.6	58.2	65.3	71.0	59.7
Total valid votes	739,653	2,557,827	566,483	117,507	1,858,847	1,427,939	184,962	612,841	1,965,452	666,834
Invalid votes	36,187	89,855	32,942	10,227	110,451	85,835	18,132	54,174	155,935	28,147
% of invalid votes/voters	4.7	3.4	5.5	8.0	5.6	5.7	8.9	8.1	7.3	4.0
of which blank ballots	26,955	41,664	23,073	7,945	84,945	64,619	13,868	38,904	104,262	20,258
% of blank ballots/invalid votes	74.5	46.4	70.0	77.7	76.9	75.3	76.5	71.8	66.9	72.0

Source: Calculated from data provided by Ministero dell'Interno- Direzione centrale per i servizi elettorali.

*"The sum valid votes" of "invalid votes" sometime differs from voters because of a negligible amount of contested votes.

TABLE B8-11 Popular Referendum June 11, 1995 n.11: "Ban Commercial Advertising During Broadcasting of Films." Regional and National Returns.

	Valle D'Aosta	Piemonte	Lombardia	Liguria	Trentino A.A.	Veneto	Friuli V.G.	Emilia Romagna	Toscana	Umbria
Entitled to vote	100,944	3,683,821	7,509,878	1,477,911	752,150	3,771,080	1,081,243	3,413,315	3,032,757	706,841
Voters	56,904	2,339,369	5,061,484	917,443	451,330	2,543,728	638,384	2,396,373	1,971,030	443,016
% voters	56.4	63.5	67.4	62.1	60.0	67.5	59.0	70.2	65.0	67.2
"Yes" votes	23,967	1,008,868	2,131,485	451,113	244,346	1,170,136	271,051	1,341,235	1,076,218	209,026
%	44.6	44.7	43.2	50.6	57.1	47.6	43.7	57.8	56.4	49.0
"No" votes	29,785	1,249,711	2,800,748	440,603	183,378	1,289,900	348,588	980,913	832,770	217,317
%	55.4	55.3	56.8	49.4	42.9	52.4	56.3	42.2	43.6	51.0
Total valid votes	53,752	2,258,579	4,932,233	891,716	427,724	2,460,036	619,639	2,322,148	1,908,9880	426,343
Invalid votes	3,152	80,701	128,960	25,721	23,602	83,550	18,739	74,223	61,873	16,672
% of invalid votes/voters	5.5	3.4	2.5	2.8	5.2	3.3	2.9	3.1	3.1	3.8
of which blank ballots	2,563	57,857	84,066	19,547	20,077	65,543	13,684	57,104	45,973	11,463
% of blank ballots/invalid votes	81.3	71.7	65.2	76.0	85.1	78.4	73.0	76.9	74.3	68.8

	Marche	Lazio	Abruzzo	Molise	Campania	Puglia	Basilicata	Calabria	Sicilia	Sardegna	Total Italy
Entitled to vote	1,242,148	4,414,698	1,157,881	319,004	4,616,981	3,335,480	521,790	1,772,684	4,338,240	1,381,882	48,630,728
Voters	775,901	2,648,231	598,247	127,767	1,969,866	1,513,798	203,277	666,987	2,121,728	695,048	28,139,920
% voters	62.5	60.0	51.7	40.1	42.7	45.4	39.0	37.6	48.9	50.3	57.9
"Yes" votes	370,616	1,055,084	222,888	45,627	706,336	494,542	79,332	220,208	588,562	275,785	11,986,425
%	50.0	41.2	39.0	38.7	37.9	34.5	42.7	35.8	29.8	41.2	44.3
"No" votes	370,854	1,505,831	348,249	72,222	1,158,317	937,727	106,435	395,713	1,387,167	393,028	15,049,256
%	50.0	58.8	61.0	61.3	62.1	65.5	57.3	64.2	70.2	58.8	55.7
Total valid votes	741,470	2,560,915	571,137	117,849	1,864,653	1,432,269	185,767	615,921	1,975,729	668,813	27,035,681
Invalid votes	34,427	86,834	27,110	9,875	105,189	81,519	17,507	50,793	145,537	26,217	1,102,201
% of invalid votes/voters	4.4	3.3	4.5	7.7	5.3	5.4	8.6	7.6	6.9	3.8	3.9
of which blank ballots	26,334	39,623	22,379	7,725	77,194	62,004	13,556	37,138	106,774	19,129	789,733
% of blank ballots/invalid votes	76.5	45.6	82.5	78.2	73.4	76.1	77.4	73.1	73.4	73.0	71.7

Source: Calculated from data provided by Ministero dell'Interno- Direzione centrale per i servizi elettorali,

*"The sum valid votes" of "invalid votes" sometime differs from voters because of a negligible amount of contested votes,

TABLE B8-12 Popular Referendum June 11, 1995 n.12: "Limit a Single Company's Faculty to Sell Advertising to no More than Two National Tv Channels". Regional and National Returns.

	Valle D'Aosta	Piemonte	Lombardia	Liguria	Trentino A.A.	Veneto	Friuli V.G.	Emilia Romagna	Toscana	Umbria
Entitled to vote	100,944	3,683,821	7,509,878	1,477,911	752,150	3,771,080	1,081,243	3,413,315	3,032,757	706,841
Voters	56,830	2,337,170	5,059,640	917,602	450,888	2,541,967	637,715	2,394,022	1,969,826	442,744
% voters	56.3	63.4	67.4	62.1	59.9	67.4	59.0	70.1	65.0	62.6
"Yes" votes	23,088	976,655	2,095,109	441,039	191,151	1,306,228	354,965	996,161	843,895	217,459
%	43.4	43.5	42.7	49.7	45.2	53.4	57.7	43.1	44.4	51.3
"No" votes	30,092	1,267,515	2,811,979	446,593	231,792	1,140,538	260,413	1,315,408	1,055,105	206,810
%	56.6	56.5	57.3	50.3	54.8	46.6	42.3	56.9	55.6	48.7
Total valid votes	53,180	2,244,170	4,907,088	887,632	422,943	2,446,766	615,378	2,311,569	1,899,000	424,269
Invalid votes	3,650	92,948	152,203	29,968	27,940	95,051	22,333	82,441	70,623	18,475
% of invalid votes/voters	6.4	4.0	3.0	3.3	6.2	3.7	3.5	3.4	3.6	4.2
of which blank ballots	3,028	67,297	96,782	21,911	23,868	74,352	16,330	64,269	52,221	12,463
% of blank ballots/invalid votes	83.0	72.4	63.6	73.1	85.4	78.2	73.1	78.0	73.9	67.5

	Marche	Lazio	Abruzzo	Molise	Campania	Puglia	Basilicata	Calabria	Sicilia	Sardegna	Total Italy
Entitled to vote	1,242,148	4,414,698	1,157,881	319,004	4,616,981	3,335,480	521,790	1,772,684	4,338,240	1,381,882	48,630,728
Voters	775,629	2,647,544	598,260	127,724	1,968,908	1,512,947	203,218	667,153	2,122,028	694,757	28,126,572
% voters	62.4	60.0	51.7	40.0	42.6	45.4	38.9	37.6	48.9	50.3	57.8
"Yes" votes	365,953	1,045,035	218,263	44,795	694,458	482,285	77,282	212,186	569,311	269,400	11,730,479
%	49.6	41.0	38.5	38.1	37.4	33.8	41.8	34.6	28.9	40.5	43.6
"No" votes	371,972	1,506,505	347,979	72,699	1,163,260	943,288	107,807	401,866	1,399,657	396,373	15,171,890
%	50.4	59.0	61.5	61.9	62.6	66.2	58.2	65.4	71.1	59.5	56.4
Total valid votes	737,925	2,551,540	566,242	117,494	1,857,718	1,425,573	185,089	614,052	1,968,968	665,773	26,902,369
Invalid votes	37,704	95,465	32,018	10,174	111,160	87,356	18,126	53,082	152,497	28,979	1,222,193
% of invalid votes/voters	4.9	3.6	5.4	8.0	5.6	5.8	8.9	8.0	7.2	4.2	4.3
of which blank ballots	28,651	41,121	23,450	7,872	83,541	65,678	13,693	38,073	101,804	20,897	857,301
% of blank ballots/invalid votes	76.0	43.1	73.2	77.4	75.2	75.2	75.5	71.7	66.8	72.1	70.1

Source: Calculated from data provided by Ministero dell'Interno- Direzione centrale per i servizi elettorali.

*"The sum valid votes" of "invalid votes" sometime differs from voters because of a negligible amount of contested votes.

TABLE C1 Balance-Sheet of Official Party Budget, 1994.

	Revenues				Expenses	Balance	
	Membership Dues	State Contributions	Other Revenues	Total Revenues	Total Expenses	Operating Surplus-Deficit	Accumulating Surplus-Deficit (Including Previous Years)
PPI	1,525,743,000	15,109,496,472	402,437,609	17,037,677,081	31,278,374,998	-14,240,697,917	45,850,467,135
PDS	6,862,104,834	26,882,109,727	24,404,933,039	58,149,147,600	55,016,866,156	3,132,281,444	41,231,409,835
Rifondazione Comunista	871,570,520	8,215,262,860	5,342,670,130	14,429,503,510	10,254,526,830	4,174,976,680	3,070,656,786
Forza Italia	510,100,000	33,745,315,824	4,322,894,196	38,578,310,020	35,793,589,780	2,784,720,240	2,784,720,240
Green Federation	120,000,000	2,818,458,431	1,152,051,832	4,090,510,263	2,622,643,253	1,467,867,010	2,588,647,820
PRI	97,656,000	340,167,643	2,839,784,195	3,277,607,838	2,634,506,942	643,100,896	-1,532,910,073
Lega Nord	2,278,624,846	11,860,003,225	10,855,140,497	24,993,768,568	22,904,338,602	2,089,429,966	8,014,514,627
MSI	477,715,600	20,061,093,382	4,629,826,330	25,168,635,312	11,577,694,965	13,590,940,347	10,689,050,174

Source: Data supplied by parties

TABLE C2   Balance-Sheet of Official Party Budget, 1992-1994.

	Revenues	Expenses	Operating Surplus-Deficit	Accumulating Surplus-Deficit (including Previous Years)
DC/PPI				
1992	107,334,589,538	107,325,911,575	8,677,963	-12,352,386,087
1993	23,437,893,107	42,695,276,238	-19,257,383,131	-31,609,769,218
1994	17,037,677,081	31,278,374,998	-14,240,697,917	-45,850,467,135
PDS				
1992	49,815,322,828	50,383,026,259	-567,703,431	-44,019,318,235
1993	31,528,208,101	31,872,581,145	-344,373,044	-44,363,691,279
1994	58,149,147,600	55,016,866,156	3,132,281,444	-41,231,409,835
Rifondazione Comunista				
1992[a]	7,284,206,346	8,518,556,830	-1,234,350,484	-1,234,350,484
1993	11,366,176,679	11,236,146,089	130,030,590	-1,104,319,894
1994	14,429,503,510	10,254,526,830	4,174,976,680	3,070,656,786
Forza Italia				
1994[b]	38,578,310,020	35,793,589,780	2,784,720,240	2,784,720,240
PRI				
1992	11,829,583,353	12,213,332,229	-383,748,876	-3,671,478,296
1993	6,327,233,240	4,831,765,913	1,495,467,327	-2,176,010,969
1994	3,277,607,838	2,634,506,942	643,100,896	-1,532,910,073
Federazione dei Verdi				
1992	5,337,064,972	5,236,323,644	100,741,328	232,781,944
1993	3,995,323,560	3,107,324,694	947,998,866	1,120,780,810
1994	4,090,510,263	2,622,643,253	1,467,867,010	2,588,647,820
Lega				
1992	12,564,616,843	10,373,661,781	2,190,955,062	2,385,162,392
1993	22,970,666,098	19,430,743,829	3,539,922,269	5,925,084,661
1994	24,993,768,568	22,904,338,602	2,089,429,966	8,014,514,627
MSI				
1992	9,656,503,952	10,233,358,795	-576,854,843	-4,883,346,016
1993	11,720,894,589	9,739,438,756	1,981,455,833	-2,901,890,183
1994	25,168,635,312	11,577,694,965	13,590,940,347	10,689,050,174

[a] The 1991 budget refers to the *Movimento per la Rifondazione Comunista* which was transformed into the *Partito della Rifondazione Comunista* on December, 15, 1991. The 1992 and the 1993 budgets, do not includ the *Movimento*'s deficit.

[b] It born on 1994.

Source: Data supplied by parties

TABLE C3 Reported Membership of the Main Parties, 1986-1995.

	Rifondaz. Comunista	PCI/PDS	DC/PPI	CDU	Lega Nord[a]	Forza Italia	MSI/AN	Liberali	Repubblicani	Radicali
1986	-	1,551,576	1,395,239	-	-	-	156,520	36,931	-	11,010
1987	-	1,508,140	1,812,201	-	-	-	165,427	26,439	117,031	11,822
1988	-	1,462,281	1,887,615	-	-	-	151,444	17,768	107,949	5,750
1989	-	1,417,182	1,862,426	-	-	-	166,162	19,121	99,386	3,199
1990	-	1,319,305	2,109,670	-	-	-	142,344	44,732	83,498	4,287
1991	112,278	989,708	1,390,918	-	-	-	150,147	50,327	72,175	4,296
1992	119,094	769,944	-	-	140,000	-	181,243	18,731	71,886	10,474
1993	121,055	690,414	813,753	-	-	-	202,715	-	-	42,676
1994	120,000	700,000	233,377	-	-	300,000	250,000	-	20,916	5,281
1995	115,537	693,000	160,000	205,923	-	-	280,316	-	3,995	-

[a] Data 1993, 1994, 1995 not available.

About the Editors
and Contributors

Michael Braun, formerly researcher in political science at the University of Duisburg, is currently a free-lance writer.

Mario Caciagli is Professor of Comparative Politics at the University of Florence.

Onorato Castellino is Professor of Political Economy at the University of Turin.

Pier Virgilio Dastoli is the secretary general of the European International Movement.

Aldo Di Virgilio is researcher in political science at the University of Calabria.

Roberto Fideli has a research doctorate in social and political science methodology.

Mark Gilbert is visiting Assistant Professor of Political Science and International Relations at Dickinson College, in Carlisle, Pennsylvania.

David I. Kertzer is Dupee Professor of Social Science at Brown University, where he is also Professor of Antropology and History.

Sandro Magister is a specialist on Vatican affairs and correspondent for the weekly magazine l'*Espresso*.

Marco Maraffi is a researcher in the Department of Sociology at the University of Milan.

David Nelken is Distinguished Professor of Sociology at the University of Macerata, Italy and Distinguished Research Professor of Law, University of Wales at Cardiff.

Gianfranco Pasquino is Professor of Political Science at the University of Bologna.

Pier Vincenzo Uleri is a researcher in the Department of Political Science and Political Sociology at the University of Florence.

Marzia Zannini is engaged in research at the Istituto Cattaneo, Bologna.

Index